PERSUASION

Volume 122, Sage Library of Social Research

RECENT VOLUMES IN
SAGE LIBRARY OF SOCIAL RESEARCH

PERSUASION
Theory and Context

Kathleen Kelley Reardon
Foreword by Gerald R. Miller

GAIL THEUS FAIRHURST
Contributing Author, Chapter 10

Volume 122
SAGE LIBRARY OF
SOCIAL RESEARCH

SAGE PUBLICATIONS   Beverly Hills   London

To

Christopher T. Noblet

*for his constructive criticism
and invaluable friendship*

Copyright © 1981 by Sage Publications, Inc.

For information address:

SAGE Publications, Inc.
275 South Beverly Drive
Beverly Hills, California 90212

SAGE Publications Ltd
28 Banner Street
London EC1Y 8QE, England

Printed in the United States of America

Library of Congress Cataloging in Publication Data

Reardon, Kathleen Kelley.
    Persuasion, theory and context.

    (Sage library of social research ; v. 122)
    Bibliography: p.
    Includes index.
    1. Persuasion (Psychology) I. Title. II. Se-
ries.
BF637.P4R34   303.3'4   81-1892
ISBN 0-8039-1615-9   AACR2
ISBN 0-8039-1616-7 (pbk.)

THIRD PRINTING, 1984

CONTENTS

FOREWORD

In the past decade, the once unchallenged hegemony of persuasion as the primary process for communication study has been severely shaken. While the reasons for this apparent decline of interest in the symbolic strategies used by individuals to control and manage their environments are various and complex, Michael Burgoon and I argued in *Communication Yearbook 2* that one possible reason lies in the myopic view of the social influence process held by many students of persuasive communication: *"Students of persuasion may have fallen captive to the limits imposed by their own operational definitions of the area"* (p. 31). More specifically, we suggested four potential shortcomings of the traditional approach to persuasion research: a tendency to treat persuasion as a linear, unidirectional communicative activity; an overriding concern with persuasive discourse as it occurs in a one-persuader-to-many-persuadees situational context; a preoccupation with perusasion as an action-centered or issue-centered activity, rather than a process that frequently has as its *end* the enhancement of personal credibility or self-esteem; and a widespread allegiance to the view that persuasion is an attitude change-centered activity, rather than a process that often seeks behavioral modification and realignment.

Although Burgoon and I were commenting primarily on the working prejudices of persuasion researchers, similar conceptions of the persuasion process are readily identifiable in many of the texts used in persuasion classrooms. Happily, Reardon's book departs from this mold, providing an expanded conceptualization of persuasion which places it squarely in the center of people's daily communicative transactions. Persuasive discourse is treated as an invaluable tool not only for selling aspirin or E.R.A., but also for defining one's social identity and desirability; to a large extent, people's self-conceptions are shaped by a subtle mixture of influencing and being influenced. Stated differently, the "Who?" of the elusive "Who am

I?" is powerfully determined by the individual's skill in directing the actions of others, as well as his or her susceptibility to the persuasive wiles of other would-be persuaders.

Several features of this volume underscore Reardon's commitment to a more robust, more universally relevant notion of persuasive communication. Separate chapters are devoted to analyzing carefully the dynamics of persuasion in interpersonal, organizational, and mass media settings. The author's concern with the differing rule logics that prevail in these settings conveys a flavor of the situational complexities of persuasive communication and strongly reinforces the need to adapt audience analysis and strategy selection to the demands imposed by the particular situation. For example, Reardon argues cogently that interpersonal persuasion is governed by a behavioral logic stressing intrinsic definition and negotiation of rules by the communicators themselves, whereas persuasive messages emanating from the mass media are tailored primarily to conform with a set of extrinsic rules imposed on heterogeneous media audiences by prevailing cultural and social norms. It follows, then, that what is persuasively good for General Motors in its efforts to sell cars to its potential customers may fail dismally for Gerald Miller in his efforts to sell his children on the wisdom of abstaining from drug usage. The "G.M. mark" of persuasive excellence is simply not the same for all situational contexts.

Throughout the volume, the author also stresses consistently the inevitable reciprocity of persuasive influence. To return to the previous illustration, both my definition of the role position, parent, and my perceived adequacy in fulfilling this role are strongly impacted by my children's responses to my persuasive messages. Such a view is, of course, entirely congruent with the current emphasis placed on the transactional nature of communication and is unlikely to strike readers as revolutionary or earthshaking. Be that as it may, communication scholars have not always practiced what they have preached in their writing, and it is encouraging to encounter a book that pays more than metatheoretical lip service to underlying assumptions about the nature of persuasive exchange.

Lest I overemphasize the new and rediscovered friends Reardon brings to the volume, I should also note that the theoretical and empirical staples of previous persuasion books have not been neglected. Chapter 4 describes some of the frequently used theoretical vantage points for investigating the persuasion process, while Chapter 6 presents a census of a number of persuasion variables examined by researchers. Chapter 10, an invited contribution by Gail Theus Fairhurst on the kinds of empirical methods used by persuasion researchers, serves the valuable function of acquainting beginning students with the argot and the design of persuasion research. To capitalize on this contribution, some instructors may prefer to have students read the chapter early so that they may better understand descriptions of research occurring in other chapters.

Those readers acquainted with my own theoretical and research biases will predict that my reactions to this book are neither totally positive nor completely sanguine. While this is so, it is as it should be. If this were my book, I would not so readily embrace the rule-following model as the keenest scalpel for dissecting the persuasion process. But this is Reardon's book, not mine, and as I have sought to convey in these remarks, she has set forth her perspective thoughtfully, clearly, and consistently. As a consequence, this volume constitutes a useful and needed addition to the basic literature on persuasive communication, one that largely circumvents the conceptual shortcomings mentioned at the outset of this foreword.

—Gerald R. Miller
East Lansing, Michigan

ACKNOWLEDGMENTS

This text was written to encourage the revitalization of an area of study important to communication scholars. To accomplish this task I drew upon the works of many colleagues who may not have seen their work as particularly relevant to the study of persuasion. However, revitalization requires the relinquishment of labels that inhibit cooperation and complementarity of thought. It requires fresh ideas and sound reasoning. I have borrowed from the best. The act of borrowing is itself an acknowledgment of respect. However, to add the explicitness of the verbal to the implicitness of the nonverbal, I wish to acknowledge the contributions of my colleagues, especially those whose work appears in this text.

To Gerald Miller I owe special thanks. His work has had a significant impact on my thinking about persuasion. Few have contributed with such consistent high quality to the study of this phenomonon. His decision to write the forward of this book was therefore most gratifying. On a more personal level, I am grateful for his encouragement and comments on the manuscript.

I also wish to thank Gail Fairhurst for her contribution of Chapter 10. My respect for her work is only equalled by my appreciation for her friendship.

My gratitude is extended to James H. Watt and Sjef van den Berg for sharing their expertise in mass media and organizational communication respectively. Their comments influenced my thoughts concerning the role of persuasion in these two contexts.

A special thanks is extended to Paula Beaudette for her assistance in the preparation of the bibliography and for her inimitable style of subdued, ever-present moral support.

I'd like to thank Jenny Boomer for her perfection and perseverance in the typing of this manuscript.

Finally, and foremost, I'd like to thank Christopher Noblet for his editing. His temperament, tenacity, and talent as a writer served me well. I also wish to thank him for his patience with my occasional bouts of insecurity and equally frequent moments of elation.

A book is a journey over peaks and through valleys. I am glad that all of these people were with me.

Chapter 1

INTRODUCTION

The past ten years have witnessed a dramatic decline in the import attributed to the study of persuasion. Miller and Burgoon (1978) suggest that traditional methods of persussion research have been "swimming against both the ideological and scholarly currents of the past decade." Yet they consider a pessimistic prognosis unjustified.

Eagly and Himmelfarb (1978) have observed a recent recovery of interest in attitude, which they attribute to the new, widely shared interest in information-processing views about attitude formation and change. Their message to researchers is also that persuasion research is still alive and recuperating nicely from its ten-year decline.

While it is true that a computer search for persuasion literature covering the last ten years would reflect a decline in the number of studies that have included the term *persuasion* in the title, a closer look at the literature of that decade reveals no lack of studies on the process of influence, which, by any other name, is still persuasion. It appears, then, that despite any dissatisfaction the study of this phenomena may have engendered, it has not been summarily dismissed from consideration by communication scholars.

Perhaps the late 1960s' disdain for anything that implied an attempt to manipulate others created some embarrassment for the already frustrated persuasion researchers, whose attempts to link attitude and behavior continued to fail. Whatever the reason, in one sense, at least, the resulting decline of that which was once called "persuasion research" has been a good thing. It has given us the time necessary to move ourselves from among the trees to see the forest with renewed objectivity. We are now ready for a persuasion renaissance, the beginnings of which must be characterized by a loosening of the fetters that have bound the phenomenon to undeserved negative attributions.

The accomplishment of this objective does not require a condemnation of previous persuasion theory and research. On the contrary, if we assume that a phenomenon has a life of its own beyond that which the researcher breathes into it, all attempts to understand that phenomenon are worthy of our attention.

In the next several chapters, then, a rigorous exercise in eclecticism will be conducted. The best of many schools of thought will be conjoined to lend support to a perspective on persuasion that defines subject and scientist as cohorts in an overdue revitalization effort. The blueprints have been in my mind for some time now. The materials for this theoretical edifice, however, have only recently become sufficient to begin building. Those who enter will find some corners reminiscent of the past, others a reflection of the present. It is hoped that each visitor will leave with, at the very least, the sense that an engaging harmony is possible, though some areas must, at this time, remain unfashioned.

Before embarking on this experience it seems appropriate to introduce some of the basic tenets of the perspective to be advanced in the next several chapters. Behaviorism, the major "world view" of the first half of this century, focused on the observation of human behavior as the only clue to cognitive processes such as attitude. Actually, little has changed in this regard. What has changed is the amount of "subjective" input researchers allow to influence their interpretations of behavior. Rules theory and constructivism, for example, represent a belief in one's subjects as the creators of their own versions of reality and thus the best sources of explanation for their own behavior. Behaviorists harbored a deep apprehension concerning their subjects' ability to interpret the causes of their own behaviors. They looked with some disfavor on the individual differences that increased error variance. Were they wrong? As we shall see, the answer is, "That depends."

Much self-report literature indicates that we should not be too quick to place explicit trust in the subject. A statement by Duck (1980: 117) indicates that some caution is especially advisable when we study the transactional nature of communication: "My own team has found that partners often have such widely different views of the state or future of their relationship that it is hard to believe they are really in the same one."

Given the limitations of both imposed and induced perspectives, the choice becomes very difficult (see Hewes, 1978). The researcher is thus "between a rock and a hard place" unless he or she can locate some justification for a preference. In this book, the context of interaction and the amount of autonomous behavior it affords its occupants will be defined as that attribute which can serve to justify the researcher's decision.

People have versions of reality imposed upon them at least as often as they create their own. In this sense, conceptualizations of reality are both "borrowed" and "owned." Whether individuals decide to allow their personal versions of a situation to guide their behavior, decide to accept borrowed versions, or find a combination of the two preferable is largely a function of the level of autonomy they believe the context affords. When behavior selected on the basis of personal rules is perceived by the actor as potentially generative of undesirable returns, "borrowed" versions of reality (e.g., role prescriptions) may be construed as the safer generative mechanism of behavior selection. This will be discussed at greater length in future chapters. For now it is important to recognize the implications this perspective has for persuasion research.

First, no longer can we afford to study persuasion in terms of message strategies without regard for the individuals who use them and their perceptions of the contextual constraints on their behavioral choices. People differ in the extent to which they feel free to apply their "owned" rather than "borrowed" rules. Like equity, attraction, homophily, and so many other communication concepts, self-autonomy is in the eyes of the beholder. A person with a strong internal locus of control (Rotter, 1966) may define a situation, typically construed as very constraining, as one conducive to self-autonomy.

A second implication of this perspective is that persuasion is not something one person does to another. It is a means by which persons assist each other in the shaping of their private and shared versions of reality. As such, it involves reciprocated changes in attitudes and behavior. The degree of reciprocity varies in relation to the potential for feedback afforded by the context of interaction.

Third, the choice of an effective message strategy requires that persuaders estimate the amount of persuadee-perceived self-autonomy. One of the major premises of the theoretical model to be introduced here is that persons generally prefer to be viewed as consistent, appropriate, and effective. Often they will sacrifice one of these preferences to meet the others. For example, when in Rome, they do as the Romans do. Such behavior may be inconsistent with one's own view of self, but appropriate and effective in that context.

This tripartite view of the motivation behind human behavioral choice leads to a rather simple persuasion rule of thumb: To the extent that the self is allowed to serve as a generative mechanism of persuadee behavior, appeals to personal rule consistency are useful. To the extent that the self is submerged by the demands of the context (other persons and other goals), appeals to behavioral appropriateness and/or effectiveness are more likely to generate success. Personal rules may still operate to guide behavior, but they are not of paramount concern in such situations. In Chapter 5 this perspective will be examined at greater length, and in later chapters the implications for research will be explored.

It seems reasonable to begin the introduction of an alternative perspective on persuasion by focusing on the human mind. The question of whether thought precedes behavior or vice versa will be addressed in later chapters. Thought and behavior are, in any case, inextricably related. Thus, this text begins with a focus on human logic and its relationship to communication behavior. Then we will journey through the annals of persuasion literature and research, stopping at those points having the most relevance for the perspective on persuasion to be advanced in Chapter 5. The next several stops will focus on those interpersonal and noninterpersonal contexts of persuasion that differ in the amount of self-autonomy they afford. Finally, the subject of past and future research directions will be addressed.

If we do not linger long at some of your favorite spots, it is not because they do not belong to a theory of persuasion, but because any theory of human behavior is, by nature, an exercise in selective perception. It is only one version of reality. I have attempted to borrow freely from the works of many fine minds in our field. The result is an eclectic approach to persuasion that seeks to reevaluate and reconstruct rather than replace prior theory. Kuhn (1975) advises that such endeavors inevitably meet with resistance. Such resistance compels us to provide good reasons for the acceptance of anything new. It requires that knowledge remain a process of accretion rather than sporadic replacement.

Whether or not the perspective advanced herein will meet that challenge, persuasion will remain a pervasive process of human communication. Our task as social scientists must be to model that reality so that we may comprehend it. The remaining chapters take a step in that direction.

Chapter 2

LOGIC AND PERSUASION

Through frequent associations with ulterior motives for human behavior, "persuasion" has come to be considered by many an activity reserved for the unethical. On the contrary, persuasion is a form of communication in which every person who ventures forth into the company of others must participate. Persuasion is necessitated by the single fact that all of us differ in our goals and the means by which we achieve them. The inevitable result is that we often get in each other's way. The goal-seeking behavior of one person is often at cross purposes with that of another. When one person's goal achievement is blocked by the goal-seeking behaviors of another, persuasion is used to convince the offender to redefine his or her goal or alter the means to it.

The fact that people rely on each other for approval requires that they find ways to make their goal-seeking behavior appear sensible to others. Our lifestyles indicate that we are social beings in need of the company and approval of others. These needs could not be fulfilled if behaviors were forever at cross purposes. Through persuasion, an activity in which we attempt to change the behavior of those whose goals impede our own, we reduce the natural conditions of estrangement which separate us and thereby foster the development of what we know as "society."

The term *society* implies some level of agreement among its members concerning what behaviors are appropriate. There is never total agreement among societal members concerning appropriate behavior, but mass media and interpersonal communication and persuasion foster consensus on issues that threaten the society's existence. If this were sufficient to create conditions of total agreement, persuasion would be of little use. However, societies also encourage divisions of labor to keep them intact. Persons with similar goals form subgroups which, while serving the needs of the society, also threaten it by encouraging members to focus their efforts on what often results in conflicting goals. Thus, societies simultaneously create conditions of inclusion and exclusion for members. Being in one group or relationship automatically implies exclusion from another.

To prevent disagreements among group members from becoming a threat to society, explicit and implicit rules of conduct are generated and sanctions are introduced to ensure adherence. Within-group dissention is also controlled through the creation of roles varying in status. Roles are essentially well defined, consensually shared clusters of rules for behavior. Rites of passage characterized by promotions, raises, and changes of office serve to indicate clearly when and to what extent one may alter these rule clusters.

While society provides rules for behavior, the rational nature of the human mind allows individuals to be critical of these rules and thereby affords opportunities to change and violate them. People's behaviors are constrained by rules but not determined by them. Even within groups, people criticize their own rules and elicit change. Betty Cogswell (1979) has shown that while persons may agree on the definitions of particular roles, they often develop their own variant forms of these roles.

Thus, the existence of a society does not alone guarantee harmony among its members, who are always pulled toward adopting some modes of behavior and pushed to reject others. This pushing and pulling is accomplished through communication and persuasion.

THE LEARNING OF RULES

There are at least four means whereby people learn appropriate modes of behavior: association, imitation, communication, and persuasion. Association and imitation are learning activities in which even lower forms of life may participate. Dogs learn to associate their actions with certain rewards or punishments. They are also capable of imitating each other's behavior. Communication and persuasion require higher levels of cognitive functioning and consciousness. It is through these two activities that people learn what constitutes appropriate behavior as well as the reasons for such behavior. Unlike lower forms of life, humans are responsible for their behaviors and therefore need to know what is expected of them. Furthermore, given the potential for variation among learning experiences, people also need to know why a particular behavior is expected in order to defend their choices. Rules and their logic are not learned through association and imitation alone. Knowing why a behavior is appropriate requires a form of learning that must be accomplished through symbolic interaction.

If all human behavior were the product of association and imitation, persuasion would be confined to fostering new associations and providing opportunities for novel imitations. Although much human behavior results from learned associations between phenomena, the teaching of behavioral rules and their logic is achieved through communication and persuasion. These two activities are the means whereby human behavioral regularities are created and altered. Without them society as we know it would not be possible.

COMMUNICATION

If humans are social creatures concerned with eliciting the company and appreciation of others, then we may assume that they seek to understand what behaviors will facilitate this process. Communication is one means of discovering and demonstrating the appropriateness of our behavioral choices. We can learn behavioral associations and imitative behaviors without engaging in communication, but only through communication can we determine the appropriateness of such behaviors. Even a simple "hello" conveys to the recipient of that greeting the knowledge that she "counts" as a person to be recognized—perhaps that her past behaviors are generally acceptable or that there is insufficient evidence to indicate otherwise. Similarly, a professor's frown can be interpreted by a student as dissatisfaction with the student's work. The message conveyed to the student is, "What you have done is not appropriate, given my standards."

Through communication we can facilitate each other's growth or destroy each other. George Gerbner (1978) refers to the latter as "symbolic annihilation." As social beings we require the appreciation of those persons we consider significant in our lives. The adage, "Sticks and stones can break my bones but names can never hurt me," is one of the most deceptive pieces of defensive communication ever passed from generation to generation. The words others use to describe our relationships to them can inflate or devastate our egos. Through communication we weave the webs of significance that define our own selves. Through communication we learn to whom we are to be compared and to what positions we may reasonably aspire. We learn who to admire and in so doing grant these persons the power to make us feel important or irrelevant to the maintenance of their particular webs of significance.

Commnication, then, is more than the conveyance of ideas from one person to another. It is the means whereby we learn who we are and who we might become. Moreover, it is our vehicle for demonstrating how well we have accommodated our previously inappropriate modes of behavior to meet the standards of the present.

Given the power others have over one's definition of self, it is easy to understand why people seek to establish some confidence in their ability to deal with the messages of those with whom they interact. Confidence is largely a function of knowing what to expect. Several communication theorists have advocated a discovery emphasis in their description of communication. George Kelly (1955) has told us that persons are in the "business of prediction." The uncertainty reduction theory advocated by Charles Berger and Richard Calabrese (1975: 100) proposes that "when strangers meet, their primary concern is one of uncertainty reduction or increasing predictability about the behavior of both themselves and others in the interaction." Finally, rules theorists (Pearce and Cronen, 1978; Cushman, 1977; Reardon-Boynton, 1978, 1979; Shimanoff, 1980) have proposed that people develop cognitive schemas that prescribe and/or describe what "should" occur in interactions. Each of these perspectives implies that much conscious planning and executing goes into our communication. Kathleen Reardon (1981) has attempted to modify that impression by recognizing that the repeatable nature of the contexts in which we interact allows us to behave much of each day with little conscious self-monitoring. Gail Fairhurst (1980) has drawn a distinction between the roles of the rule activator, whose behavioral selection is below consciousness, and the rule applicator, who views the context as sufficiently problematic to require conscious behavioral selection.

On the surface it may appear that the perspective on communication offered in this text also ascribes to an image of the communicator as consistently conscientious in his or her pursuit of, in this case, appropriate behavior. It should be noted that while I see the discovery and demonstration of one's appropriateness to be a product of communication, I do not believe that it is generally the conscious purpose of communication. Furthermore, some interactions provide more information about one's appropriateness than others. Most of us have had the experience of communicating merely to avoid the discomfort of silence in an elevator or to be sociable at a party of strangers. In both cases we were, in a sense, attempting to do what was appropriate, but it is unlikely that we discovered much about ourselves. Similarly, in our interactions with familiar persons, much of what we do is redundant. Behavior that has become expected is often performed without conscious monitoring. In such cases only deviation from the expected will elicit conscious behavioral choice and appraisal. Hence, while one of the major by-products of communication is discovering appropriate behavior, both the amount discovered and the degree of consciousness involved are influenced by features of the context.

Demonstration of behavioral appropriateness, an accomplishment of communication, is an activity primarily studied by developmentalists. Demonstration has been treated as an activity reserved for children. It seems unreasonable, however, to conclude from the dearth of developmental research focusing on postadolescent subjects that only children have the need to demonstrate their progress as socially competent beings. All human beings need to be advised of how well they are accepted and appreciated by others.

Donald Cushman et al. (1980: 6-7) consider the self-concept a generative mechanism of interpersonal communication. Their perspective on the role of self-concept in communication contributes to explanations of both the discovery and the demonstration functions of communication. They see the self-concept as "capable of governing and directing human action." Moreover, they view self-concept as consisting of rules that generate action and are maintained or changed through feedback about action. Feedback allows the actor to determine "the 'goodness-of-fit' between his/her belief about the appropriate choice and his/her progress toward attainment of his/her purpose."

The Cushman et al. perspective is consistent with that advanced in this text concerning the desire of individuals to see themselves as doing what is appropriate by some set of preferred rules. However, their perspective does not emphasize the context of communication as influencing the degree of conscious self-monitoring, nor do they describe the self-concept as multifaceted.

Cushman et al. propose that the self-concept has two dimensions, the idealized and the real. In actuality, individuals may have several facets of self, each having an idealized and a real version. David Swanson and Jesse Delia (1976: 19) contend that, "just as the diamond is multifaceted, so is the self multidimensional. Thus, in communication, we are not bound to a narrow range of ways of behaving and presenting ourselves; instead, we have a diversity of 'facets,' any one of which might be 'turned toward' a particular social situation."

While the perspective on communication in this text concurs with the Cushman et al. definition of self-concept as a generative mechanism of interpersonal communication, in place of their perception of the self-concept as "the" rationale for choices of action, I see self-concept as one very important rationale which, as evidenced by its multifaceted nature, derives part of its definition from the context of interaction. A reciprocal relationship exists between the self and the context. As mentioned earlier, the familiarity of the context influences the extent to which conscious rule selection and behavioral monitoring are required.

PERSUASION

Given the foregoing discussion, the question to be addressed now is, What is the relationship between persuasion and communication? As mentioned earlier, they are both means of learning appropriate behavior. The most important distinction between the two, however, is that persuasion is always a conscious activity. Gerald Miller and Michael Burgoon (1973) advocate this position. While they would not deny that people can unintentionally influence, their perspective implies that it is impossible unintentionally to persuade. Persuasion involves conscious intent.

A necessary but not sufficient condition of persuasion not applicable to communication is the perception by one individual that the behavior of at least one other is inconsistent, inappropriate, or ineffective by some set of standards. If this behavioral inpropriety is perceived by the observer as sufficiently threatening to his or her goals to warrant the effort, attempts to persuade the offender may follow. A second condition of persuasion, then, is the perception of a threat to one's own goals. The threat need not be explicit—merely sufficient in the eyes of one individual to warrant an attempt to change the behavior of the other(s).

A third difference between persuasion and communication involves self-concept. Self-concept plays a much more central role in interpersonal persuasion than it does in communication. The suggestion that one should change always implies some level of inadequacy on the part of the persuadee. Also, persuaders do not seek to change the behavior of others unless such change has implications for their own self-concepts. It is important to remember that self-concept is defined herein as a set of rules that not only guide one's own behavior but also tell people how they can expect others to behave toward or with them in a particular context. If these important expectations are violated and no account is provided, then the occurrence of persuasion becomes probable.

Noninterpersonal persuasion is often less immediately self-concept-generated for the persuader than is interpersonal persuasion. For example, while mass media advertisements may appeal to dimensions of the persuadee's ideal self-concept, there is little immediate feedback to the advertisement agency (persuader) concerning its image. So we may assume that the primary generative mechanism of mass media advertising is more extrinsic in nature than can be explained by reference to self-concept alone. Monetary profits are often the most obvious and most intensive generative mechanism of advertising behavior. For the persuadee, self-concept enhancement may be as important a reason to buy a product as monetary gain is a reason to advertise it.

Despite the differences in generative mechanisms operating in interpersonal and noninterpersonal modes of persuasion, the definition and preconditions of persuasion as defined in this text apply to both. Persuasion is, in all cases, the activity of demonstrating and attempting to change the behavior of at least one person through symbolic interaction. It is conscious and occurs (a) when a threat to at least one person's goals is observed and (b) when the source and degree of this threat are sufficiently important to warrant the expenditure of effort involved in persuasion.

This definition excludes those situations in which an individual convinces himself or herself that someone's behavior has changed in the desired direction without symbolic interaction. Convincing oneself that some person or condition has changed is self-persuasion. It is an *intra*personal activity which, while important, is not the focus of this text. Interpersonal and mass persuasion involving verbal and/or nonverbal symbol exchange will be of primary interest in the next several chapters.

It is important to note that the term *persuasion*, like *communication*, is not used in this text as an implication of success. Persuasion and communication are activities involving at least two persons whose joint actions determine the outcome. Persuasion is not something one person does *to* another but something he or she does *with* another. Even if the persuader does not feel that the goal of changing the behavior of another has been accomplished, persuasion, as an activity, has still occurred. Use of the terms *persuader* and *persuadee* in this text is not intended to imply that persuasion is a unidirectional activity. A person rarely changes another individual's perspective or behavior without altering some of his or her own rules in the process.

The acceptance of the communication and persuasion perspective introduced in this chapter requires a subject and context orientation. *Consistency, appropriateness,* and *effectiveness* cannot be defined without considering when, where, and for whom. The next section focuses on how people's perceptions of context influence their behavioral choices as well as how those perceptions can be used to alter rule repertoires and their accompanying logics.

THE LOGIC OF BEHAVIORAL CHOICE

When individuals perceive the behavior of others as threatening to their goals, two conditions may be faulted: (a) These persons do not share the same rules, and/or (b) while they may share the same rules, their logics for rule application differ. When both conditions are present, persuasion becomes a twofold process. The persuadee's rule repertoire must be altered, and a logic must be provided which makes the application of the preferred rule sensible.

Given this perspective on persuasion, an understanding of the relationship between rules and their logic is imperative. A logic for rule usage consists of those conditions that make the rule sensible. As Gottlieb (1968: 41) explains, "the internal structure of rules does not indicate all the conditions which must be satisfied for a rule to operate as a rule." He adds that rules that might operate quite satisfactorily in one context may not do so in others. Rules are stored in the minds of the individuals who use them to guide their behavioral choices. As indicated in Figure 2.1, each rule consists of conditions for its usage, and behavioral options varying in normative force and desired consequent(s). A particular behavior is sensible to the actors if they perceive a high degree of correspondence between their perceptions of the context and the antecedent conditions specified in the rule that guided the behavioral choice. For example, if a policeman stops a vehicle and informs the driver that he was speeding, that information about the antecedent conditions makes the stopping of the car sensible. Imagine for a moment a driver being advised by a police officer that he was speeding. If the driver informs the policeman that the only reason he exceeded the speed limit was to get his pregnant wife to the hospital, we may assume that the driver expects the policeman to redefine the action of speeding as sensible in this emergency situation. This redefinition of the antecedent conditions, if accepted by the policeman, could render the assignment of a ticket inappropriate. Should the policeman hand the driver a ticket anyway, we may assume that while a pregnant wife in labor may be a sufficient reason for a husband to violate a speeding rule, it is insufficient grounds for policemen, in general or in this particular situation, to apply another rule.

Gottlieb (1968: 41) describes this situation as a lack of correspondence between the full account of the events in the case and the "protasis" of a rule—that part which specifies the circumstances in which it operates. The policeman and the driver may have agreed that speeding usually results in a ticket, but the driver considered the additional condition of his wife's

Figure 2.1   Regulative Rule Model (Reardon, 1979)
NOTE: See T. J. Smith (1976) for an explanation of preference as a normative force.

pregnancy to be a reason for not applying that rule. The policeman, however, saw only that the man was speeding—the major condition making the rule application sensible to him.

Thus, people can agree that a rule should exist but can disagree on the logic of its application. Persuasion in such circumstances requires attempts by the persuader to create in the mind of the persuadee a new perception of the antecedent conditions (protasis) that make sensible the application of the preferred rule.

Shimanoff (1980: 57) defines a rule as "a followable prescription that indicates what behavior is obligated, preferred, or prohibited in certain contexts." She considers rules to be contextual and shares the contention of others (Snyder, 1971; Pearce, 1976; Phillipsen, 1977) that rules should cover types of acts rather than specific acts. Since rules imply regularities of behavioral choice, it is reasonable to insist that their scope conditions be sufficiently broad to apply in many situations. This characteristic of rules leaves considerable room for differing interpretations concerning the degree of correspondence between those scope conditions specified in the rule and actor perceptions of the actual situation. It is this potential for disagreement over interpretations of correspondence that makes the role of persuasion so important. If we had a rule for every situation rather than for types of situations, consensus concerning correspondence would be increased. The opportunities for persuasion would be limited because judgment and reasoning would only occasionally be needed to defend interpretations.

The fact is that we do not live in a world characterized by a rationality afforded by a near-perfect correspondence between the scope conditions of rules and actual events. Rules are necessarily generalizations. As Gottlieb (1968) explains, the protasis of a rule must necessarily be more general than the facts of the case; otherwise rules would lose their utility for further applications. Moreover, it is impossible for anyone to know the "actual event." People must interpret events and in so doing only recognize and use for rule selection a subset of the "actual" conditions.

Accepting that rules must necessarily be general paves the way for a perspective which proposes that participation in persuasion requires both the ability to (a) recognize what rule a persuadee is following, and (b) determine which conditions of the actual event he or she used to render the application of that rule sensible. It is not sufficient to know the rules others possess in their repertoire. To be persuasive one must also be sensitive to the logic that makes those rules applicable.

To this point the logic of rule application has been defined as the perceived correspondence between the antecedent conditions of a rule and actor perceptions of the actual situation. It is important to include in that definition of logic some consideration of actor's desired consequents as well. The term *antecedent conditions* implies that some perception of the context comes before the application of a rule which makes it the sensible thing to do. Most rules researchers give little attention to the fact that contextual conditions existing outside of the individual are not the only consideration preceding behavioral selection. Humans are capable of thinking beyond their behaviors to the consequences. They are also capable of using past experiences to determine the probability that a particular behavior performed in a given context will lead to a desired consequent. So it is not merely the correspondence between the present context and the antecedent conditions of the rule, but also the actor's perception of the correspondence between the conditions that successfully led to the desired consequents in the past and the present situation.

This form of correspondence provides another area of potential disagreement between interactants—disagreement over which rule is appropriate. Once again, opportunities for persuasion obtain. Convincing a persuadee that an alternative desired consequent is more appropriate given the context encourages a revision of rule application in future situations of that type. As mentioned earlier, people generally prefer to do what is consistent, appropriate, and effective. The persuader's task is to determine whether the persuadee will be more influenced by appeals to societal standards, relationship standards, or personal standards when demonstrating the superiority of an alternative desired consequent.

In the policeman example, the driver could suggest explicitly or by implication that the helpful thing to do would be to skip the ticket. In this instance, he would be suggesting that the desired consequent of punishing a lawbreaker, given the pregnant wife's condition, is not as appropriate as helping in an emergency. If the policeman sees the desired consequent of enforcing the law as more important than helping the person on the street, then rule revision is unlikely. However, if he accepts helping behavior as a means of being both a good policeman and a nice guy, then he may accept the wife's condition as a reason to redefine the context as an emergency and apply a helping rule.

This example suggests the value of perceiving desired consequents as separate from antecedent conditions in the study of persuasion. Persuaders can use what they think the desired consequent(s) of the persuadee should be in the particular context as another correspondence strategy. Should they also provide an alternative rule that is sensible to the persuadee, the chances of rule application revision are enhanced.

The major proposition to be derived from the foregoing description of the role of persuasion is that it requires some sensitivity to the logic of others. The well-accepted "common ground" perspective on persuasion, which suggests that persuaders locate some point of agreement between themselves and those they wish to influence, evidences a similar philosophy. Establishing common ground is, however, at best a first step. Persuasion involves more than demonstrating an appreciation for the persuadee's rules. A necessary prerequisite to persuasion is a sensitivity to the cognitive construal processes of others. Much like the debate coach who insists that his or her negative team learn to think as if they were an affirmative team, communicators who wish to improve their ability to alter rule repertoires and logics must sensitize themselves to the thought processes of others. In future chapters, those abilities that influence competence in persuasion will be discussed at greater length. However, the next section of this chapter will be devoted to an understanding of those cognitive processes that influence behavioral choice.

CONSTRUCTS AND RULES:
THE FOUNDATIONS OF BEHAVIORAL LOGIC

The very fact that people interpret events means that they can never experience reality directly. They must create their own reality through the application of cognitive schemas which are at once the product of and the foundation for communication and persuasion. These cognitive associations take the form of constructs and behavioral rules. Since the perspective on persuasion advanced in the text relies heavily on the logic of rule application, an understanding of the relationship of rules to constructs is important.

Personal Construct Theory

According to George Kelly (1955), people strive to make their worlds predictable. They develop constructs to interpret phenomena. According to Kelly, constructs are analogous to yardsticks. They serve to measure the meaning of an object, action, or context. They operate much like bipolar adjectival scales. Consider, for example, the characteristics one must have to be a friend. Some of them might be a sense of humor, talkativeness, consideration for others, and punctuality. Kelly contends that each adjective one uses to describe a person or object or an event has a bipolar opposite. The above set of constructs, then, reflects the following set of opposites for a friend: sense of humor/morbid, talkative/quiet, considerate/inconsiderate, punctual/tardy.

Constructs are developed by individuals to assist them in their interpretations of their world. They differ from person to person because different experiences generate different constructs. Yet in all cases they operate to make the relationship events more predictable. The amount of predictability required for comfort is a personal matter. We do know from the works of Berlyne (1960, 1963), de Charmes (1968), and others that some novelty is required by the human mind to keep it alert. Humans are "driven" to explore. Too much novelty, however, is dysfunctional to productive thought and behavior. Since the world we live in provides many opportunities to experience novelty, people expend much of their mental energy searching for and maintaining order and predictability.

It is not motives or drives alone that impel persons to action. Kelly (1955) states: "Suppose we began by assuming that the fundamental thing about life is that it goes on; the going on is the thing itself. It isn't that motives make a man come alert and do things; his alertness is an aspect of his very being." In essence, Kelly implies that people do not react to the past but seek accurately to address the problems of the future. They seek to develop cognitive schemas that will facilitate their ability to anticipate the future. The following fundamental postulate and corollaries constitute the central tenets of Kelly's Personal Construct Theory:

> Fundamental Postulate: A person's processes are psychologically channeled by the way he or she anticipates events.

This fundamental postulate indicates that a person's main purpose in life is to make sense of the world and to test conclusions on the basis of their predictive capacities. Like scientists, all people construct hypotheses on the basis of past experiences and then proceed to test those hypotheses by applying them to the world. This fundamental postulate is elaborated in the following eleven corollaries:

> Construction Corollary: A person anticipates events by construing their replications.

People do not live in a world of consistently different happenings. On the contrary, much of what is done one day (getting out of bed, getting dressed for work, eating breakfast, and so forth) will be repeated the next. Bannister and Fransella (1977: 20) interpret Kelly's construction corollary as meaning that "basic to our making sense of our world and of our lives is our continual detection of repeated themes, our categorizing of these themes and our segmenting of the world in terms of them." There would be no attempt to predict accurately if we could not detect replications of events. Unlike most animals, we are creatures of the future, a time period given meaning by our interpretations of it in light of our past.

> Individuality Corollary: People differ from each other in their construction of events.

No two persons ever see a single event in exactly the same way. Their past experiences, even for two identical twins residing in the same womb, are not equivalent. Since it is our past which gives meaning to the present and future, our interpretations and anticipations are never identical with those of others, a fact that exacerbates the problems of communication.

> Organization Corollary: Each person characteristically evolves, for convenience in anticipating events, a construction system embracing ordinal relationships between constructs.

This corollary implies that a person's constructs are interrelated. Larger, more abstract constructs subsume more concrete constructs. For some people "persuasion" is a construct that may be subsumed by the construct "communication." The subordination of some constructs by others formulates within the human mind a logic system used primarily to anticipate the future.

> Dichotomy Corollary: a person's construction system is composed of a finite number of dichotomous constructs.

Kelly considers it useful to see constructs as having two poles, affirmative and negative. For every positive descriptive term in a person's repertoire, a negative counterpart exists. As Kelly explains, even when we are unable to provide a label for contrast, we do not affirm without implicitly negating. In other words, to state that a person is attractive is to imply that he or she is not unattractive.

> Choice Corollary: People choose for themselves that alternative in a dichotomized construct through which they anticiapte the greater possibility for the elaboration of their own system.

People do not become permanently imprisoned by a construct system. On the contrary, these systems are elaborated upon and occasionally disconfirmed over the course of many years. Popular books such as *The Women's Room*, by French, *The Seasons of a Man's Life* by Levinson et al., and *Passages* by Gail Sheahy suggest the occurrence of evolution and revolutionary changes of evaluative schema throughout the life cycle. In contrast to the Freudians, who view people as the victims of their infancies, Kelly argues that people are not the victims of their pasts, though they may enslave themselves by adhering to unalterable visions of what the past means, thereby fixating the present (see Bannister and Fransella, 1979: 19). The change of a construct system, then, is a matter of choice, an action rather than a reaction.

> Range Corollary: A construct is convenient for the anticipation of a finite range of events only.

The "range of convenience" of any construct is all those things to which one might eventually find that construct applicable. The construct *girl*, for example, is used by many persons to refer to all females. The individual who has been sensitized to the inequities inherent in our language might use *girl* as the child female equivalent of *boy* and *woman* as the adult female equivalent of *man*, thereby limiting the range of convenience of each construct.

> Experience Corrollary: A person's construction system varies as he or she successively construes the replication of events.

This corollary is related to the choice corollary in that it implies change. It steps beyond that corollary, however, by positing that such change is a result of successful and unsuccessful validation of constructs. Constructs are predictive, not merely ways of labeling objects and events in our world. If predictions prove accurate, then it is likely that a construct will be retained. However, if a construct leads consistently to inaccurate predictions, we may feel compelled to dispense with it or modify the overall construct subsystem in which it resides (see Bannister, 1966: 366).

> Modulation Corollary: The variation in a person's construction system is limited by the permeability of the constructs within whose range of convenience the variants lie.

In this corollary Kelly implies that each person has a more or less rigid construct system. It is likely that rigidity of constructions will lead to more frequent invalidation of predictions, thus requiring more frequent change. The person whose construct system includes permeable constructs may comfortably assimilate the slightly unexpected as a variation upon rather than an invalidation of a construct. The construct *permeable-impermeable* refers to the degree to which a construct can assimilate new experiences into its range of convenience, thereby generating new implications. It may be that *cognitive complexity* is in large part a function of one's range of convenience and construct permeability.

> Fragmentation Corollary: A person may successively employ a variety of construction subsystems that are inferentially incompatible with each other.

This corollary merely indicates that the construing of events is a personal matter. Successful usage of one construct or construct system to explain an event and generate behavior does not guarantee that the same construction of that type of event will occur in the future. The degree of consistency demonstrated by an individual is a matter of personal choice.

> Commonality Corollary: To the extent that one person employs a construction of experience similar to that employed by another, his or her processes are psychologically similar to those of the other person.

This corollary specifies that people are similar to the extent that they construe events in similar ways. Communication is facilitated by similarity and inhibited by differences in construal processes. The next and final corollary indicates, however, that we need not possess the same construct systems to understand each other.

> Sociality Corollary: To the extent that one person construes the construction processes of another, he or she may play a role in a social process involving the other person.

Our interpretation of others' construct systems provides the foundation for our influence on others. People recognize that they are not the same as others. They attempt, with more or less success, to understand just where the other individual is "coming from." The success or failure of attempts to persuade another are to a large degree a function of the accuracy with which one can construe the construct system of another. To be able to do so successfully provides persuaders with an understanding of what persuadees expect of them. This social perspective-taking is an invaluable communication skill.

CONSTRUCTIVISM

The work of communication theorists influenced by Kelly's perspective on human cognitive processes has developed into a coherent theoretical framework referred to as *constructivism*. Although constructivism is essentially consistent with Kelly's formulation, Barbara O'Keefe (1978) indicates that a communication focus has led to some important departures.

First, Kelly proposes that people behave like scientists, imposing patterns on undefined events. O'Keefe (1978: 5) rejects this interpretation, stating, "In fact, people erect interpretive systems principally through communication with and accommodation to the meaningful, pervasive, and enduring social world into which they are born." This perspective is consistent with the view advanced in this text: Communication is an activity in which we discover and demonstrate the appropriateness of our behavioral choices.

O'Keefe adds that Kelly's "man-versus-scientist" perspective implies that people consciously apply their interpretive schemas to the world. She explains that constructivist research explicitly emphasizes the *nonconscious* nature of interpretive processes. O'Keefe considers conscious attention to and examination of constructs to be an occasional occurrence.

This nonconscious view has become widely shared of late by communication theorists (Berger, 1980; Delia, 1980; Duck, 1980). While in total agreement with O'Keefe on the necessity of both departures from Kelly when studying communication, this text proposes that making the nonconscious logic of choice conscious is the first step in persuading someone to change a behavior. Although there is little evidence to suggest that people can report the logic behind their behavioral choices, it is conceivable that they can recognize a logic proposed by the persuader as a probable or improbable explantory framework for their actions. If the persuader is familiar with those construals of antecedent conditions and desired consequents that typically activate the inappropriate rule, his or her chances of proposing an alternative logic are enhanced. Hence, while conscious considerations of the cognitive construals that activate rules do not usually precede behavioral choice, bringing them to a conscious level *after* the choice is the first step in preventing future inappropriate activation of the same rule.

Jesse Delia (1977) encourages a perspective on effective communication as heavily reliant on reciprocal perspective-taking. He shares with Feffer and this author (1970) the idea that communication behavior is fundamentally involved with taking the other's viewpoint. Feffer (1970: 204) explains, "This serves to generate anticipations as to the other's complementary response to an intended action and, in turn, serves to correct or modulate the intended behavior."

Whether we can nonconsciously take the perspective of another individual is debatable. It seems more likely that some level of consciousness is required to engage in types of communication that are more than simple pattern adherence. Persuasion is one such type. It requires conscious social perspective-taking. Thus, while the communicator may not typically operate as a scientist consciously manipulating the interpretive processes of self and others, persuasion requires conscious activity.

Fortunately, through everyday communication with others the persuader has stored in his mind regularities of behavior that "fit" with certain construct clusters. Interpretations alone are insufficient to guide action. Context-specific desired consequents and construals of antecedent conditions are linked to behaviors in the form of cognitive schema referred to as *rules*. These rules and their underlying logic are discussed in subsequent sections of this chapter.

BEHAVIORAL RULES

Once constructs have been established for the interpretation of a given context, behavioral responses must be determined. The translation of impressions into behavior requires regulative rules.

As Figure 2.1 indicates, regulative rules consist of four components: antecedent conditions, behavioral options, behavioral force, and desired consequents (Reardon-Boynton, 1978). *Antecedent conditions* are all those aspects of the present situation to which the individual attends, and all his or her memories of past successes and failures in such situations. *Behavioral options* are those particular behaviors from which the individual communicator may select. The level of *behavioral force* assigned to each behavioral option indicates how necessary it is to the enactment of the episode, given the desired consequents. For example, in greeting episodes it is usually obligatory for men who meet each other for the first time to shake hands if they wish to be considered courteous. It is not generally acceptable, however, to shake hands with one's roommate upon awakening each morning. Such behavior is prohibited. Likewise, most persons consider it rude to stand close to another individual in an elevator unless the elevator is crowded, in which case such behavior is permissible. Finally, *desired consequents* are the goals of the communicator. If a person wishes to influence a friend to assist in carrying a heavy couch up to his apartment, certain forms of request, such as the addition of "please," will benefit the cause. A communicator considers the consequence in light of the antecedent conditions before slecting from the behavioral options. It would not behoove anyone to formulate rules on the basis of consequent attainment alone. The context in which the conversation occurs and past successes and failures in achieving the same or similar consequents are considered.

CONSTITUTIVE AND REGULATIVE RULES

Just as regulative rules may provide several behavioral options from which a person may select, constitutive rules may afford several contextual impressions. As mentioned earlier, the correspondence between actual reality and the antecedent conditions of a rule can never be perfect, because reality is never experienced directly; it is interpreted.

Several scholars have questioned the value of distinguishing between constitutive and regulative rules. When people perceive certain familiar contextual features and observe recognizable behaviors, they can infer that a type of activity is taking place. For example, handshaking alone may be sufficient to suggest that what is being observed "counts as " a greeting episode. Constitutive rules tell persons what certain actions within given contexts "count as." Shimanoff (1980) suggests that we discard the concept of constitutive rules since they can easily be converted to regulative rules. For example, the regulative rule derived from observing several handshaking incidents is, "If one wishes to perform a greeting ritual in this society, one should shake hands." This is a regulative rule, the existence of which informs observers that a greeting ritual is probably occurring when they see people shaking hands.

This conversion of constitutive rules to regulative rules works quite well if one infers from an observed action (handshaking) an episode (greeting ritual). However, in everyday communication, people often have to determine if the contextual features constitute an opportunity for a greeting ritual. In short, they must decide whether the conditions in the context match any of the antecedent conditions of those rules typically followed in a greeting episode. If, so, then handshaking is appropriate.

In this example, the constitutive rule for a greeting episode, which would logically imply a set of rules, makes the application of the regulative rule for handshaking sensible. People must interpret their surroundings before they can hope to know the sensible rules to apply. In the policeman example, recognizing that certain actions constitute law violation made the application of the ticketing rule sensible. The driver provided additional information about the conditions surrounding the speeding so that the policeman might define the situation as an emergency, which could render the ticketing rule inoperative.

It is not very important that communication scholars quibble over whether to discard or to retain the concept of constitutive rule. If one is not interested in knowing why a particular rule was selected over other alternative rules, then constitutive rules may be of little interest. The perspective on persuasion introduced in this text, however, is predicated on the assumption that cognitive interpretations of the context provide a rational base for the application of particular regulative rules.

Barbara O'Keefe (1978: 6) explains this relationship between context interpretation and regulative rule when she states, "The choice of strategy rests on the individual's predictions about the future from events in the past, and his strategically organized behavior serves as an implicit test of those predictions. Present action permits validation or modification of interpretive processes; future choices will reflect the success or failure of the present choice. In this way, every act collapses past, present, and future; and thus every act emerges from a new past into a new future."

The result is a reflexive relationship between constitutive and regulative rules. Cronen and Reardon (1981) provide support for the perspective that people use impressions of what episode is occurring (i.e., a fight) to interpret actions. When those actions do not confirm the episode impressions, then individual acts are observed until the pattern they form can be

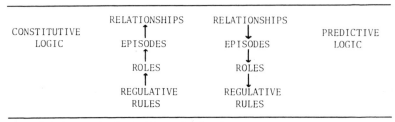

Figure 2.2   Interaction Logic Abstraction Levels

identified as an episode. Humans seek to establish a logic of action so that they can interpret and anticipate behaviors. They create logics of interaction that consist of several levels of abstraction. If, for example, an individual observes that another person is following a certain set of rules that he or she has observed used together in the past, that individual can subsume these rules under a role. Similarly, the conjunction of certain roles can constitute an episode, and episode groupings can constitute a relationship. Figure 2.2 depicts these connections between levels and demonstrates how recognizing a higher-level schema can facilitate the prediction of certain occurrences at lower levels, beyond those used as evidence for the existence at the higher level. For example, if I know that Mary has a violent relationship with Bill, I can anticipate that certain episodes will occur when they are together beyond those that I have already observed and used as evidence for labeling their relationship "violent."

Cronen, Pearce, and Harris (1980: 15) define constitutive rules as specifying "how meanings at one level of abstraction 'count as' meaningful at another." Using the statement "You are beautiful," they explain that in the context of a dating episode this speech act can be interpreted as a compliment. However, given the context of an argument, this same comment might evoke a very different relationship meaning and thus elicit very different subsequent actions. Using the Cronen and Reardon theoretical model, should the intonations accompanying this statement deviate from expected intonations, a revised episode definition may be in order.

Constitutive rules, then, specify the relationships between components at one level of abstraction which constitute another level. The observation of an individual following a certain cluster of rules constitutes the existence of a particular role. Knowing what role is being used to guide behavior then provides one portion of the contextual information which, together with other contextual features, may correspond to the antecedent conditions of a particular regulative rule. For example, certain behaviors (dress, demeanor, and so on) may indicate that someone is a policeman, a Republican, or a "preppy." Knowing that a person fits one of these roles may provide sufficient information to determine what other rules he or she is likely to follow.

People prefer to develop logics that consist of high levels of abstraction so that they can predict behavior. Seeing an individual perform a behavior may tell me that he or she is following a given rule. Knowing that the individual follows this rule does not tell me what other rules the same individual might follow. If I observe a number of the person's behaviors, however, and infer the existence of a number of rules, I can impose a logic on those rules in the form of a role. Once I know the person's role, I may make predictions about other rules he or she is likely to follow, assuming that I have had prior experiences with persons in that role.

Constitutive rules, then, are logics that tell the individual what combination of components on one level of abstraction constitutes another. Unlike regulative rules, they do not prescribe action but are used to interpret action. Once an individual knows what actions mean, he or she can use this information to activate or apply regulative rules.

A close analogy to constitutive rules found in the natural sciences is the concept of gravity. Gravity cannot be seen. It is a fiction created in Newton's mind to explain certain mathematical relations that hold between points in motion (see Rychlak, 1977). It is now a widely shared fiction. It allows us to make sense out of a number of occurrences and to predict many more. Constitutive rules are also fictions, which make sensible certain relations between (in the case of episodes) regulative rules. Knowing that a certain episode is occurring explains the presence of certain behaviors and allows the prediction of others.

The constitutive rule is a useful concept in the study of persuasion. It is important that a persuader know not only what rules exist in an individual's repertoire, but also what logic renders their activation or application sensible.

CONCLUSION

In the next two chapters we will look at how the theoretical model introduced in this chapter relates to traditional perspectives on persuasion.

This chapter has focused on introducing a perspective on persuasion, one that does not depend on attitudes and beliefs for its foundation. However, it will become obvious that the work done over the last four decades, while originating from a very different root metaphor called *behaviorism,* laid the groundwork for many of the integrations and extensions of ideas found throughout this text.

Chapter 3

THE ATTITUDE-BEHAVIOR RELATIONSHIP

Persuasion is a form of communication. As discussed in Chapter 2, it is also more conscious than other forms of communication and has as its main purpose changing the behavior of others. In this age, governed by a "You do your thing and I'll do mine" philosophy, it is natural that negative connotations should become associated with an activity engaged in to change others. However, as mentioned earlier, we deceive ourselves if we believe that a society can exist without this activity. If society is a good thing, then persuasion must be a healthy activity.

Be that as it may, the disguising of intentions is a prevalent communication behavior in our society. It is an accepted and often expected means of avoiding conflict. Even young children learn that saying what one means can sometimes be a very sure way of not getting what one wants. Recognizing the prevalence of deception in communication can be disturbing unless we consider what life would be like if all were to say what they mean. Once again, the need for rules becomes apparent. Economizing of truth is a necessity, especially when the truth might hurt. If each of us were always motivated by selfless concerns, then this might not be the case. Given that selflessness is not the norm, a certain amount of restraint is appropriate when dishing out truth. To assure our cooperation, rules have been developed to assist us in the restraint effort.

DECEPTION IN INTERPERSONAL AND
MASS MEDIA COMMUNICATION

Deception is especially prevalent in our everyday interpersonal communication. Here, too, disguised purpose is the norm. Terms like *hidden agenda* and *ulterior motive* carry negative connotations because they suggest that people may hide their true purposes. Actually, people often collaborate in deception. Mark Knapp and Mark Comadena (1979: 272) consider deception, like other forms of communication, to be mutually negotiated. These authors hit us between the eyes with our own potential for self-deception when they state, "Sometimes we consider ourselves innocent recipients of another's deceipt, but even then it is difficult to discount the role our own needs, values, and expectations play in another's message decisions."

Truth-restraining rules are so frequently applied that, to a certain extent, we have as a society developed a noncritical acceptance of deception. Many advertisements exemplify this. Gorgeous models, who may have never used a mop in their lives, show women how to change from housewife to vixen with a simple squirt of cologne. Whitened teeth are introduced as a prerequisite for sex appeal. Actors who play the role of doctors or detectives on television programs are accepted as experts on the dangers of caffeine and the benefits of travelers checks. Age appears to be something we will never experience, since the mass media's nearly exclusive emphasis on youth denies its existence.

Mass media, especially, have been given the license to deceive. According to Leo Rosten (1960: 40), they merely provide for us what we wish to see and hear: "The deficiencies of the mass media are a function, in part at least, of the deficiencies of the masses." The intellectual's disdain for the low caliber of television's content is not shared by the majority. Intellectuals "cannot believe that the subjects dear to their hearts bore or repel or overtax the capacities of their fellow citizens."

Despite the prevalence of imposed and jointly negotiated deception, few of us wish to admit that we communicate to others in order to change them. We prefer to disguise this intention. Is this unnecessary deception? Does this make us a society of liars? If taken to extreme, perhaps it does, but more often it merely reflects the fact that most people do not wish to lose the rewards that relationships with others provide. There are certain things we cannot say we are trying to do. It is impolite to say to someone, "I am trying to show you how superior I am to you in ability." Similarly, the woman who wishes to say, "I am your equal," would be wise to "dress for success" and use assertive gestures rather than state her actual purpose for doing so, if she wishes to maintain a good relationship with colleagues. Does this make her a liar? That is a tough question. If members of a society agree that the absence of certain amounts of garnishing would spoil the interpersonal stew or ruin the persuasive campaign, who can be at fault?

Debating the question of who is at fault for our acceptance of media and interpersonal deception would not prove profitable to the study of persuasion. The more important question is, How much is too much? Gumpert (1979) explains that people are not even concerned with the matter of accurate labeling in the case of television recording. To Gumpert this is an appalling situation: "Even minor or insignificant confusion of authenticity should be important. There is a need to be able to tell the difference between real and artificial, between a creation of nature and an artifact of man, between fantasy and reality, between what was, what is, and what will be". (1977: 297). Gumpert accuses us of abdicating our sensory responsibility when we do not care whether something was recorded "live" or taped. We are not "driven to authenticate mediated events," but instead naively sit back as the producer transcends the boundaries of our reality.

The student of communication must be alert to instances of deception, while recognizing that people who attempt to rid their interpersonal communication of all forms of deception will soon find themselves without friends. Even the 1970s' emphasis on self-worth has not altered that fact. Assertiveness training and books that tell us we are "O.K." or "worth it" began to grace many bookshelves during that decade. Our courts furthered the recognition of the value of an individual. "No-fault" divorce, E.R.A., nondiscrimination laws, and debates over the legality of abortion and capital punishment indicate that societal construct-system changes occurred. The effects these changes have had on interpersonal communication are far-reaching. It is acceptable to have self-oriented goals. We are in an era of greater assertiveness and more direct communication. A father of this decade need not ask the man dating his daughter, "Just what are you intentions, son?" Chances are she will already have asked that question herself.

Despite these changes, intentions cannot always be expressed. On the contrary, the overt expression of intention in interpersonal communication is still a delicate issue. In his book, *Interaction Ritual,* Erving Goffman (1967) explains how people engage in "facework" to avoid too much truth. They often cooperate in interactions to protect each other's "face" from threat. Whenever people engage in conversation they place their "faces," which Goffman defines as the positive social value people effectively claim for themselves, in jeopardy. The individual expects that others will not purposely attempt to place his or her social worth in question. Perhaps this is where deception becomes "too much"—when it is used purposely to humiliate others or to produce some threat to their self-images. In this case the regulative rule that exists to restrain the conveyance of potentially harmful truths has been misused.

People do not always live up to this obligation to save the face of another. However, we often find that no matter how angry we are at someone, a heartfelt apology leads to a face-saving response: "Oh, I hardly noticed. Don't worry about it. I do the same thing sometimes." In like manner, those who try to raise the value of their own faces by bragging will probably find others making remarks that bring them back into line: "Well, I guess you're pretty pleased with yourself, huh?"

Sometimes it is necessary to attempt to tell someone the truth about some negative trait. To do so directly is not usually acceptable. Goffman (1967: 30) points out that we tend to prefer tactful communication. Tact, in regard to facework, depends on the tacit agreement to communicate via hint: "The *rule* here is that the sender ought not to act as if he had officially conveyed the message he has hinted at, while the recipients have the right and obligation to act as if they have not officially received the message contained in the hint." Goffman further explains that people find communication through hint useful because hintable communication is deniable and can be used to warn others that, should they persist in the annoying behavior, they may lose face. Rather tricky, you say? Surely, but also extremely important to competent communication in a society where people do not expect direct communication of unpleasant intentions.

Given the fact that telling the "whole truth and nothing but the truth" is reserved for courtrooms and not conversations, it is easy to see why persuasion is such a complex activity. The task of discovering why individuals decide to behave in a certain manner is quite formidable if they actively engage in efforts to disguise their true purpose. Research provides little reason for optimism in this matter. It appears that members of our culture are not very good at detecting lying strangers (Hocking, Bauchner, Kaminski, and Miller, 1979; Bauchner, Brandt, and Miller, 1977; Ekman and Friesen, 1974a; Shulman, 1973). Moreover, familiarity does not always increase detection ability (Bauchner, 1978), and we may therefore assume that in contexts where deception is the rule, the identification of constitutive and regulative rules is likely to be quite difficult.

Perhaps the best defense in such cases is a good offense. Persuaders must put themselves into a discovery frame of mind. They must attend to those deviations from normal communication which they typically ignore. Self-monitoring research (Snyder, 1974) indirectly supports this idea. It appears that high self-monitors are more accurate at identifying deceivers than are low self-monitors. It seems reasonable to assume that a shift to a higher level of self-monitoring when engaging in the conscious activity of persuasion may facilitate the identification of those behavioral rules which are embedded in deceptive nonverbal and verbal action. Thus, while deception poses a problem for persuaders, it is not a formidable obstacle.

RESPONSIBILITY: THE REASON FOR RULE-FOLLOWING

The prevalence of deception in our daily communication is indicative of the lengths to which people will go to maintain their self-images and relationships. As noted previously, research indicates that most people are not especially proficient at detecting deception. Our skill at creating conditions of deception seems unmatched by our ability to recognize it.

In any case, it is clear that to engage successfully in social interaction one cannot merely tell the truth. As Knapp and Comadena (1979: 271) point out, truth is relative. Everything that can be true can also be false, given the right people and circumstances. What is a vicious, harmful lie for one person may be an act of loving kindness for another: "Definitions of truth and deception, then, are person- and context-dependent. They are not, in terms of social interaction, at opposite ends of a continuum but appear as close and inseparable cousins."

The importance of discretion to social interaction has far-reaching implications for the study of persuasion. Literally centuries of study have been devoted to uncovering the necessary linkages between cognitive appraisals of persons, objects and events, and associated behavior. Yet, even today, little can be said with confidence about the connection of attitudes and behavior. If, however, one looks at the attitude research of the last several decades, one very important aspect of human activity seems to have been sorely neglected—those rules that prohibit the behavioral demonstration of attitudes that could threaten social interactions, relationships, and society.

As long as people are held responsible for their behaviors and are capable of monitoring those behaviors, there can be little hope of finding necessary relationships between attitudes and behavior, beliefs and behavior, and intentions and behavior, without considering the context of such action and the associated rules. Even very young children recognize that they and others are responsible for their behaviors and that the accidental and the intentional require quite different motive attributions.

Piaget (1932), in his book *The Moral Judgment of the Child,* subsumed both intention and motive under the broader concept of subjective responsibility. *Subjective responsibility* refers to the child's attention to internal and hence subjective processes in other people, the child's judgment about the intentional or accidental nature of an individual's overt behavior, and the child's conclusions about the underlying motive for that behavior. *Objective responsibility,* on the .other hand, refers to a focus on the external, observable features of an action, such as its consequences. Developmental theories of intention indicate that children learn to formulate attributions of causality as part of the process of socialization. According to Piaget (1954), a notion of causality appears to be present even at the level of sensorimotor intelligence. Piaget (1969) explained that up to the age of 4 or 5, the child assigns a psychological purpose to everything, even inanimate objects. Around the age of 5 or 6 the child begins to apply the concept of purpose to humans only.

Despite conflicting literature on the age at which children come to recognize purposeful behavior in others, most studies indicate an increasing capacity with age to assign intentions and motives to the agent of observed action. The former deals with whether the action was purposeful or accidental, the latter with the reasons for the purposeful action. Keasey (1977) explains that motives and intentionality are quite different, in that it is only when an act has been judged intentional that motives need come into consideration.

In later chapters the concept of motive will be discussed in terms of accounts for action. For now, it is important to realize that people learn to differentiate between the accidental and the intentional. The concurrent realization that they too are judged by their intentional actions makes them cautious in their behavioral choices, a fact frequently neglected in early twentieth-century persuasion research.

THE AGE OF ATTITUDE RESEARCH

Before plunging headlong into the maze of attitude research filling library shelves, it seems useful to point out a few characteristics of social science which may at times have led researchers astray. *Attitude* is a hypothetical construct. This means that while we firmly believe that it exists, it cannot be directly measured. Can you touch or see an attitude? If so, you are one up on the rest of us. The only thing we can do is look for something that reflects attitude. Behavior was once the most obvious choice. It was assumed that changing one's behavior implied a change in attitude as well.

It may be apparent already that this linkage might not be as direct as once hypothesized. However, it must be remembered that a majority of the research of the 1950s and 1960s was rooted in a traditional behaviorist paradigm. In the quest to locate a measurable manifestation of attitude, some researchers closed their minds to cognitive influence on behavior. They categorized the world into the observable and the worthless. The student of this era was taught to consider anything that could not be observed as not worth bothering about. The result was a generation of bright minds suffering from a dysfunctional ailment that Kelly (1955) referred to as a "hardening of the categories." Before we come down too hard on behaviorism, however, we should consider our own present-day perspectives. Perhaps they too limit our abilities to see clearly and respond critically to our own work. Bannister and Fransella's (1977) opinion of such uncritical thinking sponsored in the name of scientific rigor is apparent in their discussion of memory research. As a result of the influence of faculty psychology, researchers insisted on studying human functions separately, in spite of the fact that they cannot be lived separately. They explain, with a touch of sarcasm, that "any experimental psychologist who has ever done a study of, say, memory, has watched his stubborn subjects continue to cognize, emote, perceive, sense and so on, even though the experiment only called upon them to remember" (1977: 52).

Even today, researchers often insist on taking the person out of the context in which he or she exists. Bannister (1968) reminds us that a person is no more his cerebral cortex than he is his left earhole. It might also be worth considering the unpleasant thought that there may be some things worth studying that may not be observable. Even more painful is the recognition that there may be some human activities outside the grasp of scientific analysis.

It is easy to be critical now; hindsight is 20-20. One lesson we may glean from this unfortunate segmentation of the individual is that any particular view of human behavior is subject to error. Maintaining an open mind when studying human behavior is imperative. As early as 1947, Doob, despite the fact that he had contributed significantly to the analysis of the concept of attitude, proposed that it be dropped from social science. LaPiere (1934: 102-111), an attitude researcher himself, discussed the problems inherent in attitude measurement. He explained, "Whatever our attitude on the validity of 'verbalization' may be, it must be recognized that any study of attitudes through direct questioning is open to serious objection, both because of the limitations of the sampling method and because in classifying attitudes the inaccuracy of human judgment is an inevitably variable."

Many attitude researchers of the 1940s were aware of the problems of definition and measurement. Yet over twenty years later, during the 1960s and 1970s, when this author was a young undergraduate behaviorist, attitude was still the focus of communication research. A waste of time? Not likely. In defense of the diligent attitude researcher, Isidor Chein's (1967) attempt to ebb the tide of criticism aimed at the ambiguous term *attitude* is quoted here:

> The present writer, at least, does not consider the demonstration that a term is ambiguously and inconsistently used as sufficient reason for discrediting it on scientific discourse. Words that have real referents are necessarily as ambiguous as their referents are vaguely apprehended. To abandon a word because it is not precisely defined is to give up the scientific quest before it has begun. One begins by vaguely observing something (whether it be matter, or intelligence, or attitude) and gradually sharpens one's observation until the word designating this observed something is more and more precisely defined. Science, after all, begins in ignorance [1967: 51].

It can probably be safely said that the study of attitude was not abandoned too soon. We social scientists do not give up easily. As Duck (1980) states, journal articles do not conclude with the suggestion that "less work needs to be done." However, the final rejection of attitude research was not a unanimous announcement of the end of forty or more years of wasted research. It was as Doob (1967) intended it to be, "a happy day for social science," since this event signified "the emergence of a more integrated and scientific system of human behavior."

Learning through science is neither rapid nor always pleasant. It would be less painful, however, if we could recognize that insisting upon "hardening one's categories" slows the wheels of progress. Critical thinking is always necessary. Without it we become the victims of trained incapacities. One example of this from present-day science is our uncritical emphasis on reliability. Kelly (1955) defines reliability as "a measure of the extent to which a test is insensitive to change. Bannister and Fransella (1977: 76) contend that instead of expecting a measure to yield near-identical scores on all occasions, one should decide whether a change should be expected. The aim of the social scientist should be to understand the meaning of change, not to merely pass it off as an initial interference with reliability of tests by an irresponsible subject, to be regarded as error variance.

Recognizing the tentative nature of any perspective, we are now ready to embark on a voyage through attitude theory and research.

THE ATTITUDE-BEHAVIOR DILEMMA

In a 1975 article, "Faith, Mystery, and Data: An Analysis of 'Scientific' Studies of Persuasion," Charles Larson and Robert Sanders bring into serious question the conclusions derived from several decades of scientific investigations of persuasion. Larson and Sanders (1975: 178) pose two major questions: "(a) Why has persuasion been treated as an independent research topic, rather than as a sub-species of communication? and (b) Why has the most typical experimental procedure been to assess the effect of isolated variables on respondents' attitudes; do persuasion variables affect nothing but attitudes?"

To answer these questions, they direct us to three propositions implicit in persuasion research:

[1] Persuasion brings about changes in people's attitudes.

[2] Attitudes are constraints on behavior, or predispositions to respond.

[3] Persuasion brings about changes in what people will (or will not) do, because it affects attitudes which in turn affect behavior [1975: 178].

Larson and Sanders contend that past general commitment to these propositions is questionable, since there has been little direct effort to prove them. They claim that these propositions, the foundation of persuasion research, have been treated like axioms rather than as the "empirical claims they really are."

While proposition 1 appears reasonable enough, proposition 2, that attitudes constrain behavior, is questionable in light of the fact that little correspondence between attitude and behavior has been found. Larson and Sanders suggest that rather than question such a strong foundation for research, two rationalizations can be offered. Larson and Sanders may be a bit strong in their claim that no one other than they have had the temerity to suggest that attitudes do not affect behavior. It is true, however, that even those who have questioned the relationship have not done so with sufficient vehemence. As a result, at least two rationalizations persist for accepting proposition 2. One is that "there has been little attitude-behavior correspondence because of a general failure to accurately measure attitudes." The other is that the paucity of evidence for attitude-behavior correspondence shows the relationship to be "more complex and indirect than has been thought" (Larson and Sanders, 1975: 179).

Larson and Sanders consider these arguments unconvincing and propose that an examination of them is needed. They reason that such a probe could undermine the justification for the past conduct of scientific studies of persuasion. While no new knowledge can ever render past efforts useless, it is reasonable to expect that few people would wish to rock the boat until its sinking is inevitable. Still, as Larson and Sanders maintain, it is the role of the scientist to avoid embracing any proposition as "an article of faith."

Larson and Sanders (1975: 180) reexamined existing research in persuasion and found that "data are not consistent with the assumptions that led to the undertaking in the first place—and what is worse, those inconsistencies were not noted when the research was reported." They ultimately suggest that the necessary relationship between internal states and behavior be reconstructed. They propose an alignment hypothesis that states, basically, that suasory discourse affects what people *say* rather than what they *do*. They provide an example of a man who adjusts his verbal behavior in terms of the social function it serves. If a man wishes to impress his boss, what he says may have no connection with what he really feels. If so, then there is no reason to examine any hypothesized predispositions the man might have.

Although Larson and Sanders find more support in the literature for the alignment hypothesis than for proposition 2, this does not mean that people always compromise themselves in light of situational demands. Some individuals may indeed tell the boss just exactly how they feel. In such cases it may be helpful to know what "feelings" an individual has about the subject in question as well as his or her relationship to the person(s) with whom he or she is communicating.

Larson and Sanders's strongest contribution may not lie so much in their willingness to "rock the boat" as in their conclusion that persuasion is a "psychosocial" act. This view implies a new view of persuasion as a means by which people adjust to each other. It is a relational perspective rather than predominantly source- or receiver-oriented. Further, as they suggest, a psychosocial perspective of persuasion refocuses our research efforts on discovering "how such acts are constructed and understood rather than which elements of such acts elicit which response" (1975: 193).

In Chapter 1, persuasion was defined as an attempt to change the inappropriate, inconsistent, or ineffective behaviors of others. It is possible to consider the source and receiver as equal participants in this process as they adjust their construals of the context and their behavior in it to meet or conflict with the expectations of other and self. This appears on especially useful perspective for interpersonal persuasion, where reciprocity facilitates mutual change in perspective and/or behavior.

The question to be asked at this point, however, is what is to be gained by exploring past theory and research if the propositions on which these rest are faulty? Well, first of all, as mentioned before, new knowledge never renders past thinking obsolete. While the behaviorist paradigm has recently come into question because of an increasing recognition of the role of choice in human behavior, the work that came out of that era has much to offer the student of persuasion. A sense of history can be used not only to avoid similar mistakes but also to clarify how we got where we are today. Most important, it is likely that we will find treasures of self-erudition among the antique shops of past theory and research that, if restored and placed in a context complementing their original grandeur, may render even greater our understanding of the process of persuasion. For these reasons, the next section is devoted to an examination of behavioristic conceptualizations of the concept "attitude" and its relationship to a new contextualist model of persuasion.

ATTITUDE: AN ALTERNATIVE VIEW

Richard LaPiere (1934) extracted from the diversity of opinion surrounding attitude the points of agreement among attitude theorists. They generally agreed that attitudes are "acquired out of social experience and provide the individual organism with some degree of preparation to adjust, in a well-defined way, to certain types of social situations if and when these situations arise" (1934: 26).

He added, however, that the popular questionnaire method of eliciting attitudes ignores the quite obvious absence of a necessary correlation between symbolic (speech) and nonsymbolic (action) behavior. His classic study of American attitudes toward Chinese people substantiates this claim. In a ten-thousand-mile motor trip across the United States with a Chinese couple, LaPiere reported that, despite strong anti-Chinese sentiment characteristic of that decade, they were received at 66 hotels, auto camps, and tourist homes, and were turned away at only one. They were served in 184 restaurants and cafes scattered throughout the country and treated with "more than ordinary consideration" at 72 of them. After six months had elapsed between the overt acceptance of the Chinese couple, LaPiere "questionnaired" the establishments. His results indicate a wide discrepancy between nonsymbolic and symbolic behavior. Of the 128 establishments that responded—81 restaurants and 47 hotels, auto camps, and tourist homes—92 percent of the respondents from the former and 91 percent from the latter stated that they would not accept members of the Chinese race as guests of their establishment.

LaPiere (1934: 31) concluded that situational factors must be considered when studying the impact of attitude on behavior: "If social attitudes are to be conceptualized as partially integrated habit sets which will become operative under specific circumstances and lead to a particular pattern of adjustment, they must, in the main, be derived from a study of humans behaving in actual social situations. They must not be imputed on the basis of questionnaire data."

The absence of a direct relationship between attitude and behavior led to much confusion surrounding the definition of attitude. Leonard W. Doob provided a behavioral definition of attitude. He considered this effort an advance beyond definitions of attitude as the subjective counterpart of something in the environment, as a predisposition within the organism, or as what the attitude scale measures. Doob (1947: 43) defined attitudes as "an implicit, drive-producing response considered socially significant in the individual's society." He elaborated on this definition for discussion purposes. The result was a definition of attitude as

[1] an implicit response
[2] which is both (a) anticipatory and (b) mediating in reference to patterns of overt responses,
[3] which is evoked (a) by a variety of stimulus patterns (b) as a result of previous learning of gradients of generalization and discrimination,
[4] which is itself cue- and drive-producing,
[5] and which is considered socially significant in the individual's society [1947: 42].

This is one of the most inclusive definitions to come out of early attitude theory. It is inclusive in the sense that it accounts for the origins, functions, and consequences of attitudes. Doob's definition can be used as a point of departure for discussing past and present-day justifications for accepting the existence of some mental constructs that influence behavior.

Early theorists did not, however, pay sufficient attention to the contextual, or what Larson and Sanders refer to as the social, aspect of the psychosocial act of persuasion. In reviewing Doob's contribution, keep in mind the importance of contextual considerations to the study of attitude and behavior change. While the last section of Doob's definition indicates a recognition on his part of constraints imposed on the individual from external sources, criticism of his work by Isidor Chein reveals the problems inherent in giving contextual considerations less emphasis than they deserve. As we review segments of Doob's definition, the problems inherent in this shortcoming should become more apparent.

(1) "Attitude is an implicit response." An implicit response is one which occurs within the individual. It is an intrapersonal response not observable to others. This perspective on attitude has led many to consider its major role one of predisposing the individual to act in a certain manner: an immediate response to a stimulus pattern that sets the tone, so to speak, for further responses.

(2a) "An attitude is an implicit response which is . . . anticipatory . . . in reference to patterns of overt responses." This perspective follows from a probability conceptualization of attitude (see Wicker, 1969). Attitude is credited with the recurrences of behavior of a given type or direction. Furthermore, some degree of organization, structure, or predictability is expected. This perspective seems to have influenced Doob to place temporal constraints on the occurrence of attitude. Consistent with Hull's conceptualization of antedating responses, attitude from this perspective precedes another rewarding response and by its association with that rewarded response has also been reinforced, so that it occurs before its "original time in the response series" (1947: 49).

Doob is essentially suggesting that all responses have antecedents, even if they cannot be consciously recalled. Through the process of socialization, for example, women learn to view sexual activity differently from men. While a young woman may have a physical need for sexual activity as strong as that of her male counterpart, her avoidance of it at a young age or prior to marriage is a function, in part at least, of her anticipation of sanctions for participating or reward for waiting. She may not recall anyone ever telling her directly about the sanctions surrounding female sexual involvement, but vague memories of the story of Hester Prynne and other subtle incremental teachings of cultural taboos have probably left an impact that forms what Doob referred to as an implicit anticipatory response. This woman thus becomes predictable. Doob does admit that "exceptions under different psychological conditions must be noted." In other words, the woman harboring this anticipatory response may never-theless engage in premarital sexual relations if persuaded by social circum-stances or physical desires. This allowance on Doob's part for circum-stantial interference is important. It separates his perspective from the purists of stimulus-response advocates.

Isidor Chein (1967), while giving Doob credit for such allowances, questioned his emphasis on the temporal sequence of attitude attributes. He explained:

> Doob's formulation raises the problem which confronts all attempts to deal with dynamics in historical, as distinguished from ahistorical terms, namely how something which no longer exists (and it no longer exists because it antedates its effects) can influence something which is now going on [1948: 54].

Chein's criticism introduces for deliberation and debate the entire question of the relationship of time and thought. The rule model introduced in Chapter 2 specifies the importance of antecedent conditions that precede the selection of a behavioral option. Chein's criticism implies that revised selection on the basis of new or further retrieval of stored information is also quite feasible.

(2b) "An attitude is an implicit response which is . . . mediating in reference to patterns of overt responses." This aspect of Doob's definition reflects the latent process view of attitude. Attitude is treated as a hidden or hypothetical variable, shaping, acting upon, or mediating observable behavior (see Wicker, 1969). This perspective has been even more popular than probability conceptions of attitude. The attitude is not considered to consist of the behavioral responses themselves or their probability, but is instead an intervening variable, occurring between the stimulus and the response, that can be inferred only from overt behavior. Unlike the probability conception of attitude, which by definition indicates that for any issue the absence of empirical evidence for a predictable relationship between attitude and behavior is sufficient to assume that an attitude on that issue is nonexistent, the latent process view implies that the attitude is there, but that our measurement techniques are not sufficiently adequate to locate it. Larson and Sanders (1975) have objected to the latter view because, in the absence of empirical evidence, latent process advocates must rely on faith to support their belief in the existence of attitudes.

Doob combined the probability and latent process views in his defi-nition of attitude. Its anticipatory nature is a reflection of the former view and its mediating nature originates from the latter. As such, it is difficult to conceive of an empirical test that would support or reject Doob's definition. Thus, while Doob's definition may be one of the most inclusive to come out of attitude theory, it may have added to the demise of attitude research by setting up incompatible research demands.

(3a) *"An attitude is an implicit response . . . which is evoked by a variety of stimulus patterns."* Just as it is possible for an attitude to evoke a repertoire of alternative behaviors, one attitude can be evoked by a variety of stimulus patterns, as depicted in Figure 3.1.

Doob (1967) explains that perception and learning influence these connections. Agreeing with theories of selective attention, he states, "Perception indicates that the individual is responding because he has previously paid attention to or been oriented toward certain stimuli which then affect his sense organs and thus evoke his attitude."

The context of behavioral selection can be very complex. Under such conditions it is likely that *choice* rather than conditioning determines behavior. Doob's attachment to a behaviorist paradigm precludes the discussion of choice as anything other than interference with the normal course of events, a sort of error variance. In contrast, the position taken in this text is that most human communication is too complex to rely on conditioning. The totally conditioned communicator is also the noncompetent communicator. Choice is the norm rather than the exception. This does not, however, preclude the possibility that selective perception

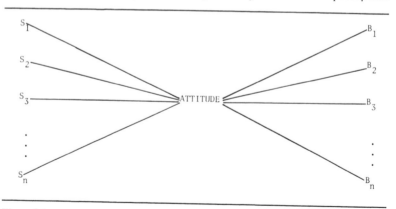

Figure 3.1

and learned connections between contextual exigencies, behavior, and reward influence behavioral selection. Constructs and rules are partially a function of selective attention processes. People cannot develop rules for every occasion; they must find novel events sufficiently similar to familiar contexts to justify the operation of old rules or face the often stressful activity of generating new rules (see Reardon et al., 1980). In any event, choice is required in exigent situations described by Doob as having multiple stimulus patterns.

(3b) "An attitude is an implicit response . . . which is evoked . . . as a result of previous learning or of gradients of generalization and discrimination." Doob preferred to explain the complex nature of responding to contextual exigencies (stimuli) in terms of gradients of generalization and discrimination. If, for example, the stimulus "poodle" fails to elicit an anticipatory response of dislike mediating a goal response of running away, whereas a bulldog elicits a running response, we can assume that the individual discriminates among types of dogs. If the individual runs from all dogs, then we can consider stimulus generalization accountable for that behavior.

Doob did not indicate that people *choose* to respond or not to respond on the basis of generalizations and discriminations, but that they merely respond. Cogitation over alternatives and just exactly how similar the confronted animal is to the bulldog was not considered. Instead, in line with Hull's (1943: 185) description of response amplitude as "diminishing steadily with the increase in the extent of deviation . . . of the evocation stimulus . . . from the stimulus originally conditioned," Doob proposed that we are conditioned to deviations from previously experienced events in the same way, but with less intensity than conditioning with presently experienced events.

He described the strength of an attitude as divisable into at least two types. The strength of the bond between attitude and the stimulus pattern evoking it is referred to as "afferent-habit strength." Attitude was considered a function of the number of previous reinforcements and the position on the discrimination-generalization gradient occupied by a particular stimulus pattern. Like Bateson (1972), Doob obviously considered experience to consist of repeatable patterns which lend certainty to what would otherwise be a very chaotic environment.

(4) "An attitude is an implicit response . . . which is itself cue- and drive-producing." According to Doob, attitudes, like all other responses, have stimulus value. They arouse other responses. Overt behavior is one type of response aroused by an attitude. Doob referred to the bond between attitude and behavior as "efferent-habit strength." He viewed this bond as influenced by the cue and drive strength of a given attitude. As he explained, "an attitude has cue value in the sense that it acts as a stimulus

to produce another response, but it also is a drive in the sense that tension is reduced through subsequent behavior leading to a reward" (1947: 47).

Although afferent- and efferent-habit strength are theoretically intriguing concepts, the latter especially fails to account adequately for the linkage between an attitude and a given response in those instances where many responses are possible and equally rewarding. Chein (1967: 55) proposed that "conditions (inner and outer) surrounding the bond are different from time to time. It follows that the relative frequency of evocation is a function of the surrounding conditions rather than of 'the strength of the bond' and that, in this respect at least, all bonds are equally strong."

It does not seem useful to take sides with either Chein or Doob on this issue. Both acknowledged the existence of an attachment between attitude and behavior. Chein placed primary emphasis on external forces influencing the strength of the bond, whereas Doob favored an internal orientation. It seems feasible to consider both frequency and conditions of occurrence as factors influencing the connection between attitude and behavior. In terms of constructs and rules, we can consider the former to be more resistant to external constraints than the latter. For example, while it is possible to construe women as inferior, changing social norms have influenced male behavior in public places to conform to demands for equality. It seems reasonable to assume that many people retain the afferent-habit strength between the stimulus woman and the negative constructs, but adjust the rules to conform to societal pressures, thereby weakening the consistency between afferent (stimulus-attitude) and efferent (attitude-behavior) bonds. It may be very useful to view afferent bonds as consisting of linkages between constructs and superordinate construct(s), attitude as one or more superordinate constructs, and efferent bonds as linkages between superordinate constructs and regulative rules. The new model that emerges from this perspective appears in Figure 3.2.

This model suggests that persuasive communication can be used to change constructs, rules, or both. If one seeks to change both, the result is more likely to be private acceptance of the persuasive message rather than mere compliance (behavior change alone). For example, assume that a particular man normally construes all suggestions offered by female colleagues as worthless and so ignores them. If a persuasive message merely altered his image of female competence but did not provide any face-saving ways whereby he could also change his behavior, the result could be inconsistency between the superordinate construct "female colleague" and the behavior toward female colleagues. If, on the other hand, pressure through affirmative action programs, superiors, or peers influenced this

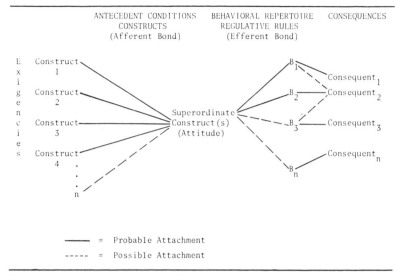

Figure 3.2   Construct-Rule Linkage Model

man to change his overt behavior toward female colleagues but did not influence his construal of their competence, compliance alone would result. Finally, should he be influenced to reconstrue the value of female competence and, on his own or through a persuasive message, find face-saving ways of revising his behavior accordingly, then private acceptance is more likely to be secured.

As discussed in Chapter 2, actor construals of a situation influence rule activation or application. Thus, changing the constructs used in reference to women colleagues could also lead to a change in behavior toward them. It is possible, however, for an individual not to have in his repertoire a rule for behavior toward female colleagues which is consistent with his other rules. In this case the persuader must assist him in the generation of a new rule. We shall return to this conceptualization of the persuasion process. For now let us turn to Doob's final description of attitude.

(5) "An attitude is an implicit response . . . which is significant in the individual's society." This aspect of Doob's definition is consistent with the concept of normative constraints. In Chapter 2 the rule model behavioral repertoire is accompanied by normative forces. Although many behaviors might be feasible in a given situation, some are obligatory, others are prohibited, preferable, permissible, or irrelevant to the enactment of a particular episode. It is possible to construe what Doob refers to as "drive

strength" as a partially normative force operating as an external constraint on the behavior of the individual. The word *partially* is used here because individuals can exert pressure on themselves as well.

In conclusion, it should be noted that constructs do not exert equal influence on a superordinate construct. Constructs are hierarchically ordered by the individual. Chein's example of stereotypes provides clarification. To him stereotypes are not attitudes but "conditions of attitudes." They have afferent-habit strength. That is to say, while you may consider a certain type of person to be slovenly, you may be indifferent to slovenliness. The result is an absence of action implications and hence no attitude. Actually, the absence of prescribed action in itself prescribes inaction, and even inaction is an action implication. Thus, while I agree with Chein that some stereotypes do not have strong implications for behavior, it is likely that even weak afferent and efferent bonds influence an individual's selection from his or her behavioral repertoire. It is also likely, however, that the higher the construct is in the individual hierarchical construct system, the more likely it is to influence the superordinate construct (attitude), the regulative rule, and the urge to translate that rule into behavior.

CONCLUSION

The concept of attitude may have lost its predictive and explanatory power merely because we attempted to make it all things to all scientists. Very few communication scholars would argue that people do not form cognitive associations that carry some evaluative component. The question is, To what extent can recognition of these cognitive associations facilitate behavioral prediction? The concept of superordinate construct is used in Figure 3.2 to indicate that cognitive associations influence the activation and application of regulative rules. They can be defined as an integration of context-specific constructs and their associated affects used in connection with desired consequents to select and order behavioral options. The term *context* is used broadly here to refer to persons, objects, and events considered potentially relevant to behavioral choice.

Superordinate constructs limit regulative rule options. As discussed in Chapter 2, people match them with the antecedent conditions of rules within their repertoire. With the additional influence of desired consequent(s), these rules are then ordered. If the context is very familiar, the rule that has proven most effective will be activated. As familiarity diminishes, superordinate constructs are derived more consciously, as are their associated rules.

The construct-rule linkage model is not intended to suggest that people are never irrational. It is intended to imply that they do seek to select behaviors consistent with their past behaviors and also appropriate and/or effective by some set of standards derived from associations with others. Knowing that people prefer to be consistent in their rule-following behavior and desire to be perceived as doing what is appropriate and effective, persuaders can create conditions for change by bringing into question the consistency, appropriateness, or effectiveness of persuadee behavior(s). Sometimes people will sacrifice consistency for appropriateness/effectiveness and vice versa, thereby facilitating behavioral change. In the selection of appeals the persuader must decide whether, given the specific contextual conditions, consistency, appropriateness, or effectiveness holds the highest priority in the mind of the persuadee.

In Chapter 2, "appropriateness" was described as having an important role in communication and persuasion. Chapter 4 will focus on consistency and those theories which established a place for it in the study of persuasion. Later chapters will combine what we know of the human concern for appropriateness, consistency, and effectiveness in an effort to identify characteristics of successful persuasion.

Chapter 4

THEORETICAL ORIENTATIONS OF

PERSUASION RESEARCH

In the previous chapter we examined Doob's definition of attitude. Although Doob's conceptualization of attitude encompasses most of what we knew about the concept at that time, with the assistance of Isidor Chein we found several aspects of the definition in need of reconstruction. The construct-rule change model provides a type of reconstruction that focuses on persuadee logic as a cause of behavioral choice and the guide to persuasive appeal selection. The importance of choice to this model suggests what has been referred to of late as an "actionist" perspective. Essentially, the actionists perceive people as choice makers in their environments. Some do not ignore the possibility of conditioning as a form of learning, but emphasis is placed on the individual's ability to select from among behavioral options.

As we shall see in this chapter, theoretical perspectives on persuasion have moved toward a recognition of environmental contingencies as factors operating to influence the behavioral choices of persuadees. Yet, even today we do not have a model of persuasive communication that provides a general explanation for the successes and failures of persuasive messages in changing attitudes and behaviors. Jeanne Herman (1977: 127) explains that "to understand the impact (or lack thereof) of a persuasive communication on a person's belief and attitude system, it is necessary to delineate a complex model of cognitive processing." She adds that persuasive communications are processed through several stages before being integrated into an individual's belief and attitude system. Furthermore, the persuasive potential of any message can be thwarted or nullified at any of the processing stages. Accepting Herman's claim implies that simple conditioning models cannot possibly capture the complexity of the persuasive process. The construct-rule linkage model, introduced in Chapter 3, attempts to represent this complexity. In the next section we shall trace the steps that brought us to the metatheoretical perspective supporting this cognitive model of persuasion.

LANDMARK THEORIES OF PERSUASION

Before plunging into a review of theories of persuasion, we are well advised to stop to consider just what a theory should look like. Essentially, any theory is "an abstract, symbolic representation of what is conceived to be reality" (Zimbardo et al., 1977: 53). Theories consist of two types of rules· correspondence rules and functional rules. The former relates the independent variables introduced in a theory to the dependent variables. In terms of attitude theory, correspondence rules relate source and message variables to measures of behavioral and/or verbal report changes. Functional rules, on the other hand, tell us how to manipulate the concepts (variables) of the theory so that hypotheses may be formulated.

A theory tells us how events in the world ought to be related. It is one human being's construal of some aspect of the world. As such, it is subject to human error. No theory can explain everything. All theories have scope conditions or parameters beyond which they cannot provide reliable explanations (see Reynolds, 1975). One of the most common problems associated with attitude theory is the absence of specified scope conditions. The attitude theorists' disregard for contextual considerations set them up for failure; they were looking for one theory to explain all types of persuasion. They did not see the necessity for limiting the scope of their theories to, for example, interpersonal, dyadic, group, or mass persuasion, or for explaining how these theories applied differentially to each context.

A good theory, then, specifies the scope conditions. It provides us some way of explaining some portion of reality. Furthermore, theories are vital to understanding any complex phenomenon because they can

(1) generate predictions about complex functional relationships between variables;
(2) integrate many empirical observations that, on the surface, may appear to be dissimilar;
(3) separate relevant from irrelevant variables, and provide schemes for organizing the relevant ones;
(4) allow for the derivation of nonobvious predictions (that is, statements about reality that one would not make on the basis of intuition); and
(5) explain why variables function as they do, often by postulating hypothetical processes (Zimbardo et al., 1977: 55).

Unfortunately, the communication scientist and many other social scientists, in their zeal to prove themselves true scientists, have often opted to emphasize measurement over theory. Quantitative and qualitative measures are to theory as a horse is to a carriage. A theory can provide very little if it remains untested, but variable testing with little regard for theory can only serve to confuse us. While it may be true that some persons are more adept at conceptualization than measurement or vice versa, the student of communication must learn both or risk the possibility of inhibiting progress (see McCroskey, 1979). Theories are inextricably associated with measurement. As such they are "intellectual tools for organizing data in such a way that one can make inferences or logical transitions from one set of data to another; they serve as guidelines to investigation, explanation, organization, and discovery of observable facts" (Deutsch and Krauss, 1965: 4). In the next section we shall trace the history of persuasion theory and the inferences that guided research.

LEARNING THEORY

The most basic and long-lasting paradigm influencing persuasion theory and research was classical conditioning. According to this perspective, when a particular response follows a given stimulus, the repeated pairing of this (conditioned) stimulus with a neutral (unconditioned) stimulus will eventually result in the elicitation of the response from the sole presence of the neutral stimulus. Every student of general psychology encounters the classic example of this paradigm. Pavlov conducted an experiment in which he rang a bell shortly before blowing meat powder into a dog's mouth. The dog initially salivated in response to the meat powder but later came to salivate in response to the bell alone.

Staats (1967, 1968) tells us that all attitudes are acquired through classical conditioning. Watson and Johnson (1972) explain that a word, such as *dangerous,* that generally elicits a negative response when paired with another word, such as *noxious,* can lead to the same negative response to *noxious.* They refer to this transference of response tendencies from one word to another as "higher-order conditioning."

The process of persuasion often involves influencing a person to respond to one object or word in the same negative or positive way in which he or she typically responds to another object or word. However, sometimes there is a need to change previous associations. This is achieved through "counter-conditioning." Counter-conditioning involves pairing a stimulus that evokes a negative response with one that evokes a positive response. As long as the positive stimulus-response linkage is stronger than the negative stimulus-response linkage, counter-conditioning is possible. For example, if the word *child* elicits a slightly negative response for someone, the pairing of that stimulus with *cute* or *refreshing* or *warm* will increase the likelihood of *child* eliciting a positive response in the future. The new stimulus must be strong enough to discredit the person's previously negative connotation of the original stimulus.

Classical conditioning has come to be viewed as too simplistic an explanation for all types of learning. However, one of the most common persuasive techniques is to associate the object of change with some other positive or negative stimulus. Source credibility essentially works on this principle of association. High source credibility, when associated with a message, increases the likelihood of message acceptance. For example, advertisers believe that the association of Farah Fawcett or Cheryl Tiegs with cosmetics increases the likelihood of a person responding positively to the advertised product. Similarly, subliminal messages conveyed in grocery store music or embedded in advertisements can quietly and surreptitiously influence cognitive associations.

While few deny the effectiveness of forming associations as a means of persuasion, the same types of learning appear to involve much more than mere association. Teaching a dog to salivate at the sound of a bell is certainly not in the same league as teaching a person to chew with the mouth closed. Also, even if associations constitute the basis of all learning and hence all persuasion, humans can identify and choose to accept or reject those associations that are inappropriate or inconsistent when considered against other societal and personal rules. In short, humans can change their own associations through a higher-level cogitation than Pavlov's dog ever devoted to the experiment.

Operant conditioning is a second form of learning, stemming from an emphasis on response reinforcement. The main principle here is that responses become stronger and more resistant to change the more they are associated with rewards. In contrast to classical conditioning, operants are behaviors emitted by the organism, not elicited by a known stimulus. The important link is between the response and the reinforcement. The stimulus is often irrelevant and sometimes unknown.

An example of operant conditioning is seen often in newly "liberated" marriages. When the man of the family who is used to the traditional division of domestic labor decides to cook his first meal and is reinforced for such behavior by praise, the chances of his repeating that behavior are increased. The stimulus for such behavior is not considered important from this perspective. However, it seems reasonable to conclude that recognizing the conditions that lead to a desired response provides an edge for the person who wishes to increase the likelihood of response repetition. In other words, if the spouse can determine what she may have said or done to encourage this new behavior, she may be able to repeat that behavior and encourage the same response. However, researchers who concern themselves with operant conditioning realize that the husband's behavior might be the result of several unidentifiable experiences, such as hearing that his boss is a great cook. Therefore, instead of attempting to identify the stimuli, we focus on the response-reinforcement connection.

The influence of learning theory on persuasion research was prevalent during the mid-twentieth century and is still obvious in today's research. During World War II, Carl Hovland, a psychology professor at Yale University, and his associates were concerned with influencing the morale of soldiers and with changing civilian attitudes toward the war effort. After the war, he and several students developed an approach to attitude change that has come to be known as The Yale Communication and Attitude Change Program. Much of their work centered around learning theory. To them, attitude is an implicit approach or avoidance response to some object. As such, it is an emotional reaction. The Yale group focused on belief as the change agent of attitude. Beliefs were defined as the cognitive or knowledge component of attitude. Zimbardo et al. (1977: 57) explain this association:

> Thus we should be able to change people's attitudes toward abortion by changing their beliefs about the age at which a fetus becomes a living human being or by altering their beliefs concerning the right of a pregnant woman to decide what to do with her own body. It is further assumed that the learning of new information in a persuasive communication will change beliefs. An effective communication will raise questions about abortion ("Is a three-month old fetus human?") and provide whatever answers support the appropriate belief.

In 1953, Hovland et al. reported much of the Yale program results in their book, *Communication and Persuasion*. They explained that attitude change depends on the "rehearsing" or "practicing" of mental and verbal responses. Furthermore, incentives and motivation are needed to encourage the acceptance of the new response over the old one. In terms of the abortion example, it is not sufficient to rehearse in one's mind the new perspective on abortion as a woman's means of deciding what is right for her. The individual must perceive this change of belief and attitude as potentially rewarding (incentives) and must find the change environment (opinions of others, appeals used, source characteristics, and so on) favorable (motivation).

Fishbein (1963) focused upon the relationship of belief and attitude as part of his theory thereby extending the conditioning paradigm into the 1960s and 1970s. Unlike Doob (1947) and other theorists who left the exact nature of attitude unspecified, Fishbein utilized the concept of belief as a foundation for attitude. He viewed beliefs about some object, concept, or goal in terms of their relationship to some attribute (i.e., to some other object, concept or goal). Attitude was viewed as the evaluation associated with the belief. As Fishbein and Ajzen (1975: 29) explain, "some of the implicit evaluation associated with a response constitutes an attitude which may have been formed as the result of prior conditioning."

To Fishbein, then, attitudes are a function of beliefs and associated evaluative responses. Fishbein's model will be explained at greater length later in the chapter. It is one of the classics of persuasion models originating from a learning theory perspective. As early as 1932, however, Tolman was emphasizing the importance of considering human needs as the foundation of attitude and belief. He contended that people learn expectations and perform behaviors that they believe will lead to valued results. Despite the apparent emphasis on learning, this perspective suggests the existence of choice among alternatives rather than rigid stimulus-response associations. Inherent in this emphasis on valued consequences is the implication that there is not necessarily a direct association between attitudes and behaviors. While it is likely that a person associates several attitudes with a given object or event, not all of these attitudes are equally likely to be conducive to obtaining a valued consequent. Before elaborating on this variation of the influence of desired consequents, let us look at some related perspectives.

FUNCTIONAL PARADIGM

According to McGuire (1973), the functional paradigm represents a less "intellectual" stance than learning theory. It stresses that people have many needs which attitudes must gratify. Fishbein and Ajzen (1975) refer to this line of thought as "expectancy-value theories." They point to the work of Tolman (1932), Rotter (1954), and Atkinson (1957) as representing a theoretical perspective which proposes that people hold certain attitudes because those attitudes facilitate the attainment of valued consequences.

One of the most well-known functional theories was developed by Katz (1960). According to Katz, we develop favorable attitudes toward those things in our environment which bring satisfaction, and unfavorable attitudes toward dissatisfaction-producing aspects of our world. This satisfaction-seeking behavior has been referred to as the *instrumental, adjustment,* or *utilitarians, function of attitudes.*

A second function of attitude introduced by Katz (1960) is *ego-defensive.* We refuse to harbor attitudes that force us to admit to discrediting information about ourselves. Ego-defensive attitudes are defense mechanisms. Prejudiced attitudes are ego-defensive. They secure our superiority over others. For example, by refusing to admit to the equality of women in the business world, some men protect themselves from the competition that such an admission might create. By suppressing minority groups some individuals reinforce their own sense of superiority. While such attitudes are dysfunctional to social relation, they protect what such individuals value most: their own self-esteem.

The *value-expressive* function of attitude allows us to appear competent, sensitive, assertive, discriminating, and so on. These attitudes are developed to foster preferred impressions. For example, the father who exclaims, "We only watch one program in this house—Masterpiece Theatre!" is not merely reporting fact but is suggesting he and his family have higher standards for entertainment than most individuals. The boss who says to the new employee, "Don't say you hope you'll do well, son. Just do well," is implying that he values competence and assertiveness.

The fourth attitude function is *knowledge.* Katz contends that we value consistency over inconsistency and certainty over uncertainty. We therefore need to establish certain frames of reference. The age-old metaphors, "There are a lot of fish in the sea" and "Never wait for a woman or a train, there will always be another one around soon," are examples of attitudes that give meaning to uncertain situations.

McGuire (1973: 228) explains the value of this theoretical approach: "To the extent that such a conceptualization is valid, communications can best reduce prejudice not so much by providing new information about the targets of those attitudes but rather by enabling the individual to deal in other ways with his underlying personality problems." McGuire is suggesting that knowing why a person holds a particular attitude puts the persuader in a better position to encourage change. This can be accom-

plished by convincing the individual that (a) his or her present attitude no
longer leads to the satisfaction sought, (b) another attitude will meet the
individual's needs more effectively, or (c) the individual should reconsider
the attitude's value in light of new information.

This perspective suggests that the ego-defensive attitude that seems to
make women more defensive with each other than with males (see Frost
and Wilmot, 1978) might be altered if women were made aware of this
tendency and were encouraged to view each other as "in the same boat"
rather than as competitors. Several women's networks have been established lately to encourage female camaraderie. If successful, these groups
will redefine female collegial relationships as sources of support rather
than challenges to self-esteem, thus removing the threat that makes ego-
defensiveness necessary. Similarly, if the person who will not wait for a
train or a woman is encouraged to consider that "all good things are worth
waiting for," the proven functional worth of this attitude across situations
may lead him to reconsider the value of the more situation-specific
attitude that precludes waiting for a woman.

McGuire tells us that the functional approach offers insights ignored by
other theories, but the theory has been generally neglected and therefore
its success has been limited. Perhaps its simple logic does not sufficiently
challenge our social scientific minds. Nevertheless, it is one theory that can
be converted into action. Unlike several other theories which speculate
about the nature of attitudes with little reference to techniques for
changing them, Katz's approach provides both theory and technique. As
such, it is worthy of more attention than it has received by those who wish
to practice persuasion as well as study it.

COGNITIVE CONSISTENCY APPROACHES

Basic to cognitive consistency theories is the perspective that new
information disrupts the cognitive organization developed by an individual. Such disruption is intolerable and therefore tension results. This
tension drives the individual toward consistency. A way to assimilate or
accommodate the new information into the existing cognitive structure
must be located. McGuire (1973: 227-228) refers to these approaches as
representative of a conflict-resolving paradigm. The communication recipient is viewed as a "harassed honest broker, trying to find resolution
among many conflicting demands. He feels his attitude toward the object
must take into account his own information, his self-interest, the demands

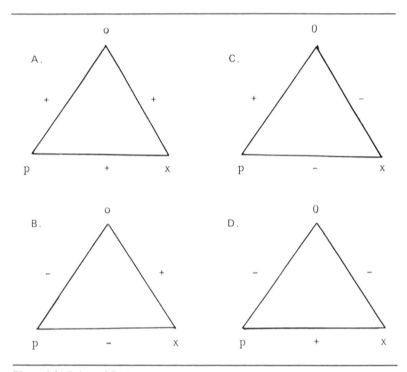

Figure 4.1   Balanced States

of other people, and this new communication. In the end, he adjusts his attitude to keep from getting too far out of line with any one of these demands."

The work of Fritz Heider (1946, 1958) on balanced configurations reflects the consistency principle. Heider was concerned with a person's perceptions of the relationships between himself (p), another person (o), and an object or event (x). A balanced state is assumed to exist when the relationships between p, x, and o depicted in Figure 4.1 obtain. Imbalanced states exist when the relationships between p, x, and o depicted in Figure 4.2 obtain.

Heider (1946: 110-111) summarizes these relationships by stating, "In the case of two entities, a balanced state exists if the relation between them is positive (or negative) in all respects, i.e., in regard to all meanings of L and U. . . . In the case of three entities, a balanced state exists if all three relations are positive in all respects or if two are negative and one

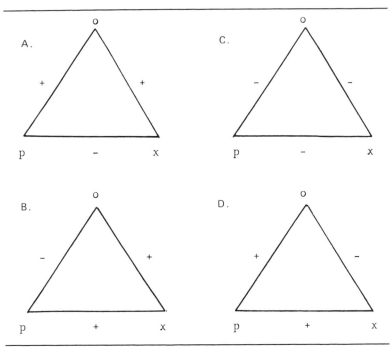

Figure 4.2 Imbalanced States

positive." In this statement, L refers to liking and I refers to person p's perception of the (causal) unit relation between himself and person o or object x (e.g., ownership, similarity, membership).

Balanced states are not conducive to change. That is to say, unless tension exists in the relationship, change is not considered necessary. Successful persuasion, from this perspective, requires as a prerequisite some degree of imbalance. One limitation of Heider's conceptualization, however, is that his relationships are more akin to preferences than to intense forces such as hatred and love (see Zajonc, 1968). Furthermore, balance theory is limited to the relationships between a maximum of three entities.

Other theorists have extended Heider's works (Newcomb, 1953; Cartwright and Harary, 1956; Abelsen and Rosenberg, 1958). Actually, Heider's early conceptualizations of balance have given impetus to an age of persuasion research based on what might be labeled harmony and disharmony in the cognitive organization of the individual. In a sense, these theoretical perspectives draw upon learning theory and its less intellectual counterpart, expectancy theory. In terms of learning theory, the imbalanced state can be viewed as unrewarding, balance as rewarding. Although expectancy does not appear as a central concept in Heider's theory, it seems reasonable to assume that the cognitive structure (belief) and attitude (evaluation) of a given relationship sets up certain expectations for behavior that are utilized to reinforce or weaken the unit bond. These expectations might be based on different perceptions of the relationships under different contextual conditions. Although Heider mentions the possibility of multiple relations between two entities, he does not deal with the strength of bonds and degree of balance. Should the degree of balance be offset by some unexpected behavior on the part of person o, an alteration in the beliefs and/or attitude about o and x is conceivable. Person p, for example, may dislike person o's mother, x, and may therefore dislike person o also. Should person p find person o arguing with his mother x one day, person p may find himself appreciating person o much more. He may realize that person o is obligated to like his own mother and so an indication that given no obligation to mother x, o might then agree with p, may be sufficient reason for p to revaluate his feelings about o. Person p may perceive o as trapped in an obligatory relationship. In other words, p is expected to like his mother x. The triangle in this case would have originally been as shown in Figure 4.1B, where p dislikes person o and mother x. After person p observes person o violating the obligatory rule, "Be nice to your mother," he may decide to like person o but still dislike his mother. The result is the triangle shown in Figure 4.2A, which, according to Heider, is an imbalanced configuration but one which is justified by reference to the rules impinging on o as x's son.

When this much qualification must accompany a theory, it should lead to some skepticism about the value of its usage. The above example indicates that rules may exist that relieve o from full responsibility for his behavior. Simple triangular configurations that do not specify degrees of balance are limiting. Subsequent theories of cognitive organization attempted to deal with the limitations of Heider's perspective. In any case, Heider's interest in consistency did set persuasion research on a path that still exists today.

CONGRUITY PRINCIPLE

Osgood and Tannenbaum's (1955) congruity principle, like Heider's balance model, is based on the associative or disassociative nature of

assertions. However, Osgood and Tannebaum (1955: 43) were also interested in the degree of polarization between concepts that are related
through assertions. They consider extreme concept polarization as a manifestation of unsophisticated or emotional thinking: "The most simple-
minded evaluative frame of reference is therefore one in which a tight
cluster of highly polarized and undifferentiated good concepts is diamet-
rically opposed in meaning to an equally tight and polarized cluster of
undifferentiated bad concepts." General sematicists refer to this type of
thinking as "two-valued." Osgood and Tannenbaum consider it characteristics of lay thinking in any period of conflict and emotional stress.

   According to Osgood and Tannenbaum (1955: 43) the principle of
congruity can be stated succinctly: "Changes in evaluation are always in
the direction of increased congruity with the existing frame of reference."
It is only when two or more concepts are associated by an assertion that
congruity becomes an issue. In other words, we may entertain two logically incompatible attitudes toward objects, persons, or events in our
society (e.g., Christianity and prejudice) but experience little if any stress
until they are brought into association (e.g., Christians are not prejudiced).

   To determine the direction of attitude change resulting from an incon-
gruous assertion, it is necessary to consider the existing attitudes prior to
the reception of the message as well as the nature of the assertion.
Attitudes can be favorable, neutral, or unfavorable; assertions can be
positive or associative or negative or disassociative. When attitudes toward
both objects of judgment are polar, the nature of the assertion determines
congruence or incongruence. When one attitude is neutral and the other is
negative we can expect "guilt or praise by association" to rule. For
example, the statement, "Mary is a Mormon," may result in negative
feelings about Mormonism (neutral concept) if Mary is disliked (negative
concept), but positive evaluations of Mormonism if Mary is well liked.

   The general principle is that when a state of incongruity exists, the
evaluations of the two objects will tend to change in the direction of
congruity. This is best viewed as a compromise response (see Fishbein and
Ajzen, 1975). If an individual with whom you share a friendship (+2 on a
scale of −3 to +3) is in favor of abortion, whereas you are opposed to it
(−1), incongruity exists whenever the subject arises in conversation.
According to the principle of congruity, both the friend and abortion will
come to have congruent evaluations (both will be +1).

   A major criticism of the Osgood and Tannenbaum perspective is that it
does not account for the situation referred to by Rokeach and Rothman
(1965) as "overassimilation." According to Rokeach and Rothman, an

assertion elicits a unique cognitive configuration representing a character-ized subject (CS). The characterized subject is a person, thing, or idea that is described or qualified. The CS has two components, a subject (S) which is capable of being characterized and a characterization (C) capable of being applied to the subject.

When an individual encounters a CS he or she must first decide whether or not the C and S are relevant to each other. Then the relative importance of C and S must be determined. Finally, the relative importance of the combined CS with C and S individually is assessed. It is in this final step that Rokeach and Rothman move beyond Osgood and Tannenbaum by suggesting that the evaluation of CS may be even more polarized than C or S alone. For example, an individual may have very positive feelings about the term *mother* and very negative feelings about *negligence*. But the combination of these terms into *negligent mother* may result in a stronger reaction than C or S could elicit singly. Rokeach and Rothman refer to this situation as *overassimilation* (as opposed to assimilation) when the evaluation of CS more clearly conforms to the evaluation of C or S.

Rokeach and Rothman developed the belief congruence theory to resolve some of the problems inherent in congruity theory. However, both theories focus on evaluations of attitudes only, and both subscribe to the perspective that information aggregates as a function of simple mathe-matical, noncontextual laws. Before responding to the latter, let us look at one theoretical model focusing on belief more than attitude.

COGNITIVE DISSONANCE THEORY

The theory of cognitive dissonance, developed by Leon Festinger (1957), is another variation on the consistency perspective of attitude change. Like Rokeach and Rothman's (1965) belief congruence theory, Festinger's approach focuses on the relationship between "knowledges" about objects, persons, events, and so on. However, Festinger narrows his focus to include only two types of relevant relations, dissonant and consonant. According to Festinger (1957: 13), "two elements are in a dissonant relation if, considering these two alone, the obverse of one element would follow from the other." For example, if a person in debt bought a car, a dissonant relation between the two cognitive elements "buying a car" and "being in debt" would result (see Insko, 1967: 199). A consonant relation, on the other hand, implies an appropriate match of two cognitive elements or that one "follows from" the other. For example, not buying a car follows from being in debt.

Obviously, not all dissonant cognitive relations elicit the same degree of felt dissonance. The importance of the cognitive elements is one factor influencing dissonance magnitude. The person who recognizes that he or she must save money to survive the winter should experience more dissonance upon the purchase of a new car than the individual who just likes to be thrifty. The magnitude of dissonance also increases with an increase in the proportion of dissonant to consonant cognitions. The more reasons one has for not spending money, the greater is the dissonance created by behaving as a spendthrift. Finally the "cognitive overlap" or similarity among the dissonant elements influences the magnitude of dissonance. Greater dissonance should result from the selection of a boat over a car (low similarity) than that which results from the selection of one type of car over another.

According to Festinger, people seek to reduce dissonance in one of four ways: revoking the decision, increasing the attractiveness of the chosen alternative, decreasing the attractiveness of the unchosen alternative, or creating cognitive overlap between the items in question. The magnitude of that dissonance is a function of the extent of reward or punishment used to induce the behavior. The rule is that the greater is the reward or punishment used to induce the behavior the less is the felt dissonance. If, for example, an individual is offered $25.00 to state that she likes vanilla ice cream when in actuality she abhors it, we can expect less dissonance than if she is offered ten cents to induce the same behavior. Obviously the importance of the issue must be considered as well. For example, a hostage being offered $25.00 to insult his country should experience more dissonance than the woman who for $25.00 claims to like vanilla ice cream.

According to Festinger, forced compliance situations can be equally as dissonant-producing as "free choice" situations (see Brehm and Cohen, 1962). In forced compliance situations, however, typical dissonance reduction behaviors are: reducing the importance of the induced behavior, changing one's private opinion to be consistent with the behavior (e.g., "I really do like vanilla ice cream"), or magnifying the reward or punishment used to induce the behavior.

It is interesting to note that Festinger does not view intention as crucial to the production of dissonance. On the contrary, he posits that even involuntary exposure to information that is somehow inconsistent with established cognitions results in dissonance. Even the individual who overhears dissonant information must engage in dissonance-reducing activities. Festinger would add that should a large number of persons agree with the overheard information, dissonance will be exacerbated.

The effects of volition (Brehm and Cohen, 1962), self-involvement (Deutsch et al., 1962), cognitive overlap (Brock, 1963), regret (Festinger and Walster, 1964; Walster, 1964), the greater importance of postdecisional processes over predecisional processes in producing alternative revaluation (Davidson and Kiesler, 1969; Jecker, 1964), and several other variables are exhaustive and well documented in other texts (see Insko, 1967; Fishbein, 1963, and Fishbein and Azjen, 1975). The amont of literature on dissonance theory indicates that its effects were far-reaching in the field of attitude change. Rather than balance theory and other consistency theories, Festinger focused on choice from among alternatives. Instead of imprisoning the individual in a triangle of likes and dislikes or entrapping him by assertions linking otherwise unrelated cognitive elements, he presented the individual as a choice maker in the environment. However, once the choice is made the individual is seen as obligated to defend it, a condition that may not obtain in the real world (see Chapanis and Chapanis, 1964; Elms, 1967; Bem, 1965; Eagly and Himmelfarb, 1978; Aronson, 1968; and Fishbein and Ajzen, 1975).

COUNTERATTITUDINAL ADVOCACY

A derivation of dissonance theory is found in counterattitudinal behavior research. Miller and Burgoon (1973) define the counterattitudinal persuasion technique as the preparation and presentation by the persuadee of a belief-discrepant message for some real or ostensible audience. The example they give involves a father asking his son to prepare a message containing "all the arguments he can muster" against smoking marijuana. The father is hoping that the son will convince himself to stop smoking marijuana.

According to dissonance theory, if the reward for engaging in counterattitudinal advocacy is low, individuals are more likely to construe their own behavior as indicative of their own attitudes than when they are paid handsomely to say things in contrast to their prior beliefs. In other words, if the father does not threaten the son with punishment or offer him excessive reward for preparing the belief-discrepant message, the likelihood of self-persuasion is enhanced. This perspective stands in direct contrast to incentive theory, which posits greater self-persuasion when rewards are offered (see Miller and Burgoon, 1973).

INOCULATION THEORY

Another second cousin to the straight dissonance approach to persuasion is McGuire's inoculation theory. Relying on the metaphor of immunization against the possibility of future disease, McGuire posits that persuadees can be inoculated against the possibility of encountering counterarguments in the future. McGuire (1961) and Tannenbaum and Norris (1966) have demonstrated that the most effective form of inoculation is combining supportive and refutational messages rather than merely loading the persuadee with supportive arguments. It appears that it is better to arm the persuadee with arguments with which to fight counter-persuasion attempts. For example, if the father who sends his son off to college with much evidence against marijuana-smoking also tells his son (1) to expect that others will disagree and (2) how to deal with such arguments, the likelihood of the son retaining his initial antimarijuana position is enhanced. Essentially the young man has been armed to resist the dissonance-producing capacity of counterarguments.

The decline of cognitive dissonance theory was probably due to its simplicity. Each research study evolving from a cognitive dissonance perspective added new variables that qualified the claims of Festinger's work. Too many qualifications soon render a theory obsolete. Social situations involve numerous variables in consistent interaction. Any attempt to reduce such complexity to a simple, all-encompassing law of information-processing is open to challenge.

Kuhn (1975) in *The Structure of Scientific Revolutions,* describes this theory-obsolescence process as beginning with the awareness of an anomaly (i.e., that expectations have somehow been violated) and then continues with an exploration of the anomaly. It is "only when the paradigm theory has been adjusted so that the anomalous has become the expected" (1975: 53) that a perspective is ripe for change. Kuhn explains that "novelty emerges only with difficulty, manifested by resistance, against a background provided by expectation." When sufficient evidence exists, however, to indicate that something is wrong, a period follows in which "conceptual categories are adjusted until the initially anamalous has become the anticiapted" (1975: 64).

Cognitive dissonance theory resisted the anomalous for many years. It is still alive today. The reason may lie in Kuhn's (1975: 77) description of the resilience of paradigmatic scientific theory as likely to be declared invalid "only if an alternate candidate is available to take its place." He adds that even the obvious mismatch between theory and the real world is not sufficient reason to discard a theory: "The decision to reject one paradigm is always simultaneously the decision to accept another, and the judgment leading to that decision involves the comparison of both paradigms with nature and with each other." Rather than discard a theory, its scientist defenders will devise numerous ad hoc alterations and qualifications to reduce the conflict. Hence, cognitive dissonance theory has not been rejected. Such rejection requires a new paradigm, not merely a new theory. By the time researchers were ready to question cognitive dissonance theory, they were becoming prepared to reject behaviorism altogether. To date no perspective has been offered that has generated the enthusiasm and intersubjective agreement among scientists necessary for a paradigm shift. It may be only a matter of time before one will meet the test. Perhaps then some of the theories described in this chapter will be relinquished to a reversed position in history.

In the next section we will look at a theory that applies indirectly to the process of persuasion. More than any of the perspectives previously presented in this chapter, the next perspective focuses on the formation of cognitions about persons as well as their potential for change in terms of contextual contingencies. Furthermore, we will finally return to a focus on intention, which has generally been ignored by consistency theorists.

ATTRIBUTION THEORY

According to Heider (1946, 1958) the human mind seeks sufficient reasons or explanations for the behavior of others. These take the form of causal attributions. People do this to "make possible a more or less stable, predictable, and controllable world" (1958: 80).

The concept *intention* becomes important to Heider's theory when he distinguishes between personal and impersonal causality. Personal attributions are formulated only when the individual observed appears to have performed a purposive action. Impersonal causality refers to forces outside the actor's control. Jones and Davis (1965) elaborate this perspective by suggesting that there are two prerequisites for intentionality, the knowledge that the effects of an action will result, and the ability to produce the effects. For example, a three-year-old who announces that your favorite painting is ugly may elicit laughter rather than the assignment of negative attributions (e.g., "little brat"), since the child may not realize the importance of the painting to you and her age suggests that she may not know how hurt you may feel when someone insults your taste in paintings. The

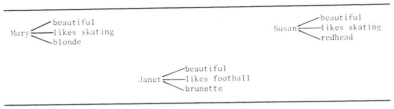

Figure 4.3

assumed absence of both malicious intention and an awareness that hurt feelings might result from her actions excuses the child from responsibility. In this case, then, the normal assignment of negative dispositions is curtailed. Should the child make a series of similar remarks at ages 10 and 16, negative attributions will probably be assigned (e.g., "thoughtless, insensitive twirp").

Jones and Davis (1965) took an interest in the degree of certainty associated with an assigned disposition. They contend that certainty depends upon the desirability of the effect resulting from an action and the extent to which these effects are common to other behavioral alternatives available to the actor. For example, if Mike decides to date a particular woman named Mary on Saturday rather than two others who are also available, it is likely that she has at least one unique characteristic. A closer look at Mary as compared to the other two women appears in Figure 4.3.

All three women are beautiful. We can conclude that Mike's selection of Mary indicates that either he prefers blondes or he prefers skating over football. If Susan also liked skating instead of football, we could be more certain that Mike prefers blondes, since the only difference among the three women would then be their hair color. If Mary turns out to be a boring date but he asks her out again, we can then assume with greater certainty that blonde hair is really very important to him.

In each case what the observer is formulating is a correspondent inference (Jones and Davis, 1965). To the extent that several plausible explanations of the observed behavior exist, certainty of attributions decreases. This perspective is consistent with Kelly's (1955) discounting principle, whereby he describes the condition of multiple causality of messages. Kelly emphasizes the importance of behavioral consistency across situations to attribution. If an individual always insists upon having the last word in a discussion, observers might conclude that he is "into power." To the extent that others in the group(s) do not behave in the same manner (distinctiveness) the likelihood of the attribution is increased. In other words, if everyone tries to have the last word, the individual in question will not stand out as being more "into power" than any other individual. Acording to Kelly, low-level consensus (the degree to which everyone performs in the same manner) also influences the likelihood of an attribution.

The work of Heider (1944, 1958), Jones and Davis (1965), Jones and Nisbett (1971), and others also point to the characteristics of the observer as influencing attributions. For example, some people are inclined to blame the environment for their own actions, whereas others always blame themselves. The poem "A woman thinks about her faults until they seem like double, a man he just forgives himself and saves the Lord the trouble" (Brooks, 1971: 214) points to this difference. A bit sexist perhaps, but it does point out the difference between defining the world in terms of external versus internal events.

Most theories of message acceptance focus on internal pressures in the form of beliefs and attitudes. Attribution theory is one of the few perspectives on persuasion that also focuses on the impact of contextual cues on message acceptance. Attribution theorists suggest that perceivers are concerned with establishing the validity of the information they receive (see Eagly and Himmelfarb, 1978). Often the accomplishment of this task requires a close look at contextual rather than personal source attributes.

SELF-ATTRIBUTION AND COUNTERATTITUDINAL ADVOCACY

Attribution theory suggests that people seek reasons or justifications for the actions of others and their own actions in order to understand certain consequences. Berlyne (1960) suggests that this behavior is most pronounced under conditions of uncertainty. Furthermore, response selection appears to be dependent on inferential processes (assignment of attributes) when ambiguity is high (see Festinger, 1954; Schachter, 1959; Bem, 1972). It is through the analysis of causal relations then that the individual comes to know which behaviors are appropriate.

Bem (1965; Bem and McConnell, 1970) suggested an attribution explanation for dissonance. He explained that when internal cues are unclear, people infer *their own* attitudes and internal states from observing *their own* behavior. For example, a sense of irritability might be construed by the individual as his own jealousy over seeing a close female friend with another guy. Labeling the emotion explains it. To the extent that this man feels that jealousy is an appropriate response to the situation, dissonance will be minimal at best. To the extent that he perceives this jealous behavior as situationally inappropriate or in conflict with his self-image, dissonance is likely. In this way attribution, specifically self-attribution, can be seen as operating as either a precursor of cognitive dissonance or a means of reducing it (e.g., the labeling of the situationally appropriate emotion may justify the irritable nature of an individual who perceives himself as generally pleasant).

It is the nonspecificity of arousal (see Schachter, 1959, 1967) that requires a search for causal attributes. People appear to react physiologically to events before they assign meaning to them. According to Zillmann (1977: 4), even sensitive individuals follow this pattern:

> Since the arousal is said to be nonspecific, the individual cannot tell from his excitatory reaction alone what, exactly, caused him to become aroused. This ambiguity regarding a reaction to his world exists even if it were assumed that the individual is equipped with a sensitive introceptive system that provides him with adequate feedback of his reaction. Since the reaction is said to be diffuse, even a sensitive feedback system could convey only a diffuse arousal reaction. According to this reasoning, then, the individual is virtually forced into employing attributional processes to "understand" his reaction and to be able to select an adaptive response.

Self-attribution theory has been used to explain counterattitudinal advocacy. If, as Bem (1965, 1968) contends, people often make inferences about their attitudes by observing their own behavior, advocating a position discrepant with one's initial position on an issue could conceivably lead one to qualify that initial stance. Bem and McConnell (1970) consider the condition of low compensation more conducive to attitude change than that of high compensation. Miller and Burgoon (1973: 73) point out that this is consistent with the dissonance perspective on counterattitudinal advocacy. However, they specify one major distinction: "For the dissonance theorist, low justification heightens the dissonance experienced by the counterattitudinal advocate. For Bem, low justification creates an external environment that causes the advocate to infer that his behaviors are indicative of his underlying attitudes." The result, as they point out, is two distinct sets of internal processes used to explain the same behavioral consequences. Despite subtle differences, self-attribution (general or counterattitudinal) perspectives contend that diffuse arousal requires the assignment of a label which then operates to influence the individual's course of behavior.

In the next section of this chapter, dissonance, attribution, and teleological (choice) explanations of human behavior are integrated into what some may consider optimistic eclecticism. However, as Eagly and Himmelfarb (1978: 544) suggest, "each of these theories embodies some aspect of the truth as we now know it to be, and fitting them together may prove to be as stimulating and insightful as having placed them in opposition in earlier times." This justification for a combined perspective must elicit "diffuse arousal" in the bodies of some social scientists who view eclecticism as a weakness characteristic of those who refuse to make commitments and enemies. Certainly we would get nowhere in social science if all people compromised their perspectives. Yet it takes only one look at the history of the motion picture camera or the light bulb to realize the value of theoretical integration.

CONSTRUCTS, RULES, AND CONSISTENCY: A NEW APPROACH

The concepts of balance, congruity, and dissonance have in common "the notion that thoughts, beliefs, attitudes, and behavior tend to organize themselves in meaningful and sensible ways" (Zajonc, 1960: 280). This perspective presumes human rationality. Inconsistency is viewed as an uncomfortable state that imposes pressure on the individual to reduce it. While it may be true that humans prefer consistency over inconsistency, Zajonc (1960) tells us that the ways humans achieve the former manifest a striking lack of rationality. He points to Allport's (1954) example of human irrationality in inconsistency reduction:

Mr. X: The trouble with Jews is that they only take care of their own group.

Mr. Y: But the record of the community chest shows that they give more generously than non-Jews.

Mr. X: That shows that they are always trying to buy favor and intrude in Christian affairs. They think of nothing but money; that is why there are so many Jewish bankers.

Mr. Y: But a recent study shows that the percentage of Jews in banking is proportionately much smaller than the percentage of non-Jews.

Mr. X: That's just it. They don't go in for respectable business. They would rather run nightclubs.

Zajonc points out that while the concept of consistency may acknowledge man's rationality, actual observations of behavior aimed at achieving it reveal irrationality.

Zajonc's observation suggests the reason consistency, balance, and congruity theories have not proved useful in predicting behavior. While it may indeed be true that people seek to avoid inconsistency among beliefs, what they define as inconsistent and the means by which they reduce inconsistency are often influenced by idiosyncratic considerations. For example, according to balance theory, individuals do not want their good friends to be liked by their enemies. However, as Zajonc points out, an individual, concerned for a friend's welfare, may not want his or her enemies to dislike a friend. This concern for a friend creates a situation that is inconsistent with balance theory. The question is, Are these inconsistencies the exception or the rule? In other words, does the human need for consistency exist across situations while the means by which it is achieved are highly situation-dependent? If so, it should come as no surprise to find that behavior is not always consistent with attitude.

While it is true that none of the theories discussed in this chapter is presumed to account for all human behavior, the theories do suggest that when other things are held constant, the principles of consistency should provide adequate explanations. As Zajonc suggests, the question to be raised here is, Just what factors operating in the context of human interaction must be held constant?

Let us look again at an individual who does not appear to mind having her friends liked by her enemies. We could conclude that this example merely represents a long line of consistency-theory projection failures. After all, the behavior of accepting enemy and friend attraction does not correspond to the tenets of consistency theory. Instead, let us continue for a moment to accept the viability of consistency theory and focus on just what constitutes inconsistency for this individual. It is possible that individuals differ in their tolerance for inconsistency or in their definitions of what constitutes inconsistency. Perhaps the woman in our example did not perceive an inconsistency, or she may have seen a greater inconsistency problem existing in ignoring a friend's welfare by denying her the comfort of other friends (even though, to the woman of our example, these friends are enemies). The problem with inconsistency theory may not be faulty logic but the inappropriate designation of primary inconsistency. It has been demonstrated over and over that inconsistency is a troublesome

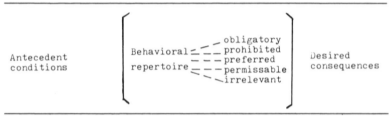

Figure 4.4

condition for people, but inconsistency as defined by whom and compared to what other possibilities of inconsistency? The behaviorist paradigm did not allow for the possibility of an experimenter-subject construct system and/or rule discrepancy. Asking the subject his or her perception of the situation was not a preferred method. What is being suggested here is that the behaviorists were not wrong about the influence of inconsistency on human behavior, but their "world view" prevented them from operationalizing inconsistency in terms of particular subjects or subject-population perceptions.

In our friend-enemy attraction situation, a higher-order inconsistency in the woman's rule system for behavior toward friends made it difficult for her to stand in the way of her friend's relationship with enemies. To be a "good friend" one must be generally concerned for the other's feelings and welfare. Requiring that a friend be disliked by an enemy when it may be to the friend's benefit to be liked by the enemy creates an uncomfortable sense of inconsistency. This is an example of the workings of what has been called "conscience" in the psychological literature. The threat of a higher-order inconsistency requires accepting a lower-order inconsistency.

Given that this explanation is feasible, let us consider how this example fits into the construct/rule model discussed in Chapter 2. The antecedent conditions shown in Figure 4.4 are person A's construals of friendship based on past behaviors or observations of "friendly" and "unfriendly" behavior. While it may be perfectly acceptable by society's standards for person A to prefer that her enemies dislike her friends, it may be prohibited to expect this. Even if society, as person A knows it, does not prohibit such expectations, person A's own idiosyncratic rules may. In the latter case, predictability as afforded by consistency theory is weakened, unless one knows the individual very well. In the former case, however, the researcher who knows the expectations of the subject population's reference groups could still retain some predictive power. This interpretation provides a place for inconsistent attitudes and behavior under the rubric of "rational." Human rationality is not merely a function of consistency but of the type and degree of consistency. An individual sees his or her behaviors as sensible if they do not challenge the validity of a high-priority rule in his or her repertoire.

Let us return for a moment to the discussion of deception in Chapter 3. Certainly, lying is inconsistent with those societal and personal rules that encourage honesty. However, it appears that most of us accept certain amounts of deception because it is consistent with higher-order rules ensuring relational and even societal maintenance. We reason our perceived inconsistency away by suggesting that particular aspects of the context account for the deception.

In terms of the correspondence between actual conditions and the rule applied, inconsistency can also only be "in the eyes of the beholder." The person whose behavior appears inconsistent may actually be unaware of those aspects of a context that would render his or her rule-following behavior inappropriate. For example, if a man is intimate with a woman who perceives intimacy as an antecedent condition for applying a rule that precludes dating other persons, does his decision to be intimate with other women make him a deceitful character? What if he does not see intimacy as an antecedent condition for exclusivity in relationships? In this case he is not likely to experience inconsistency unless she can convince him that his behavior violates another rule that is important to him.

The important question here is, What is the superordinate construct that renders the rule for exclusivity appropriate or inappropriate? For her, the relationship superordinate construct could be "lovers," whereas his superordinate construct might be "friends." Intimacy may not be an indication of love for him, whereas intimacy may imply more than friendship for her.

The question appears to be, What type of relationship does intimacy imply? Both persons recognize that they are intimate but interpret it differently in the designation of a superordinate construct—friend or lover.

It is difficult at best to capture this conflict of logics by referring to traditional consistency theories. These two persons both have positive feelings toward each other and toward intimacy. The result is a balanced configuration on this issue alone (see Figure 4.5).

Despite this balance, the relationship is in trouble. It is possible that she sees intimacy as a condition that renders the application of an exclusivity rule sensible (Figure 4.6). If he agrees that they are in love, his logic might

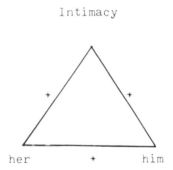

Figure 4.5

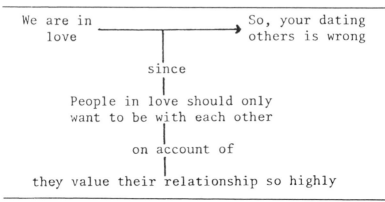

Figure 4.6

be that shown in Figure 4.7. Balance theory configurations would not provide this overall picture of logic supporting the claims. It would merely supply the configurations shown in Figure 4.8.

It is also possible that they both individuals agree on the association of love and exclusivity but differ in their definition of the relationship. This condition is not easily explained by balance theory, because perceptions of each other and exclusivity under conditions of love and friendship are

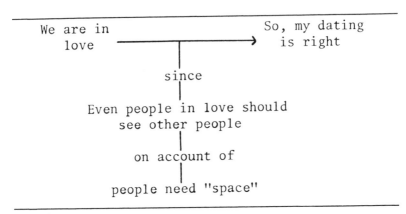

We are in   So, my dating
   love ———————————→   is right

                    since

        Even people in love should
            see other people

              on account of

          people need "space"

Figure 4.7

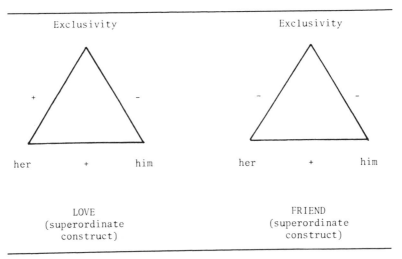

Exclusivity   Exclusivity

her   +   him   her   +   him

LOVE   FRIEND
(superordinate   (superordinate
construct)   construct)

Figure 4.8

balanced (Figure 4.9).

Apparent balance, then, is not a sufficient basis on which to conclude that all is well. In this situation, the lovers agree on the rules for exclusivity under the conditions of love and friendship but do not agree that intimacy is a sufficient condition to label the relationship one of love rather than friendship. Essentially their constitutive rules differ for loving relationships. In the previous example, they were in agreement concerning the

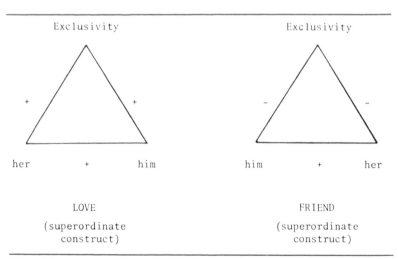

Figure 4.9

constitutive rule for love, but disagreed on the regulative rule with which this condition corresponds.

The example suggests that while inconsistency is an uncomfortable state for most of us, we differ in our tolerance for it and also in our recognition of its existence. What appears to be inconsistent behavior to one individual might be very consistent to another. The persuader must uncover the underlying logics of the involved parties to determine the origin of the perceived inconsistency.

The example also demonstrates that inconsistency is not an "out there" phenomenon. It is a function of the rule system of the actor. In Chapters 2 and 3, the concept of appropriateness was described as an additional concern of humans in their behavioral choices. Perceptions of appropriateness, like consistency, are not always shared. Unlike consistency, however, appropriateness is determined on the basis of standards external to the actor. This means that while individuals use them to guide behavior, these standards "belong" to the society, organization, group, or dyad in which the individual operates. Consistency designations are based on internal standards or what was referred to in Chapter 2 as the self-concept. It can be said that the actor perceives that he or she "owns" these standards. Hence, in order to support the claim that some behavior is inconsistent, the persuader must know the rules that define the actor's self-concept.

This differentiation in terms is important because the common usage of these words can muddle the lines of distinction between them. It is possible to consider a behavior "inappropriate" because it is inconsistent with what the actor typically does in a given situation. However, for the purposes of this text, the designation *inappropriate* will be used to refer to violations of what the persuader considers widely shared among members of the society, organization, group, or dyad. *Inconsistency* refers to the persuader's perception that some behavioral choice violates what he or she perceives to be the self-concept rules of the persuadee. *Ineffectiveness* refers to a poor choice of behavior given persuadee-desired consequences.

Persuasion, then, involves demonstrating that the logic (construct, rules, and their linkages) under which an individual is operating is (a) inappropriate, given the standards people in a particular context generally follow, (b) inconsistent, given what is known of the persuadee's past behaviors in similar situations, and/or (c) not likely to bring about the attainment of actor-desired consequences.

The friend-versus-lover example given earlier suggests that appeals to consistency, appropriateness, and/or effectiveness may fail miserably if the persuadee's superordinate constructs differ from those the persuader assumes are guiding rule application. Sometimes a persuader must demonstrate that the superordinate construct(s) being used by the persuadee are inaccurate representations of the "actual" situation before a reasonable case for inconsistency, inappropriateness, or ineffectiveness can be made. As mentioned in Chapter 3, superordinate constructs are integrations of context-specific constructs and their associated effects, used in connection with desired consequences to select and order behavioral options. Superordinate constructs, like their lower-order construct components, are interpretations. They are integrations of contextual perceptions. As such, they are subject to error. For example, the integrations may be made without consideration of all the data (as in the policeman example of Chapter 1), or the persuadee may order his or her antecedent condition constructs differently from the persuader, thus generating what the persuader sees as an inaccurate superordinate construct (e.g., lover versus friend). It is important, then, that the persuader consider the logic behind the persuadee's rule application before using one of the three approaches to persuasion.

Another complication arises from the integration of rules. For example, it is possible for an individual to derive most of his or her rules for self from a particular group. In such cases, the self-concept is not autonomous, and inconsistency is usually an indication of inappropriateness as well. Gang and cult members are characterized by this absence of autonomous selves. Most of us have multiple enmeshments in groups and relationships from which we derive some sense of self. In general, then, appeals to inconsistency and inappropriateness refer to different rules. However, in those cases in which one group defines the self, persuasion that removes the individual from the group should be directed at recalling or recreating a separate self-concept to act as a source of criticism for the group rules. This is a form of deprogramming.

The fact that groups and dyadic relationships can become the major source of self-definition for some persons requires that the persuader and the scientist treat self-autonomy as a variable influencing the selection of persuasive appeals. In general, we can assume that people perceive that some rules "belong" to them, whereas others guide their behavior from without. Persuaders must recognize the extent of perceived rule-ownership in a given context before they can determine whether appeals to behavioral appropriateness, consistency, effectiveness, or construct order or inclusion accuracy best serve their purposes.

CONCLUSION

In this chapter we traced the development of theories of persuasion. Early consistency theories became a hallmark of this field and contributed greatly to our understanding of the process of behavior change. The behaviorist paradigm, however, limited the extent to which scientists could venture into the human mind to uncover the nature of consistency. The approaches to persuasion introduced in this chapter do, however, venture down that path. The result is a tripartite perspective on rule-based persuasion appeals—consistency, appropriateness, effectiveness. In addition, we recognize that while the rules applied in a given situation may be consistent, appropriate, and effective, given the persuadee's perception of the antecedent conditions and desired consequences, those perceptions may be inaccurate (some aspects of the context may have been ignored or never seen). In such cases, the persuader must assist the persuadee in a recon-

strual of antecedent conditions before using any consistency, appropriateness, or effectiveness appeals.

The next chapter will focus on the difficulties persuader and scientist
must face in their attempts to uncover the logics behind human behavioral
choices.

Chapter 5

PERSUASION RECONSIDERED

An Exercise in Rigorous Eclecticism

The theoretical orientations of persuasion research described in Chapter 4 gave little attention to the logic behind choices and the influence of context on those choices. Today, the reader of communication, psychology, and social psychology journals can find frequent calls for movement away from noncontextual, deterministic perspectives (see Eagly and Himmelfarb, 1978; Miller et al., 1977; Rosenthal, 1972; Heath, 1976). The methodological problems posed by a theoretical base which recognizes what Rosenthal (1972) refers to as the "coalescence of source, message, and context data" are at this time very challenging. However, communication research during the last decade has made great strides toward meeting this challenge. In the next several chapters, much of that research and its relationship to a new theoretical model of persuasion will be discussed.

THE SEASON FOR CHANGE

Some of our most influential contemporary rhetoricians and scientists are calling for a movement away from purely message-centered approaches to persuasion. Rosenthal (1972) points to the limitations of the age-old rhetorical emphasis on the message as the causal agent of persuasive effect. He explains that, "when pressed, those steeped in such theory will usually assent to the proposition that there is peripheral information transmitted in a communication and that receivers do respond to this information in some way. However, as a group, rhetoricians have never interested themselves in or speculated upon this aspect of the process" (1972: 15).

Rosenthal gives some credit to modern behavioral influence for beginning to erode the rigid focus of rhetorical persuasion analyses, but adds that even this approach is based on a model that assumes message primacy. Source credibility, for example, has been treated as a facilitator of message impact rather than as a perhaps more central or significant aspect of the persuasive process. Whether this is also true of more recent studies of source credibility is questionable, but Rosenthal's position that the fixation of communication theory and research upon message effect blinds us to the complexity of human communication has important implications for future work.

Other contemporary rhetoricians have also seen the import of loosening the hold of the message-effect model. Lloyd Bitzer (1968) has described the communication context as an invitation to create a fitting response. This implies the existence of context-dependent normative forces imposing on the choices of communicators. Herbert Simons (1976: 59) contends that "meaning is always contextual" and successful communication depends on the communicator's ability to "anticipate the receiver's sense of 'logic' of the situation."

Miller et al. (1977), like Rosenthal, Bitzer, and Simons, challenge their social scientist colleagues to consider more carefully the influence of situational or context variables on the selection of persuasive strategies. They point to the abundance of empirical research showing that interactions between persons, situations, and behaviors account for at least as much total variation as any of these sources alone. They suggest a new direction: "The scope of future research on persuasive influence must be expanded from predominantly source-oriented or message-centered conceptualizations to perspectives which account for the domains of source traits, message choices, situational effects, and their interactions" (1977: 51).

The perspective of contemporary constructivists has harmonized with the increasing recognition of situational influences and contributed substantially to the acceptance of the individual as an important focus of research. Delia et al. (1979: 244), for example, add to our understanding of source impressions and message construction variations by explaining that

individuals with complex systems of interpersonal constructs tend to erect more organized, stable, and psychologically centered impressions of others. Since it is the impression one forms of another which serves as the basis for message formulation and adaptation, individuals who form more differentiated, stable, and psychologically centered impressions tend to produce more listener-adapted messages. By this reasoning the development of a complex system of interpersonal constructs is a necessary prerequisite for the formulation of sensitively adapted messages.

The work of Clark and Delia (1977) O'Keefe and Delia (1979), and other constructivists provide research support for derivations of this perspective. Eagly and Himmelfarb (1978: 553-554), representing psychological rather than communication perspectives, call for a new persuasion theoretical base:

There has been a welcome convergence of thought and empirical findings on the necessary conditions for certain attitude change phenomena. In addition, there is widespread recognition that any "simple and sovereign" explanation is likely to account for only one cell in a triple-interaction matrix. A blurring of older theoretical lines . . . has occurred. Each of these theories embodies some aspect of the truth as we know it to be, and fitting them together may prove to be as stimulating and insightful as having placed them in opposition in earlier times

Finally, in terms of human subject influences, Fishbein and Ajzen (1975), in their discussion of inference beliefs, acknowledge that researchers do not always possess the same beliefs as the subject populations they study. In reference to McGuire's logical consistency model, Fishbein and Ajzen contend that there is no reason to assume that McGuire's subjects perceived as strong a relationship between premise and conclusions as McGuire did. In addition, they conclude that taking the strength of this relationship into account could conceivably improve prediction of change in inferential belief due to change in a target belief.

In response to this widespread call for theory embracing context and subject input, a theoretical model of persuasion will be introduced in this chapter which purposely blurs fictitious and real lines of opposition to integrate the best of the old with the new.

SELF-AUTONOMY

In the final segment of Chapter 4, a new perspective on consistency was introduced. This perspective serves to separate behavioral consistency from appropriateness considerations and in so doing provides a place for self-concept in the study of persuasion. If individuals did not have a sense of identity "belonging" solely to them—establishing them as unique and influencing their actions—there would be no reason for separating consistency from appropriateness considerations. The self would be determined by the expectations of others; as it moved from group to group, it would change with each new context. Such a conceptualization does not correspond with the reality most of us experience. Attribution theory, trait theories, and a long line of first-impression studies indicate that we approach others as if they possess some characteristic modes of behavior and ways of thinking that they and others may call their own. While it may be true that we derive some aspects of ourselves from learning what behavior is appropriate in the contexts we experience, our personal cognitive assimilation and accommodation processes create a series of interpretations that are ours alone.

As mentioned in the previous chapter, cults represent the extreme of the self-autonomy continuum wherein the self is submerged in a group definition. For a cult member, that which is appropriate is also consistent. There is no identity outside the rules prescribed by the group. The multiple group enmeshments characteristic of most human activity are absent for cult members. Their lives center on the needs of the cult. Only the reemergence of an autonomous self provides a lever for extricating the self from a cult. Without a self, incorporating rules beyond those of one group, criticism is impossible. In this sense, our autonomous selves provide a check on the group pressures we all experience.

Approaches to persuasion that emphasize the inappropriateness (rather than the inconsistency or ineffectiveness) of a behavior imply that in a particular context the persuadee has not followed the rules others expect persons like him or her to follow. These rules are perceived by the persuadee as "on loan" rather than "owned" by him or her. A rejection of them indicates that adherence would violate some more valued, "owned" rule. In this case, the individual opts for consistency over appropriateness.

If people can choose to be consistent, appropriate, effective, or all three, persuaders must determine under what conditions consistency, appropriateness, or effectiveness appeals will work best. They must estimate the relative contribution of "owned" versus "borrowed" rules to behavioral selection. To the extent that personal rules predominate, appeals to consistency are warranted. Conversely, to the extent that contextual rules predominate, an appeal to appropriateness is the more sensible choice. Effectiveness combines self and other perceptions of the extent of goal achievement attainable, given the persuadee's behavioral choice.

The following persuasive conversation, involving three family members (father, mother, and bachelor daughter) exemplifies the use of effectiveness appeals:

Mom: You'd better stock up on peanut butter.

Daughter: Oh, I don't know.

Mom: There's going to be a shortage this year. It happened with lettuce and toilet paper.

Dad: She lives alone. How much peanut butter can one person eat? I wouldn't bother.

Mom: Well, she could buy a few small jars.

Dad: They go bad.

Mom: No they don't. Only the big jars go bad.

Daughter: I'll buy a couple of small jars.

Mom: I would.

Dad: Do what you want. Peanut butter isn't one of my areas of expertise.

The reason given for stocking up on peanut butter is that there may be a shortage. To avoid being left without peanut butter, the daughter is advised to buy some now. The rule implicit here is: If there is to be a product shortage, one should stock up on products likely to become scarce. Stocking up on such products may be appropriate (others think the daughter should do so) and consistent (the daughter always does so). However, it is not likely that significant others will be upset if preparation for the product shortage is not carried out, nor is there any indication in the conversation that the mother sees this action as consistent with her daughter's rules. The mother assumes that her daughter wants to have peanut butter in her house (desired consequent) and therefore considers the effective thing to do under the circumstances is to buy peanut butter before the supply runs out, a highly situation-dependent appeal.

Research focusing on the influence of situational versus personal differences variables on behavior indicates that significant main effects for situational variables are found much more often than significant individual or person effects. In many of these studies, however, the interaction (situation × person) effect is strongest (Sarason et al., 1975).

McLaughlin (1979: 4) interprets these findings as insufficient reason to disregard dispositional theories: "Whether or not it is meaningful to construe traits as 'causes' of behavior, it is nevertheless the case that individuals do behave in a consistent fashion with sufficient regularity to induce others to infer internal or intraindividual sources of motivation." She suggests that individuals are inclined to form characteristic constructions of interpersonal events and that it is therefore reasonable to assume that they adopt habits of interaction which coincide with a preferred view of self vis-à-vis social encounters.

The position adopted in this text is that people do have a sense of self, and this self is best described as a set of rules made up of those that "belong" to the individual (transcontextual) or are derived from the dyad, group, organization, or society with which the person is affiliated. The balance of "owned" rules and "borrowed" ones in any given context reflects the potential level of self-autonomy.

It is possible to construe self-autonomy as a transcontextual feature of the individual. Carl Edwards (1973) has identified three modes of adaptive interaction that appear to vary in the amount of situation versus personal behavior-selection guidance employed. He describes the cooperational mode as reflective of individuals who focus on reciprocity in interactions and are inclined to consider the needs of others when choosing behavior. People with an analytic perspective on interaction prefer to pursue non-normative courses of action in their search for a better alternative. Finally, people adopting an "instrumental" perspective are characterized by reliance on tradition or custom as guides to behavior. This perspective leads us to a variable important to cognitive theories of persuasion.

LOCUS OF CONTROL

Edward's perspective suggests that people tend to focus on others, the self, or the situation for guidance in behavioral selection. A similar perspective has been advanced by advocates of locus-of-control theory. Rotter (1966) describes individuals as either internals or externals. Internals expect to affect situations, whereas externals perceive the environment as controlling their lives. Rotter's work and subsequent research in this area treats the individual as the center of prediction and control in human interaction. There is also some evidence that locus of control influences perception of causation and responsibility in the activities of others, as well as perceptions of self-causation (Alderton, 1979).

McDermott (1974: 13) proposes that locus of control "defines the situation for an individual by providing the criteria for choice in that situation." She adds that the locus of control may be perceived in social reality, personal reality, or physical reality. An individual may perceive the locus of control for his or her behaviors as residing in social norms, especially those prescribed by significant others.

When the locus of control is perceived in personal rather than social reality, the focus is on one's expectations for self concerning what should or should not be done (Fishbein, 1967; Seibold, 1975). Finally, when the locus of control is perceived in physical reality, "information about environmental resources or physical contingencies which have been communicated to the individual determine choice by dictating means-end relationships" (McDermott, 1974: 15).

These locus-of-control perspectives suggest that the self is a powerful agent of influence on behavior. Without denying the self's contribution to behavioral choice, this text advances a context X self-interaction approach. Persuadee perceptions of self-control and situational influence are seen as variable and responsive to the competent persuader.

Self-emphasis is influenced by the nature of the context. Initial interactions are a case in point. People seem to request and convey very little personal information in these situations (Duck, 1973; Berger, 1975; Berger and Calabrese, 1975; Rubin, 1979). One interpretation of this phenomenon is that context predominance is characteristic of initial interactions. As the relationship develops, the risk involved in finding alternative approaches (analytic) is lessened. Thus, people more frequently engage in behavior reflective of self-autonomy. Context, then, is one factor that influences whether an individual will take the risk involved in nonnormative behavior. According to McLaughlin (1979), ordinary people simply do not conform unequivocally to global types. People and contexts together determine levels of self-autonomy.

Where does this leave the persuader? It should indicate that sometimes appeals to appropriateness or effectiveness are more useful than appeals to consistency, since certain contextual features can render high self-autonomy too risky. The persuader must determine what aspects of the context are likely to be interpreted by the persuadee as conducive to self-autonomy, and which ones are not. This will not provide all the information needed to determine conclusively that appeals to consistency do not constitute a viable approach to persuasion, but if, as in most advertising, time permits addressing only one issue, a person may determine on the basis of context predominance to focus on the appropriateness or effectiveness of the persuadee's behavior. To the extent that the persuader also knows the persuadee's typical locus of control, prediction may be facilitated.

What has been described above is the existence of a persuadee superordinate construct of self-autonomy that functions to limit or extend the behavioral choices available to the actor in a given situation. If the context can be so structured that very little room exists for nonnormative behavior, the persuader need not be overly concerned about persuadee perceptions of autonomy. Television advertisers devote much enegy to the creation of predominant contexts surrounding idealized role concepts. They fabricate images of proficient housewives, perfect parents, gorgeous men and women, contented marrieds, and male comaraderie, to name a few. Then, through the marvels of modern music, photography, fast-paced action and repetition, they invest these images with immediacy and importance.

Advertisers do not have time to deal with individual rules and therefore attract us with the contexts and then provide us with information on how to access them. Buying soap, toothpaste, deodorant, or beer has, as a result of advertising, become surrounded by connotations from which few of us escape untouched. Even the purchase of toilet paper has become associated with doing what is appropriate for one's family.

Although this description of advertising is not intended to exclude consistency approaches to persuasion from mass media, as later chapters will show, mass media focus less on personal rules than interpersonal, group, and organizational communication. The large audiences and minimal feedback opportunities charactertistic of the mass media require that they appeal to role expectations or, in their absence, create them.

Movement along a continuum from mass media to organizational, group, and interpersonal communication is also movement away from person-extrinsic rule predominance to person-intrinsic rule predominance. In this sense it is also a movement toward greater opportunity for effective consistency appproaches to persuasion.

CONTEXT TYPES

Throughout this and previous chapters, the influence of situation on persuader and persuadee logic has been emphasized. To this point, however, just exactly what distinguishes one context from another has not been clearly articulated. In the next sections of this chapter, the question of what constitutes "context types" and how they influence persuasion will be addressed.

The first step in the designation of context types is to establish some criteria for distinguishing among them. Several attempts to provide such criteria have already been made (Magnussen, 1971; Forgas, 1976; Miller and Steinberg, 1975; Cody, 1978; Cody and McLaughlin, 1980). Of these, a study by Cody and McLaughlin (1980) is the most relevant to persuasion and the most subject-oriented. It is important to note, however, as they do, that any attempt to specify situation types could do more harm than good if experimenters were to impose them on subjects a priori, without considering their "special" perceptions of the experimental context.

Perhaps the most impressive aspect of the Cody and McLaughlin study of compliance-gaining situations is their attention to relevance. They did not presume to "know" their subjects. They conducted two pretests using different sets of subjects in order to construct a population of relevant dyadic situations (1980: 135). They then selected three sets of twelve situations at random with replacement, for the multidimensional scaling analysis. Examples of these situations (1980: 136) include the following:

- Persuade a boy/girlfriend that there is nothing wrong in occasionally dating another person.
- Persuade your professor that a test item was ambiguous.
- Persuade your boss to let you leave work early.
- Persuade your parents to let you stay out.
- Persuade a bouncer to let you into a bar even though you have forgotten you I.D.

Subjects were asked to rate the thirty-six situations on the basis of attribute scales. Cody and McLaughlin relied on previous studies for their selection of attributes rather than on pretest. There is room for skepticism here, not because previous research is not useful, but because Cody and McLaughlin themselves considered previous research an inadequate source of situation types. The inclusion of a "miscellaneous" attribute may have allowed them to examine the exhaustiveness of their scales. They wrote them "to encompass any number of diverse types of dimensions that might emerge" (1980: 138). They used statements about the following eight attributes to rate the situations derived from pretests: superficial versus intimate; formality/status; influencability; friendly versus unfriendly; resistance; familiarity; personal benefits; miscellaneous. From their analyses, five dimensions emerged as constituting the most salient differences among situations relevant to college students: intimacy, personal benefits, resistance, dominance, and consequences. For a second study, an additional criterion was generated: rights. Then a factor analytic study was conducted to confirm the six factors and assess their internal consistency. The results were encouraging. A multiple discriminant analysis provided several significant differences between sampled situations (borrowed from previous studies by Miller et al., 1977; Cody, 1978; and Kaminski et al., 1977), indicating that the scales differentiated among situations.

Cody and McLaughlin suggest thaat we interpret their results with caution, since there is room for improving the factor structure and internal consistency through the use of additional items. Nevertheless, their results do indicate that some criteria are more salient than others in differentiating among situations. They point to a study by Ruth Anne Clark (1979b) in which Clark found that persuader self-interest and desire to maintain a liking relationship with the target influence certain characteristics of the message created by the persuader, as evidence of the potential predictive power of their factors. They suggest, on the basis of Clark's findings, that situations involving intimacy, long-term consequences, and few perceived rights "would yield messages high in statements of explicit concern for the other and low in degree of pressure exerted." They add, "Similarly, a persuader may be unlikely to use any second-order compliance-gaining strategy in situations involving few rights in which the first-attempt message failed. Personal commitment strategies could prove to be a function of intimacy and resistance. A disclaimer strategy of the form 'I don't want to appear pushy, but . . .' could turn out to be a function of intimacy, fewer rights and resistance" (Cody and McLaughlin, 1980: 147).

The work of Cody and McLaughlin (1980), and that of others interested in specifying ways of differentiating among situations, constitutes a welcome examination of a complex variable usually given some attention in the discussion sections of communication journal articles as a reason for nonsignificant findings, but rarely treated as the focus of these investigations. Their findings and the caution they encourage regarding the imposition of any situational types without regard for the subject population under observation constitute a positive step toward dealing with the unwieldly concept of context. It is with their caution in mind, and the ideas advanced in the first section of this chapter, that a model of persuadee logic is advanced in the next section.

CONTEXT PREDOMINANCE AND SUBORDINATION

Earlier in this chapter, mass media advertising was described as creating conditions of context predominance. Context predominance refers to those situations in which self-concept rules are subordinated to the demands of context rules. In such situations, persuasion appeals focusing on the appropriateness and effectiveness of people's behaviors are seen as more effective than consistency appeals, which require greater attention to the persuadee's "owned" rules. It was suggested that persuaders must determine the degree of self-autonomy afforded by the context in order to decide whether appeals focusing on the consistency, appropriateness, or effectiveness of the persuadee's behavior might prove most useful. The Cody and McLaughlin (1980) research provided dimensions to be used for differentiating among situations and predicting behavior. Their work could also provide the persuasion researcher with some guidance in determining the level of context predominance perceived by subjects. For example, the dimensions of rights, personal benefits, and resistance (see Figure 5.1) focus on self more than other or situation, as indicated by the predominance of "I" references. A closer examination of these factors might provide some clues as to the level of self-autonomy persuaders view as guiding their own and persuadee behaviors. Furthermore, the Cody and McLaughlin dimensions could be used to compare persuader-persuadee construct and rule organization.

Finally, these dimensions can be used to guide the development of questions that will clarify the superordinate constructs and rules utilized by each interactant, as well as their order. It may be a bit premature in our research on situation types to consider the Cody and McLaughlin study the final word on dimensions. However, their focus on interpersonal compliance-gaining situations and their attention to subject perceptions render it a strong candidate for guiding attempts to uncover persuader-persuadee constructs and rules.

Figure 5.1 incorporates their findings into the construct-rule linkage model. This model suggests that the type of context may influence construct and superordinate construct organization, and thus persuadee perceptions of the self-autonomy and context predominance balance. Persuasion, then, involves (a) some demonstration of the inconsistency between presumed persuadee personal construction organization and behavioral choice, (b) a demonstration of the inappropriateness of a behavioral choice, given a significant other's typical construct organization in such situations, and/or (c) a demonstration of the ineffectiveness of a behavioral choice, given the persuadee's desired consequences. Superordinate construct Z was added to indicate that A-G are not necessarily exhaustive.

The distinctions between interpersonal and noninterpersonal persuasion will be discussed at greater length in Chapters 6 and 7. For now, it is important to note that context predominance is more frequent in noninterpersonal interactions. Mass media and formal organizations are char-

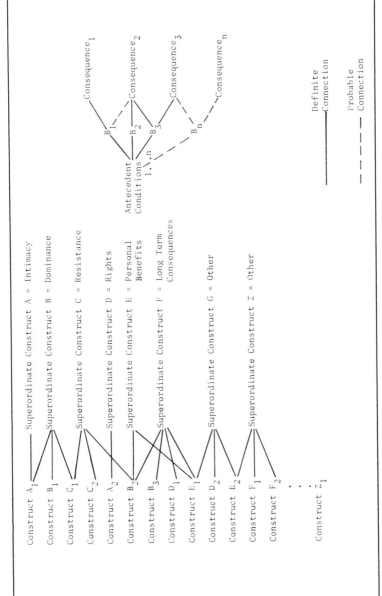

Figure 5.1 Construct–Rule Linkage for Persuadee Logic

acterized by fewer opportunities for self-autonomy on the part of inter-actants, except, as Reardon-Boynton and Fairhurst (1978) indicate, in horizontal (same-status) organizational communications. This does not mean that mass media fail to portray instances of high individual autonomy or that organizations are invariable in amount of acceptable self-autonomy. It does mean that in noninterpersonal (as opposed to interpersonal) contexts, there is generally a greater tendency to utilize (mass media) and abide by (organizations) role prescriptions rather than personal rules.

THE INFLUENCE OF STYLE AND
RELATIONSHIP TYPE

Interpersonal communication is also characterized by interaction styles such as those proposed by Edwards (1973). As mentioned earlier in this text, Edwards divided interpersonal adaptive modes into three types: cooperational, analytic, and instrumental. People's interaction-style prefer-ences can be characterized as typically cooperational, analytic, or instru-mental on the basis of how much attention they pay to others, self, or situation. If we accept Edward's division of interaction modes, then persua-dees' construct and superordinate construct orders can be said to depend on their particular interaction mode preferences. If the questions asked by a researcher reflect only situational information, then other- and self-oriented constructs will be virtually ignored. What is needed, then, is a typology of relationships that reflects an individual's position vis-à-vis another person. If the persuadee is cooperational then we should find relationship constructs higher in priority than self or situation. Similarly, persons fitting the instrumental description should give a higher priority to situation, since they are typically guided by tradition or custom rather than the needs of self or others. Finally, analytic persons pose some problems for scientists, since they prefer to pursue nonnormative courses of action. As the culprit who breeds error variance, the analytic in each of us requires that some attention be paid to individual rules, a luxury usually enjoyed only by those who engage in case studies.

Even if it is difficult to account for individual differences in our predictions, we are not relegated to using only situational information as a basis. Otherwise we would have to hope for all of our subjects to be instrumental in their modes of interaction. Instead we might look to the research on relationship types for some guidance. The Cody and McLaughlin dimensions include intimacy, resistance, and dominance. These terms are also found in relationship literature. However, the fact that intimate persons can act in a nonintimate way in situations usually considered intimate is one reason to avoid assuming that an intimate situation will necessarily elicit intimate behavior from its interactants. Relationship typologies such as those proposed by Fitzpatrick (1977) should be used along with situational types to determine the order of constructs and associated rules available to the persuadee (see Chapter 7). If the persuader recognizes that a particular view of a relationship is influencing persuadee behavior, then he or she can attempt to demonstrate the inaccuracy of that superordinate construct. Typologies such as those proposed by Fitzpatrick provide information about the typical behavior patterns of each relationship member. From this, the presence of rules may be inferred and a logic derived through account analyses. Furthermore, if a relationship type can be identified, the level of self-autonomy for both persons and thereby the potential usefulness of consistency, appropriateness, and effectiveness appeals may be predicted (on autonomy/interdependence, see Bochner, 1976; Fitzpatrick, 1976; Fitzpatrick and Best, 1979).

Given that situational as well as relational typologies may prove useful in determining the constitutive logic of superordinate constructs, it follows that other classification schemes focusing on individual differences may assist in the determination of persuadee rules. For example, Courtright et al. (1979) have described the existence of a linkage between domineeringness, dominance, and relationship satisfaction, which subjects may intuitively know and use for behavior selection. These authors explain that while domineeringness says little about one's own dominance, it does decrease the likelihood of the other's dominance. They conclude from this finding that "if you do not want to be dominated, then you should increase your own domineeringness." However, there are side effects of following such advice: "Increasing your own domineeringness . . . entails the risk of decreasing your own as well as your partner's satisfaction with the relationship" (1979: 191).

Assuming that research does reflect the "real world," then Courtright et al. (1979) have successfully uncovered a segment of the logic underlying behavioral selection by linking a behavior to desirable and undesirable consequences. If we could then determine the characteristic consequent-oriented versus antecedent-oriented level of a persuadee, the importance of focusing on the linkages between behavior and consequences could be determined. In other words, if we can determine whether a person is influenced more by what came before than what may result when selecting from behavioral options, we can also determine whether appeals emphasizing the inaccuracy of antecedent condition to "reality" correspondence will be more effective than appeals focusing on the effectiveness of persuadee means for obtaining desired consequences.

It follows from this discussion that what the model in Figure 5.1 does for researchers is provide a framework for "plugging in" their particular classification schemes while controlling for or manipulating other aspects of behavioral logic. To the extent that researchers can provide situation and relationship typologies that facilitate an understanding of the superordiante constructs guiding rule application and uncover the influence of personality or style types, predictive power is increased. It is important, however, to check our own objectivity with the subjectivity of our subjects. No typology can cover all situations or relationships, but they can give us clues concerning the constructs subjects use to activate or apply rules. What the scientist is finding in these cases are the category schemes that people use to guide behavioral selection. If the subjects do not think in terms of, or at least sense the existence of, situations or relationship "types," why should scientists do so? To borrow from Kelly (1955), if we are going to "harden our categories" purposely, we should be sure that they are representative of the "real" world. To do so requires a generally ignored necessity of true social science: checking with the subjects before the experiment to determine the "range of convenience" of our schemas.

ACCOUNTS

The model of interpersonal persuasion logic in Figure 5.1 indicates that persuader understanding of the persuadee's situational, relationship, and self-concept constructs and rules can be used to develop consistency, appropriateness, and effectiveness claims. However, this model does not indicate how the substance of these claims is derived. It merely depicts the structure of the behavioral logic in terms of the connections between constructs, superordinate constructs, and rules. To know that a person has a particular construct or rule in his or her repertoire does not provide the persuader with the information he or she needs to determine the position of that construct or rule in the persuadee's repertoire. What the persuader needs is an understanding of the persuadee's reasons for connecting particular constructs and rules. These reasons will be referred to in this text as *accounts.*

According to C. Wright Mills (1940), people only do that which they can excuse or justify. This perspective implicitly acknowledges that people recognize that they are generally responsible for their actions and that, as responsible agents of their actions, they will place their relationships and self-concepts in jeopardy if they choose to perform inappropriate, inconsistent, or ineffective behaviors.

Accounts are usually studied in situations where interaction has been disrupted by some unexpected or deviant action (Hewitt and Stokes, 1975; Scott and Lyman, 1974; Reardon, 1981). Since no two persons share the same rule repertoire or interpret reality in the same way, differences concerning appropriate and consistent behaviors and accurate constructs are likely to emerge frequently in daily conversation. Reardon (1981) suggests that, given this state of affairs, communication competence requires the ability to make seemingly illogical behavioral choices appear logical. To do so requires the development of context-specific reasons for rule application. People must have at their disposal theories about why a given rule should or should not be applied. They must know why a given behavior is appropriate, consistent, and effective. They must be able to defend the accuracy (correspondence to reality) of those superordinate constructs that give the rule in question a higher position over other alternatives. Accounts, then, are the interface between elements of behavioral logics. They are the reasons for perceived connections between those elements. As such, they constitute the "why" of construct usage, rule-ordering, and rule application.

Accounts have typically been viewed as retrospective because they are provided after an "unanticipated" or "untoward" behavior has occurred (Scott and Lyman, 1974; Hewitt and Stokes, 1975). Since persuasion is a retrospective activity, the persuader can request accounts for earlier behavior before proceeding to demonstrate the inappropriateness or inconsistency of that behavior. When this occurs, persuasion becomes a reciprocal activity, with the original persuadee attempting to convince the persuader that a particular behavior was the best choice, while the original persuader either accepts the account or attempts to establish that it is illegitimate. In dyadic persuasion, for example, there may be two persuaders and two persuadees. Each person plays both roles. One provides the account while the other attempts to demonstrate its illegitimacy. To demonstrate that an account is illegitimate, the persuader must show that the gravity of the event exceeds that of the account, or that it is not acceptable among a given circle of persons (Scott and Lyman, 1974). For example, in some relationships the account, "I'm not in a good mood today," does not provide sufficient reason for being unpleasant to other members. It is an illegitimate account.

The typical view of accounts as retrospective does not preclude the possibility that successful accounts become associated with a rule and serve to support the application of that rule in future situations. In this sense, accounts are also prospective. They are the excuses and justifications that C. Wright Mills saw as precursors to behavior. They are the reasons behind rule application and, like rules, can be revised during the activities of communication and persuasion. Their range of convenience can also be curtailed or extended by attempting to use them in those situations for which an adequate account is not readily accessible.

The ability consciously to borrow an account from a similar rule suggests that persons can fabricate accounts if they cannot locate one they believe will be accepted by other interactants. The fabrication of accounts often results in discrepancies between the prospective accounts (those that precede behavior) and retrospective accounts (those that follow behavior). This is a problem for the scientist or persuader who would like to trust the account reports of the persuadee but cannot be sure that the reported account is identical or even similar to the original reason behind the behavior in question. This suggests that account analysis must be a conjoint activity, where the subjectivity of the subject (persuadee) is checked by the objective observations of the scientist (persuader) and vice versa. Neither the objective nor the subjective approach alone is likely to be sufficient.

RULE INCOMPATIBILITY

The following conversation about why university professors and students attend conferences demonstrates how accounts can be used to justify incompatibility between two rules—one personal and the other organizational. Karen and Bill have experienced the fatigue of conferencing and are attempting to find reasons (accounts) that justify why they are willing to experience this discomfort.

> *Karen:* Sometimes I wonder why I go to these things. I really do because—I mean, you get something out of them but you get exhausted. Why do we do these things?
>
> *Bill:* To tell you what's right. To give you a context. Yeah. To see how good or bad you have it relative to [*pause*]

Karen: Really, you do. There's an awful lot to talk about—what it's like at this university versus that one.

Bill: Yeah, or "Did you hear how this university is really going down the drain?" or how it's really great.

Karen: Yeah. So part of the reason is to check. To—what do you call it? To touch base with people, to find out how bad off or how well off you are. [*pause*] But I don't know. I can't say that I've gone away from a convention in a while feeling really great. I guess there have been a lot of mixed feelings about a lot of strange happenings. I get something out of the paper presentations when they go well and listening to some of the people talk. You know, if those are good, I enjoy that. I guess it's the social part that's becoming more of a burden than a pleasure for me.

Bill: Yeah, that party last night was no fun. There were too many people. You couldn't talk.

Karen: Yeah. It was too crowded. You can't have a conversation about anything important.

Bill: No.

Karen: Or interesting. It has to be very superficial.

Bill: Boring.

Karen: And I don't know about you, but I can see myself sort of glowing. I enjoy that a little bit, but . . .

Bill: Agh! [*laugh*]

Karen: [*laugh*] It's not really me. I mean, I see when you glow, too, you know. It's not really the Bill I know. It's [*pause*]

Bill: part of me.

Karen: It's part of you. But it's not—and yet we have to do that. I don't know. I guess I'm being sour grapes or something but—

Bill: Why do you induce it upon yourself?

Karen: I don't know. [*pause*] I keep harboring the fantasy that it's going to be fun. I do enjoy seeing people I haven't seen.

Bill: That's the whole reason I think conferences should exist. It's a reunion.

Karen: Even the people on top. They come to reinforce their image too. But I think they get a little tired of it all. They go to the parties because—they make the parties. They almost have to be there. You know. Because at a conference you have "Who was there?" Wow, I talked for ten minutes with so-and-so." And that's another way of reinforcing your image. The message there is he or she listened to me for ten whole minutes.

Bill: No, the real message is, "I am so great as to be allowed . . ."

Karen: [*laughter*] Yeah, really.

Bill: " . . . to talk with someone others think is so great. Therefore, by just associating with this great person, I too am as great as I think I am great."

Karen: Right.

Bill: It's a game. It's an absolute game.

Karen: It's a marvelous game.

Karen and Bill are engaging in a form of mutual persuasion through the development of accounts. They both realize that attending conferences is compatible with some of their rules and incompatible with others. If we focus on Karen alone, the following analysis presented in Table 5.1 is possible. The conflict between these two rules was identified by Karen and Bill as a problem. Karen's violation of her personal rule is troublesome because, while her participation in conference activities is the appropriate and perhaps the effective thing to do as a professional, it is inconsistent with some of her personal rules. Bill asks her for an account: "Why do you induce this upon yourself?" Karen responds with two accounts: (1) "I keep harboring the fantasy that it's going to be fun." Perhaps as a result of recognizing that Bill will not accept this as a legitimate account, she adds (2) "I do enjoy seeing people that I haven't seen." Bill accepts this account and gives it additional force by saying, "That's the whole reason I think conventions should exist. It's a reunion." What Bill has managed to

TABLE 5.1 Regulative Rule Conflict

	Regulative Rule A	*Regulative Rule B*
Antecedent conditions	I am a member of the professional community holding	Self-concept outside of the professional "me."
Behavioral option	Attend convention parties.	Do not attend convention parties.
Desired consequent	To be percieved as an active member of that community. To prove I belong. To see how well off I am at my university.	To be appreciated for just being "me."

accomplish here is the creation of a superordinate construct, *reunion*, which gives the rule for attending conferences and parties legitimacy. It is not clear from this conversation whether or not Karen is willing to accept reunion as the superordinate construct for the conference-party-attending rule. Her subsequent comments about image management could be a reference to reunion behavior, and she may thus be reinforcing Bill's perspective. With Karen's additional input about image management, Bill concludes that they are playing a a game. Karen agrees. As a result, they grant many uncomfortable rules legitimacy, because games are not "real." They are activities that can be dismissed and so any conflict with the desire to "be accepted as 'me' " is rendered irrelevant by this construct.

This conversation segment demonstrates how people can mutually persuade in interpersonal contexts and thereby revise or replace their rules. In this conversation, the accounts for personal rule violation were co-created. The final labeling of conventions as "games" makes the continuation of the serious concern in the initial phases of the conversation inappropriate. The implied rule is that games should not be taken too seriously. This rule makes further search for reasons unnecessary and thereby negates the perception of incompatibility between Karen's personal and social rules. It is important to note that the cocreation of rule violation accounts is a form of persuasion. In this situation, it resulted in the implementation of superordinate constructs (reunion and game) which dismissed the rule inconsistency experienced by Karen and Bill. They did not change the rules but instead tried to find acceptable reasons for reordering them.

Conversations are not always characterized by the presence of explicit accounts. In such cases the observer must derive an account repertoire. Similarly, the persuader may have to reconstruct the persuadee's logic system with little overt assistance. To the extent that he or she can perceive the situation as the persuadee does (social perspective-taking), the likelihood of success is enhanced (see Reardon-Boynton, 1978; Reardon, 1981).

The foregoing dramatization demonstrates how accounts can assist in the redefinition of superordinate constructs. This is one form of persuasion that allows two previously incompatible rules to coexist. Persuasion can also involve rule change of four types, varying in the amount of change and the coactive nature of that change (Simons, 1976). These are acquiescence, accommodation, compromise, and coadjuvancy. *Acquiescence* occurs when the persuadee relinquishes the rule in question. *Accommodation* involves rule revision rather than complete acceptance. *Compromise* occurs when the persuader and the persuadee revise their rules to the satisfaction of both. *Coadjuvancy* refers to those instances when the persuader and persuadee work together to generate a mutually satisfying rule or set of rules. In the next chapter we shall look at those variables that influence the levels of self-autonomy versus context-predominance in interpersonal and noninterpersonal situations. Subsequent chapters will focus on how these levels create conditions conducive to or prohibitive of acquiescence, accommodation, compromise, and coadjuvancy.

CONCLUSION

This chapter has set forth a new theoretical model of persuasion, combining the best of the old with recent communication theory and research. The model suggests that underlying every behavior is a logic consisting of constructs and rules. This structure is supported by accounts that may take one of two forms. Prospective accounts constitute the reasoning people use to select and order their rules prior to behavior. Retrospective accounts are the reasons people give for their behavior subsequent to its occurrence. To the extent that persuaders can recognize persuadee reasoning for construct usage and rule application through their own observations and requests for retrospective accounts, their chances of bringing about acquiescence, accommodation, cooperation, or coadjuvancy are increased.

These "chances" are not, however, solely determined by the social perspective-taking abilities of the persuader. Some contexts are not conducive to coactive forms of persuasion. For example, many formal organizations, such as the military, create conditions (status, visibility, sanctions, and the like) that make acquiescence and accommodation more frequent than cooperation and coadjuvancy. (See also Simons, 1976, on combative and expressionist persuasion.)

In the next few chapters, this interaction of context, persuader characteristics, and persuasion type will be addressed as we look at the variables typically studied in persuasion and how they influence dyadic, group, organizational, and mass media persuasion.

Chapter 6

PERSUASION VARIABLES

The acceptance of Kelman's (1974: 311-312) claim that social scientists have used the study of attitude as a "cheap substitute for more elaborate studies of social behavior" challenges present-day social scientists with the task of determining what more elaborate studies should look like. Multivariate statistics now make it possible to examine the effect of a number of interrelated variables, but determining what those variables should be in persuasion research remains a problem. Also, the determination of how variables should be measured has engendered much concern among social scientists seeking to justify attitude-behavior inconsistency.

In this chapter we will look at some of the variables common to attitude change research and propose a means by which researchers may determine whether a particular study warrants their inclusion. The jargon used in this chapter will be consistent with prior theory and research rather than with the theoretical model advanced in previous chapters. When the term *attitude* is used, for example, the terms *constructs* and *superordinate constructs* are generally interchangeable with it.

The approach to be taken herein is that many of the variables considered relevant to past studies of persuasion can be utilized to alter the context- versus self-focus of the persuadee. The result is a reorganization of rules, the knowledge of which then facilitates the persuader's selection of accuracy, consistency, or appropriateness appeals. This position will become clearer as we forge our way through past research. For now it is sufficient to suggest that to the extent that a persuader can effectuate a change of persuadee focus from self to context, appropriateness appeals are rendered more useful. To the extent that self is made predominant, appeals to consistency are likely to elicit greater behavior change. Finally, in those cases where consequences are more important than appropriateness and consistency, effectiveness appeals are most useful.

VARIABLE TYPES

Clark (1979a: 55-56) has divided research variables in the study of human behavior into two types: surface-level and nonsurface-level variables. The former refers to "phenomena whose membership is determined by relatively easily observed characteristics, such as sex, race, mode of dress, lexical usage, and so forth as opposed to internal states of individuals or decision processes such as selection of message strategies, which must be studied more indirectly." Clark explains that attitude change research has generated a vast array of surface variables. Such variables have been called upon over and over to explain credibility. We have, for example, altered speakers' attire, speeded up their speech, inserted pauses, and manipulated attractiveness to discover that these variables do influence perceived credibility. However, Clark reminds us that to manipulate these variables in an effort to determine their effect on credibility, without simultaneously investigating how the message recipients' attitudes are affected, is not a particularly useful endeavor. The reasons for accepting these studies for so long is, simply, that our world view as social scientists has focused on method rather than reason. Also, our distrust of subject self-report has dissuaded us from pursuing a cognitive logic approach to persuasion.

The work of rules theorists and constructivists has responded to the need for more explanatory, indirectly verifiable variables. For example, several researchers have taken the position that children who develop social-perspective-taking skills adapt better to communication needs (Delia and Clark, 1977; Reardon-Boynton, 1978). Such research is moving us away from laboratory manipulation of experimenter-defined surface-level variables to naturalistic settings and subject input. It has also placed an increasing emphasis on the "why" of research rather than merely the "how." If we do not ask ourselves why we are studying a particular variable (i.e., where it fits in the process of human interaction), research will continue to appear like so many unattached squares in an otherwise intriguing patchwork quilt.

With that pitch for nonsurface variables in mind, we turn now to a review of some of the variables that have paved the inroads of attitude change theory and research.

SOURCE CREDIBILITY

Studies of source credibility by communication researchers have clearly demonstrated that this construct is multidimensional. Recent work also suggests that the components of credibility may not be the same across situations but instead depend on the role a communicator is expected to perform in a given context.

Anderson and Clevenger's (1972) summary of experimental research on ethos indicates that studies of source characteristics differ widely in theoretical and methodological features. Most studies prior to the mid-1960s treated ethos as a fixed characteristic. It was assumed that sources possessed characteristics that made them credible. However, later studies recognized the influence of situational factors as well as the possibility of changes occurring in the receiver's impressions during the communication act.

Early studies of source effects frequently employed sources assumed to differ in credibility. This method implies an acceptance of the experimenter's image of the source as representative of the subjects' images. Recent studies have tended to measure ethos by pretest or by checking for subject-experimenter agreement upon completion of the study. Anderson and Clevenger point out that the latter approach requires a fixed ethos perspective; for if the image of the speaker is subject to change during the speech, postmessage measures may be deceptive in terms of the ethos existing at the outset.

Credibility studies also differ in the extent of attention paid to source and audience characteristics. However, even today, credibility research reflects a tendency generally to ignore the interaction of source and subject characteristics. The few studies that have focused on audience characteristics have clearly demonstrated that communicator-audience reciprocal influence is not something researchers can afford to ignore.

More flexible perspectives on credibility than those afforded by a fixed-ethos model led to temporal considerations. Put succinctly, the question of credibility effects over time became an area of research focus in the 1950s. These studies introduced the sleeper-effect phenomenon. Hovland and Weiss (1951) found that, over a period of one month, the favorable effect of high-source-credibility attitude change diminished, and low-source-credibility negative attitude reactions became more positive. They postulated that, in the absence of further stimuli, agreement with high-credibility sources decays while agreement with low-credibility sources grows. It was Hovland's belief that the source is forgotten over time. However, a later Kelman and Hovland (1953) study provided support for a disassociation of message and source explanation. They found that reintroduction of the speaker three weeks subsequent to the initial meeting removed the sleeper effect. Also, they found that in the absence of reintroduction, those persons who best remembered the source showed the greatest sleeper effect. They assumed, therefore, that the logical explanation of sleeper effects is disassociation of message and source rather than mere forgetting of the source.

Gillig and Greenwald (1974) and Cook and Flay (1978) have seriously questioned the existence of sleeper effects. They point out that limited empirical support exists. As early as 1955, researchers questioned Hovland's experimental procedures, which failed to control for the possible experiment-related discussions of low- and high-credibility condition subjects during the time lag between experiments. Nevertheless, the sleeper effect has not been laid to rest; it lives on in most persuasion texts. It seems a reasonable explanation for the prevalence of the "they say" references to weather forecasts, news, and other low-salience issues. Perhaps what is needed is a closer look at just how important the issue is to the receiver and just how relevant his or her reference group members consider source references. The likelihood of a group of debators accepting "they" as an adequate source reference is certainly low. However, one's inability to remember who recommended the amount of salt to add to one's favorite cookie receipe is not likely to inhibit a discussion of cooking. In short, frequently in interpersonal communication, source-information connections are not required. To the extent that the contexts in which we find ourselves require acknowledgment of the source, it is likely that we train ourselves to remember sources.

Some support for this concern with issue salience can be found in studies that, unlike the bulk of attitude change research, present issues important to the subjects. McGarry and Hendrick (1974) found that when the position advocated is undesirable to subjects, variation in the perception of the communicator's characteristics will be independent of his or her persuasiveness. They claim it is only when subjects have no vested interest in an issue that credibility manipulation that minimizes negative attributes of the communicator will directly enhance persuasion. In short, subjects appear quite capable of liking and/or respecting a communicator while rejecting the communicator's message. The direct linkage between credibility and persuasion is subject to question in light of this research. McGarry and Hendrick's call for research that manipulates systematically the vested interest of subjects deserves a response.

Wheeles (1974: 278) extends his explanation of the limitations of source-credibility research beyond concern for subject involvement to a concern for message, channel, and contextual variables. He claims that lack of precision in predictions of attitude theories is not surprising, since these theories "have based predictions upon inadequate, underdeveloped concepts and have typically attempted to predict change on the basis of prior attitudes alone." A study of credibility by Greenberg and Miller (1966) demonstrates the importance of being skeptical of our own interpretations of messages, rather than those of our subjects.

Greenberg and Miller sought to determine whether a negative image of a source adversely affects receiver attitudes toward a persuasive message. The results did indicate that the positive appeal of the message was vitiated by the negative image of the source. However, Greenberg and Miller discovered that, on 7-point scales, their experimental group subjects had actually found the source generally trustworthy (4.4) and competent (4.7), despite their exposure to a seemingly negative introduction message. The introduction read as follows:

> For your information: The piece you are about to read was included in a sales brochure written and distributed in several American communities by a small group of men recently indicted for unethical business practices. The men traveled across the country trying to persuade school systems to build schools which could be used as fallout shelters. The salesmen would then offer to be "advisers" to the school board about this possibility. They charged a sizable fee for their services, and made up some kind of report without doing any work [Greenberg and Miller, 1966: 129].

The authors explained the unexpected, rather positive source impressions as resulting from a normative standard that predisposes audience members to respond somewhat positively in the absence of personal experience with the source. They added that audiences may give unfamiliar sources the "benefit of a doubt."

Rosenthal (1972) developed an alternative explanation. He held that the high source ratings given by the control group (5.1 on trustworthiness and 5.4 on competence) indicated that the content and style of the message provided sufficient information for the control subjects to glean a positive impression of the source. The experimental group received the same high-quality message and, according to Rosenthal, probably experienced some dissonance over experiencing a positive message response to a criminal source. He explained that this dissonance could account for the lower source ratings by experimental group subjects. However, the quality of the message appeared to have offset any negative feelings toward the source, since the ratings on both trustworthiness and competence on a 7-point scale were still above 4 points.

Rosenthal criticized Greenberg and Miller for their attempt to explain the absence of low source ratings by referring to the existence of a "benefit of the doubt" normative standard. Such a claim was unwarranted to Rosenthal, since Greenberg and Miller themselves concluded, on the basis of control subject ratings, that "the quality of the message was apparently sufficient to induce subjects to create a somewhat favorable perception of the source. It would appear that these subjects reasoned that such a good message could only have come from a good source" (1966: 130). Since this same high-quality message was administered to the experimental group, Rosenthal reasoned that they too experienced the favorable perceptions of the source.

Furthermore, Rosenthal disagreed with Greenberg and Miller's contention that the subjects' lack of personal experience with the source could account for their willingness to give him the benefit of a doubt. Rosenthal suggested that in the "cogitation of a persuasive message," the subjects received a direct message about facets of the source's personality. While Rosenthal acknowledged that a persuasive message cannot provide an abundance of information, it does supply some information, and subjects will use this to form impressions.

On the basis of his rejection of the Greenberg and Miller "normative standard" and "absence of personal experience with the source" explanations, Rosenthal (1972: 24) concluded that "the failure to induce a negative image of the source was the result of internal paramessage dissonance. Put succinctly, there were more source data operant in this communication than the experimenters apparently were aware of." Rosenthal's perspective emanates from his belief that people recognize some information as firsthand and therefore of a higher "evidentiary order" than "hearsay evidence," such as that provided by the Greenberg and Miller source introduction. Being confronted with information of different evidentiary orders created dissonance for the experimental group subjects, but they opted to give greater credence to their own sense experiences of the source.

If we assume, as Thibaut and Kelly (1978) contend, that people use what information they can to reduce the uncertainty in their environment by forming impressions of others, Rosenthal's explanation has a certain appeal. Yet it is not totally inconceivable that there exists a normative standard that leads subjects to give credit to individuals they do not know personally. In any case, both the Greenberg-Miller and the Rosenthal perspectives point to one very important source of error in our research practices: We would prefer to rely on our own justifications for subject behavior rather than to ask subjects for theirs. Whether the Greenberg-Miller explanation is inaccurate or accurate, their recognition of subject input gave Rosenthal (and the present author) support for the realization that "because a factual assertion is true or untrue does not mean it will be perceived as such by the receiver" (Rosenthal, 1972: 30). It questions the faith we have placed in experimenter interpretations of subject responses and, it is to be hoped, sets us on a new track of self-skepticism when determining how much we can assume to be true about audiences and subjects.

Besides encouraging some healthy skepticism about experimenter judgments of receiver reactions to source information, the Greenberg and Miller study indicates that subjects' message-based interpretations of source characteristics cannot be made with absolute confidence. Bowers and Osborn (1966) found that different types of metaphors resulted in differences in the ratings of the message source. Wheeles (1974) using scales developed by McCracken et al. (1972) found that receivers selectively expose themselves to messages based on their attitudes toward the sources and message concepts. Their results indicate that source competence is the best predictor of selective exposure, with homophily and attitude involvement "meaningfully" improving the predictive model. Even such often overlooked message aspects as speed of speaking (Miller et al., 1976), vocabulary and style (Carbone, 1975) and nonverbal expression (London, 1973) have been found to influence credibility and persuasion effects.

It is obvious then that the study of source credibility is not without its complications. Research indicates that numerous factors (including ones not anticipated by the researchers) influence credibility. McGarry and Hendrick (1974) have shown us that the assumed direct linkage between credibility ratings and message influence is mitigated by the subject's perception of message importance and direction. What is needed is a theory of persuasion that integrates the findings on source, message, and receiver influences.

Norman Anderson (1971) proposed a model of persuasive impact that treats source impressions as a weighting factor for the persuasive impact of a message. His model represents a general theory of information integration that credits the message recipient with a history impinging on his or her present judgments:

> In even the simplest investigations of attitudes and opinions, the stimuli typically carry information at a cognitive level not often reached in other areas of research. Information stimuli . . . impinge on the person, in life or in the laboratory, and he must integrate them with one another as well as with his prior opinions and attitudes [1971: 171].

Anderson's formula for information integration is

$$R = \frac{ws + (1 - 2)I}{s + (1 - w)}$$

where R is the response, s is the scale value for an item of information, I is the initial impression, w is the weight associated with the item of information, and (1-w) is the normalized weight associated with the initial impression. In attitude change research, Anderson suggests, the weight (w) and information (s) concepts should be considered analogous to the source and message. Thus, while including separate values for both the source and message, Anderson also hypothesizes a relationship between them. Eagly and Himmelfarb (1978), in their review of mathematical models of credibility effects on message acceptance, state that, in general, research supports Anderson's assumption that source credibility can be considered a weight that amplifies or multiplies the value of message information.

Donald Lumsden (1977) applied the Anderson model in a personality impression task. While his research supported the linearity of the source-message relationship (the impact of a message is a function of the strength of the message multiplied by the strength of the source), he noted three limitations of the applicability of his results. First, his study structured all the variables (source, message, and target ratings) along a likability dimension. This provided a high degree of control for the variables, but it is unreasonable to assume that likability is the only important dimension in attitude formation. Second, the context of the design—rating targets to select a method of selecting college roommates—implies some question concerning "unsuspected limitations" of likability as a criterion in this situation. Finally, a number of important variables, of which source and message are only two, were not included in the study.

Hence, while Anderson appears to have been on the right track, the application of his model to attitude change is limited to source and message characteristics. Furthermore, how applicable would his model be to situations in which the source impression is more important than the message effects? For example, political campaign messages are developed with the source impressions as the central variable and message as the weight. Whether Anderson's model is useful in such situations is open to question.

One reason that even integration approaches like the Anderson model fall short is the absence of a theoretical base explaining the functional relationships among persuasion variables. Perhaps it was necessary to generate enough conflicting evidence to call for a comprehensive theory. Whether variable testing should precede theory or vice versa is not the question to be addressed any longer. We have at our disposal research that at least indicates which variables appear to play major roles in the persuasive process. The quest now should be to determine the functional relationships among them and how they are used to create conditions conducive to persuasion. In this text, the importance of a persuasion variable is a function of the degree to which its manipulation can be expected to alter the level of self versus context predominance. Advertisers frequently use well-known sources to increase the believability of their message and to set the stage for implicit and explicit appropriateness appeals. Source credibility is important to the theoretical model proposed in previous chapters because the use of highly credible sources can (a) encourage identification, thus rendering inconsistency appeals useful, (b) lend additional validity to appropriateness claims, or (c) inform the persuadee of effective means to a desired consequent.

PERSUASIBILITY AND SEX

Rokeach's (1960) theoretical propositions about dogmatic personalities imply that people are predisposed to openness or closed-mindedness as a function of enduring personality characteristics. McCroskey and Burgoon (1974: 425) found support for Rokeach's perspective. Their research indicates that "people have relatively invariant widths of latitudes of acceptance and rejection across topics and sources." They did, however, find reason to question Rokeach's emphasis on dogmatism. They could find no evidence demonstrating that it affects latitudes of acceptance or rejection. McCroskey and Burgoon suggested that this finding may reflect a construct validity weakness in the dogmatism scale.

Research such as that discussed above has given credence to the study of personality traits as predictors of attitude change. Janis and Field (1956) set a strong precedent for looking at personality as the characteristic of being susceptible to persuasion regardless of the source or message topic. Much research in this vein attests to higher persuasibility among women than men. Some researchers, however, found that women do not seem more persuasible when the speaker is a woman. Also, researchers have suggested that differences in persuasibility between the sexes may be more culturally than biologically determined. However, Cronkhite (1975) claimed that the more dominant tendencies of males, which are culturally and perhaps hormonally induced, make men less persuasible.

The controversy over who is more persuasible continues today. In the meantime, another controversy over whom people choose for opinion leaders, males or females, has drawn attention. Research has generally suggested a male bias in our society. Richmond and McCroskey (1975), however, shed some new light on this subject. In contrast to Goldberg's (1968) finding that women are prejudiced against women, they found that, while the generalization holds true for politics, other topics, such as fashion, show a definite female preference for female opinion leaders. Richmond and McCroskey qualified their results by suggesting that their subjects were better educated than the general adult population in our society, but at least a trend toward more faith in women as opinion leaders is suggested.

It appears that we need to keep abreast with the changing times when considering sex effects. Karlins and Abelson (1970) suggest that as the American female progresses in her battle for equality, we should expect differences in persuasibility to diminish. As women enter the job force in increasing numbers, they, like men, will specialize in careers that provide them with demonstrable expertise. Furthermore, we may find upon closer scrutiny of persuasibility research that questionnaire measures that suggest women to be weak-kneed responders may actually reflect an accommodating response style that indicates women's interpersonal sensitivity. Females attempt to integrate new or opposing information into their construct systems. Message reception is followed by a period of information integration previously interpreted as an indication of successful persuasion. Women may ultimately reject as many messages as do men, but take longer to do so. Thus, the persuader who smells victory when addressing an all-female audience might be in for a big surprise.

PERSONALITY AND CONTEXT

Persuasion texts abound with evidence that personality characteristics influence attitude change. Self-esteem (see McGuire, 1969, for an explanation of conflicting findings), anxiety and insecurity (Nunally and Bobren 1959; Triandis, 1971), Machiavellianism (Christie, 1968; Guterman, 1970), and authoritarianism (Adorno, 1950; Triandis, 1971) are only a few on the long list. It is often difficult to know just how the findings of these studies can be used to facilitate our understanding of persuasion. In a nonlaboratory context it is usually considered gauche to administer a personality test to one's audience prior to message preparation. Basically, then, these studies provide evidence that personality will influence attitude change, but in our search for predictor variables that can be manipulated by persuaders, they offer little hope. One does not manipulate a personality in the same way as source credibility. Instead we may find the information these studies have provided useful in interpersonal encounters where persuasive messages can be adjusted to individual characteristics even in the course of their delivery. In fact, it may be possible to use the presence of those behaviors that researchers have considered reflective of personality types to determine the utility of consistency appeals in situation types.

Cooper and Scalise (1974: 566) interpret the conflicting literature on personality trait effects as reason for considering the interaction of personality factors and situational variables. They suggest, "It may be that people experience dissonance when an action which they commit is inconsistent with a stable personality trait." They add that what may produce dissonance for one personality type may not do so for others. On the basis of Jung's (1933) definition of introverts and extroverts, Cooper and Scalise attempted to demonstrate that introverts who learn that they have conformed to the opinions of others instead of remaining their typical independent selves should experience dissonance due to the inconsistency of their behavior with their usual lifestyle. Extroverts, they assumed, should experience dissonance when they do not conform to the opinions of others. The results supported their hypotheses. While no main effect was found either for introversion-extroversion or for conformity-independence, dissonance occurred when introverts believed they had conformed and extroverts thought they had acted independently in the face of group pressure.

Although the Cooper and Scalise definition of "situational variables" is vague, their emphasis on the personality X situation interaction is important. Unlike much previous personality research, their study reflects a recognition of the multifaceted nature of human behavior. If human behavior were influenced solely by personality and were therefore free from all situationally imposed normative constraints, chaos would obtain. It is clear that human beings are neither totally self-operative nor robots driven by societal rules. This means that any research claiming to be reflective of the "real world" cannot dwell on personality variables alone but must also consider their interaction with situational expectations.

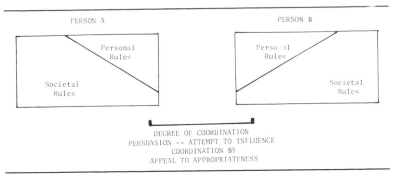

Figure 6.1 Formal Context

In previous chapters this interactional approach was discussed in terms of contextual and individual rule structures. If we view communication in general as the coordinated management of meaning (Pearce, 1976; Cronen and Pearce, 1978) between at least two individuals, and if we further construe this coordination to be influenced by personal and societal rules, each interaction becomes a matter of matching or interpenetrating rule structures (Cronen and Pearce, 1978). The extent to which personality (personal rules) influences this process is partly a function of the formal or informal nature of the context. Figure 6.1 depicts this relationship for formal contexts.

Some contexts of social interaction are highly formalized. In such cases, little room exists for personality influences. The rules are rigid and any violation of them elicits sanctions. The strongest influence on behavior here is societal rather than individual rule structures. The persuader wishing to alter the behavior of individuals in a formal context should focus on behavioral appropriateness rather than consistency, since these contexts are usually characterized by high rule consensus.

In less formal contexts, where permissible and preferred modes of behavior are at least as visible as the obligatory and prohibited ones, personality factors can exert more influence. The parameters of rule violation are wider and individual idiosyncracies are therefore given freer reign. The persuader finding herself in a flexible context may find appeals to inconsistencies between an individual's behavior and what she knows to be his personality (e.g., independence and extroversion) more effective than appeals to the inappropriateness of his behavior and what is expected of him in that context. As Figure 6.2 indicates, to the extent that a context is informal, agreement concerning expectations is reduced and

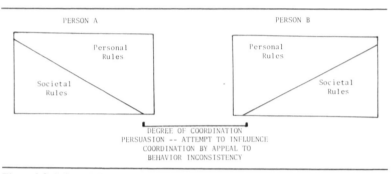

Figure 6.2 Informal Context

therefore social rules became less potent tools of persuasion. In such contexts an individual can be persuaded to alter his or her overt behavior by appeals to inconsistency between his or her personal rules and overt behavior. Conversely, formal contexts allow the individual to violate personal rules with impunity by claiming that the context rules prohibited self-autonomy. An extroverted male may refrain from telling his usual off-color jokes at a wedding because he respects the seriousness of the occasion. In such instances the formal context provides an excuse for out-of-personality behavior.

It has been suggested here that personality can be used to influence attitude and behavior change, but with less effectiveness in a formal context consisting of restrictive rules. Unless persuasion research focusing on personality includes situational variables, the results are likely to provide little useful information, because they will not reflect the interplay of societal and personal rules characteristic of real life situations.

COGNITIVE COMPLEXITY

Intelligence has received much attention in terms of its relationship to persuasibility. Indices such as mental age, chronological age, and years of schooling have yielded only minimal support for the expected negative relationship between persuasibility and intelligence. Many studies indicate a positive relationship. McGuire (1973) has suggested that intelligence may make a person more susceptible to persuasion through the increased attention and comprehension it allows, but that it reduces persuasibility through increased resistance to yielding. He adds that we can expect an overall nonmonotonic relationship of the inverted U family indicating that persons of moderate intelligence are more persuasible than persons of extremely high or low intelligence, with the level of intelligence at which maximum persuasibility occurs going up as the complexity of the communication situation increases (McGuire, 1973).

This interpretation of intelligence effects on persuasibility lends some support to the position taken earlier in this chapter—that women may appear more persuasible when, in actuality, they may be more capable of integrating interpersonal information. If so, we should expect to find, through the use of more sensitive measures than those used previously, that women struggle to integrate novel or contradictory information into their cognitive systems before deciding whether to yield a former position. We may still find that women yield more often than men, but at least we will know that it is due to their greater tendency to weigh alternative perspectives.

That women are intellectually superior is not what is being suggested here. That is a research battle most of us would just as soon avoid. However, research has indicated that females are more interpersonally sensitive than males (Gollin, 1958; Dimitrovsky, 1964; Brierly, 1966; Livesley and Bromley, 1973; Rothenberg, 1970). Intelligence tests are insensitive to this phenomenon. The study of human communication requires the development of a measure to determine how effectively people deal with information conveyed in social interaction. The measure that meets this need and has been given much attention lately is cognitive complexity.

The constructivists have provided the most communication-relevant literature on cognitive complexity. Constructivists consider interpersonal sensitivity to be a function of one's ability to interpret social situations through the application of a personal system of interpersonal constructs or cognitive structures (Delia and Clark, 1977). We can expect that some individuals will surpass others in this, merely because they place more emphasis on communication. Brian Little (1972) suggests that different people specialize in different aspects of the environment and that their cognitive structures (constructs) will therefore be extended into a highly complex system only within the domain(s) of specialization. Knapp et al. (1980) have found that people integrate prior experiences into memorable messages that they can call upon to explain certain context-specific problems and to guide action in that context. These researchers suggest memorable messages operate much like master rules that subsume more specific rules. They do so because, as limited-capacity information processors

(Shatz, 1977), people are predisposed to find rules that allow their thinking to be more abstract and integrated rather than differentiated. For example, Knapp et al. explain that the memorable message, "Never wait for a train or a woman because there will be another one around soon," is a master rule recalled by the subject who reported it because it integrated many past experiences into one overall, useful rule of thumb. It also serves to guide behavior in future relationships with women and thereby lends predictability to the individual's life. As you may recall from Chapter 2, it is Kelly's (1955) contention that we are always in the "business of prediction." Even if this is not totally accurate, we are predisposed to formulate logics or rules for our attitudes and behaviors. Master rules have the added advantage of associating disparate experiences with each other. They do so in terms of context. A woman and a train may have little in common, but in the context of a relationship rift, these two disparate objects come to be associated through the use of a master rule—a personal logic.

Constructs, rules, master rules, and the like are all methods of cognitive organization. They assist the individual in shaping expectations. They facilitate attempts to deal with novel experiences. In short, they form the logic into which the individual integrates incoming stimuli. Delia et al. (1974), Shroder et al. (1967), Crockett (1965), Werner (1957), Reardon-Boynton (1978), and others have agreed that the development of cognition involves an increased differentiation of elements and, simultaneously, an increased integration of them into a hierarchically organized system. Clark and Delia (1977), for example, supported their contention that the more differentiated are children's construct systems employed in person perception, the more effective they should be in adapting messages to others. Reardon-Boynton (1978) found that cognitively complex children are better able to provide accounts for conversational rule violations, and are more adept at providing alternative endings for incomplete conversations in which a deviation has occurred, than are their less complex peers. She introduced a computational model of cognitive complexity which, unlike previous methods of measurement, combines the dimensions differentiation, abstraction, and integration. Reardon's approach emphasizes the quality dimensions of cognitive complexity (abstraction and integration) over the quantity dimension (differentiation). She also found high construct and predictive validity for her measure when studying children's ability to account for conversational deviations and provide cooperative alternative endings for these deviant conversations. The combined computational measure correlated more highly than any other single cognitive dimension measure with these two dependent variables and with age. However, since this measure did not produce a significantly higher correlation (p < .05), Reardon-Boynton (1978) concluded that this measure may not be a better indicator of cognitive complexity in very young children, whose integration abilities are not yet developed. The face, construct, and predictive validity, however, suggests that it is a strong contender with other cognitive complexity measures (see Sypher, 1980, and Sypher and O'Keefe, 1980, for a review of other measures).

It appears, then, that cognitive complexity does play a role in human communication behavior. In terms of persuasion, complexity theory posits that more cognitively complex individuals can integrate reliable but inconsistent information into their current belief systems more readily than can less complex individuals. Herman (1977) explains that people with less complex cognitive systems may reject inconsistent information or distort it to fit into their current belief systems. Cognitively complex individuals, on the other hand, can integrate inconsistent information without attitude or behavior change by further differentiating their belief systems. Borrowing from Sears and Freedman (1967), Herman adds that cognitively complex people can be regarded as "promiscuous information gatherers" who have high rates of exposure to persuasive communications, whether consistent or inconsistent with current beliefs.

It is apparent from this discussion that cognitive complexity is one nonsurface variable that can influence the impact of persuasive messages. Although it is usually impossible to determine the cognitive complexity levels of members of a large audience, estimations of the general level of complexity may be accessible merely from premessage audience analysis typical of rhetorical perspectives. Scientific approaches may prove more useful in educational contexts where an understanding of the cognitive complexity of the child can facilitate the development of more effective educational messages and methods.

COUNTERARGUING

Festinger and Maccoby (1964) and Osterhouse and Brock (1970) have suggested that when people are exposed to persuasive attacks, they subvocalize counterarguments. Much research has focused on the role of counterarguing in attitude change. Distraction occurring simultaneously with the persuasive attack message has been described as an inhibitor of counterarguing. According to Festinger and Maccoby, the inhibition of counterarguing facilitates attitude change because the individual is left vulnerable to the message appeals. While research contradicting Festinger and Maccoby's perspective exists (Haaland and Venkatesen, 1968; Vohs and Garrett, 1968), distraction is still considered an important variable in the study of attitude change.

Miller and Burgoon (1979) concluded from the conflicting research that distraction interacts with other variables to produce attitude change. Petty et al. (1976: 883) provided support for this position. They found that "distraction inhibits the dominant cognitive response to a persuasive appeal. If the dominant cognitive response is counterargumentation, then distraction will tend to inhibit this and result in increased persuasion; but if the dominant cognitive response is favorable thoughts, distraction will tend to inhibit this and result in decreased persuasion." The nature of the message then appears to be one variable interacting with distraction to influence attitude change. Kiesler and Mathog (1968) found that source characteristics can interact with distraction to influence communication acceptance. They observed a direct relationship between distraction and attitude change only when the source credibility of the message was relatively high. They explain their findings by suggesting that a low credible source requires less counterargumentation, since resistance to the message can be obtained by simply derogating the source.

Recent distraction studies do provide support for the idea that counterarguing can inhibit attitude change. What is needed now are studies that determine whether distraction alone can intrude upon the counterarguing process so that attitude change can be facilitated.

FREE CHOICE AND FORESEEN CONSEQUENCES

Nel et al. (1969) found that delivering a counterattitudinal speech aroused dissonance in the speaker only when he thought that it was likely that the speech would convince his audience. Subsequent studies by Cooper and Worchel (1970), Goethals and Cooper (1972), Hoyt et al. (1972), Cooper et al. (1974), and others have indicated that aversive behavioral consequences are critical in determining the amount of dissonance-produced attitude change. For example, Cooper and Worchel had student subjects attempt to convince a waiting subject that a boring task was exciting and interesting. They were given only low incentive (one-half hour of extra research credit) or a high incentive (one full hour of additional credit). The results indicated that only when the attitude-discrepant speech was given for a small incentive and perceived to be accepted by the recipient did opinion change occur.

One of the most interesting results of these free choice/foreseen consequences studies is that, unlike much prior attitude change research, they give subjects some credit for evaluating their behavior. Nel et al. (1969) have suggested that dissonance is created by a discrepancy between an individual's self-concept and the knowledge that he or she has committed an indecent act. The subjects in the Cooper and Worchel study could have felt "indecent" because they lied. Since it is commonly held that decent people do not lie, dissonance was created. The need to feel decent again can be met by changing one's opinion about the lie object. In this case the dull task was perceived as more interesting than the initial opinion indicated. It is interesting to note that people feel indecent only if their lies are accepted as truths.

Cooper et al. (1974) found that the degree to which people like the individuals they mislead by lying is an important factor in attitude change. It appears that not only is a lie not indecent unless it is accepted, but it must be accepted by a liked rather than a disliked person. We can see from this type of research that science, contrary to the claims of many humanists, can uncover the intricate workings of the human mind. It is true, however, that until recent years scientific studies of human behavior have avoided such concepts as "choice" and "responsibility," resulting in somewhat stilted conceptualizations of human cognition and behavior.

When a rather simple theory like cognitive dissonance becomes subject to qualification on the basis of whether the subject is free to choose, feels responsible, and is successful in convincing others, scientists must either discard the theory altogether (because too many factors have to be taken into consideration) or become more aware of the contexts in which they study human behavior. This text and much recent research indicates a trend toward the latter approach. In the next section we shall look closely at a study that combines counterargument-distraction perspectives with a novel perspective on the importance of expectation violation, while also considering important contextual features.

EXPECTATION VIOLATION

As discussed in Chapter 1, much research points to the important influence expectations exert on behavioral choice. Miller and Burgoon (1979) examined the role of expectation violation in the process of

persuasion. While they did not ascribe to the Kellyan perspectives introduced in Chapter 2, they pointed to the work of Brooks and Scheidel
(1968), Brooks (1970), and Burgoon (1970), which concluded that the
reactions of individuals to speakers may be a function of the contrast
between speaker behavior and stereotyped expectations. Burgoon and
Chase (1973), for example, found that maximum resistance to persuasion
occurred when the pretreatment and attack messages were linguistically
similar and thus not in violation of receiver expectations.

Miller and Burgoon (1979) based their research on a model of resistance
to persuasion introduced by Burgoon, Cohen, Miller, and Montgomery
(1978). According to Burgoon et al., inoculation theory alone is not
sufficient to explain resistance to persuasion. Instead, they advanced a
communication-oriented model suggesting three primary factors that
mediate ability to resist the appeals contained in a persuasive message:
"(1) the amount of threat or motivation to counterargue the position
being advocated in the persuasive message, (2) the degree to which the
communication fulfills or violates receivers' expectations of appropriate
communication behavior, and (3) the context in which the persuasive
communication occurs" (1978: 301).

The first proposition borrows from counterargumentation perspectives
described earlier in this chapter. Miller and Burgoon (1979) explained that
individuals who perceive that their attitudes are being threatened will be
motivated to defend those attitudes. They pointed to Festinger and
Maccoby's (1964) emphasis on subvocalization of counterarguments to
explain the cognitive processes involved in responding to attitude threat.

The third proposition from Burgoon et al. (1978) refers to the interaction of such variables as distraction, threat, and task type on degree of
persuasive appeal vulnerability. Miller and Burgoon (1979: 303) explained
the Burgoon et al. interaction concept as follows:

> First, the evaluation of negative speaker characteristics should in-
> hibit the persuasive efficacy of the message and minimize threat to
> the receiver. Second, the attention to negative source characteristics
> should distract the person from counterarguing crucial arguments in
> the message. Thus, the receiver will be unprepared to defend pri-
> vately held attitudes and unmotivated to counterargue in the future.
> Conversely, attention to positive speaker attributes should enhance
> the effectiveness of an initial persuasive message and increase threat,
> given that one's attitudes are shown to be vulnerable to attack by a
> relatively effective speaker. This increase in motivation to counter-
> argue should shift attitudes back toward the initial negative position

after receipt of a second persuasive message arguing the same position as the first persuasive attack message.

Burgoon et al. (1978) provided empirical support for the above predictions. Miller and Burgoon (1979) also offered a refinement of Burgoon et al.'s second proposition through the incorporation of explicit predictions concerning the effects of confirmation or disconfirmation of receiver expectations. Referring to the work of Burgoon, Jones, and Stewart (1974), Miller and Burgoon (1979) suggested that when expectations are violated in a positive manner the effect of the initial message should be enhanced, but when a source violates expectations in a negative manner, the effect of the initial message is inhibited.

To create messages that violate expectations in positive and negative ways, Miller and Burgoon (1979) manipulated the intensity of message language. They suggested that if an individual is led to expect a highly intense counterattitudinal message but instead receives one consisting of low-intensity language, the individual's expectations will be violated in a positive manner (see Bowers, 1963; Burgoon, 1970; Burgoon et al., 1974). Miller and Burgoon added that positive violation should lead to a contrast effect that should enhance the attitude change after the receipt of the first message. However, they expected that the realization that one's beliefs can be brought into question by a moderate message would threaten the individual and increase his or her motivation to prepare counterarguments. They also expected that the exposure to a second message on the same side of the attitudinal issue would meet resistance and that attitudes would therefore revert to the original negative position (later qualified to read "revert to being more negative"). The Miller and Burgoon study warrants attention in this chapter because it exemplifies how the cognitive operations of subjects can be utilized in social science research which also incorporates more traditional variables. In the following paragraphs, that study is reviewed and alternative interpretations of its results are suggested.

The theoretical rationale advanced by Miller and Burgoon (1979) indicated that complex cognitive operations are involved in resistance to persuasion. Miller and Burgoon described their rationale and findings concerning the reversal of attitudes following a second message arguing for the same action as the first message, to be "counterintuitive." In short, popular cognitive theories do not provide a rationale for their findings. They explained further, "In fact, none of the cognitive theories reviewed by Zajonc (1969), including dissonance or attribution theory, could predict or explain the reversal of attitude data reported in this study" (1979: 312). It is obvious then that Miller and Burgoon have made a substantial contribution to our knowledge of resistance to persuasion process. They even managed to develop a theoretical rationale and research design that does not ignore the context. They did not define context-specific terms, but the concept was not ignored.

Let us look a bit closer at the Miller and Burgoon study to determine if, indeed, their explanation for the reversal phenomenon is the only possible and acceptable one.

Miller and Burgoon proposed three hypotheses:

H1: People who are initially induced to expect highly intense messages of a counterattitudinal nature, but who receive low-intensity messages, will be initially more positive toward the attitude issue; however, these individuals will revert to being more negative after receipt of a second message that argues counter to their beliefs than they were after the receipt of the initial persuasive message.

H2: People who are initially induced to expect low-intensity messages, but who receive high intense messages, will be initially relatively negative toward the attitudinal issue, but will demonstrate attitude change in the direction advocated by a second persuasive attack message on the same issue.

They explained these first two hypotheses by stating,

The rationale leading to the first two hypotheses assumes that attitudinal threat induced by exposure to a first persuasive message will motivate people to counterargue against future persuasive attacks. This assumption suggests that threat produced by exposure to a first persuasive message should be negatively related to attitude scores after a second persuasive message [1979: 305].

This reasoning leads to a third hypothesis:

H3: There will be a significant negative relationship between attitudinal threat after exposure to a first persuasive message and attitude toward the issue after receipt of a second persuasive attack.

Miller and Burgoon were also interested in the effects of the manipulation on the credibility of the communicators. They considered it necessary to collect data on credibility to determine if differences in the evaluations of communicators mediated resistance to persuasion. They did not expect such differences to obtain.

The subjects for this study were 219 undergraduate students enrolled in basic communication courses at the University of Wyoming. The subjects were randomly assigned to eight control groups (n = 144) and four experimental groups (n = 75). Each of the subjects in the four experimental groups read two messages advocating the legalization of heroin. One message argued in favor of legalization because it would reduce crime. The other argued for legalization on the basis of health and medical reasons. Before the presentation of the first message, experimental group subjects were randomly assigned to one of two expectancy sets. One set asked them to critically evaluate the low-intensity statements in the message, while the other asked them to evaluate the high-intensity statements. These subjects were then randomly exposed to either a high- or a low-intensity message. At a later experimental session, they were exposed to a moderately intense persuasive message advocating the same position as the first message but using different arguments. No expectancy sets were induced prior to the second message.

The number and type of control groups used by Miller and Burgoon indicate that they did not wish to leave any stones unturned. As Table 6.1 indicates, the control groups varied in terms of whether they received one or two messages, whether they received no expectancy set or one which asked that they focus on both high- and low-intensity statements, and whether they received a high- or low-intensity message (see Miller and Burgoon, 1979: Figure 1).

The persuasive messages used in this study were borrowed from Burgoon et al. (1978). They reported controls for comprehension, subject-predicate compatibility, abstractness, humanness, and animation. They also controlled for language intensity by avoiding highly intense metaphors, future-tense verbs, and intense levels of adverbial qualification. They deleted obscure or infrequently used words (Bowers, 1964).

Miller and Burgoon (1979) used the Burgoon et al. (1978) message as the moderate message in their investigation. To create high- and low-intensity versions of the message, they systematically varied the adverbial qualification within the message. They also varied the severity of the outcome associated with failure to accept positions advocated by the message. Male experimenters randomly distributed message treatments to the subjects. The experimental packets contained one version of the message, which subjects were asked to evaluate by underlining phrases on the basis of intensity. Measures of attitude, source credibility, and threat were then administered. Subjects receiving a second message were tested one or two class periods after the initial session. No expectancy sets were induced by the experimenters prior to the second message.

TABLE 6.1   Design of the Experiment

Group	Expectancy	Message at Time 1	Message Intensity, Time 1	Message at Time 2
Pretest posttest control	None	No	–	No
One message control I*	None	Yes	High	No
One message control II*	None	Yes	Moderate	No
One Message control III*	None	Yes	Low	No
Two message control I	None	Yes	High	Yes
Two message control II	None	Yes	Low	Yes
Distraction control I	Both	Yes	Low	Yes
Distraction control II	Both	Yes	High	Yes
Experimental I	Low	Yes	Low	Yes
Experimental II	Low	Yes	High	Yes
Experimental III	High	Yes	Low	Yes
Experimental IV	High	Yes	High	Yes

SOURCE: Miller and Burgoon (1979: 306). Published by permission of Transaction, Inc. from HUMAN COMMUNICATION RESEARCH, Vol. 5, No. 4. Copyright © 1979 by the International Communication Association.

*Even though these control groups only received one message, both experimental message topics are represented in this sample since subjects within each experimental and control group were randomly assigned to one of two message order conditions. Thus, all cells are counterbalanced for message order effect.

Miller and Burgoon (1979) found support for both Hypotheses 1 and 2, and "some support" for Hypothesis 3. In supplemental analyses computed on three dimensions of source credibility, significant time of measurement main effects were indicated for the dependent variables competence, character, and composure. The source of a second message was perceived as more competent, of higher character, and more composed. Miller and Burgoon (1979: 308) explained, "Since, however, this effect is evident in the distraction control cells as well as in the cells that received confirming and disconfirming messages, the effect cannot be attributed to the manipu-

TABLE 6.2   Experimental and Control Group Comparisons

Group	Time 1 Attitude Mean	Time 2 Attitude Mean
Pretest-posttest	6.53	6.37
One message control (High intensity)	7.06	7.24
One message control (moderate intensity)	9.88	9.81
One message control (low intensity)	7.81	8.54
Two message control (High intensity)	9.18	11.71[b]
Two message control (low intensity)	8.09	10.60[b]
Distraction control (low intensity)	7.87	9.40
Distraction control (high intensity)	7.58	10.58
Experimental I	13.18[a]	15.06[b]
Experimental II	8.68	11.73[b]
Experimental III	10.55[a]	7.68
Experimental IV	6.53	10.47

SOURCE: Miller and Burgoon (1979: 309). Published by permission of Transaction, Inc. from HUMAN COMMUNICATION RESEARCH, Vol. 5, No. 4. Copyright © 1979 by the International Communication Association.

a. Indicates significant difference from pretest-posttest control group ($p < .05$) at time 1.
b. Indicates significant difference from pretest-posttest control group ($p < .05$) at time 2.

lated independent variables. Therefore, one can logically rule out source derogation and/or praise as a competing explanation for the distraction/counterarguing hypotheses postulated in this investigation." Table 6.2 summarizes the group means as well as the comparisons between experimental and control conditions at time 1 and time 2 using Duncan's multiple-range test.

Clearly Miller and Burgoon (1979) succeeded in providing support for the distraction-counterarguing violation of receiver expectations hypotheses posited in their study. However, the validity of their claim that the results obtained are "difficult, if not impossible, to explain without reference to the extension of the Burgoon et al. (1978) model" (1979: 311) is questionable. While it may be true that the findings of their study fall outside the domain of both the inoculation analogy and congruity theory, their reasoning for rejecting these explanations points to a weakness in their own theoretical rationale. Miller and Burgoon placed much emphasis on the fact that both inoculation and congruity perspectives "deal strictly with pretreatment message strategies and make no inferences about the possibility of one persuasive message affecting resistance to subsequent persuasive messages advocating the same attitudinal position" (1979: 311). Certainly their study does deal with two messages, and the experimental group subjects had prior, experimenter-induced expectations about the first. What Miller and Burgoon did not consider, however, was that the recipients of second messages had expectations too, despite the absence of experimenter manipulations to produce them. Having had their expectations verified or violated, all subjects were thus prepared to formulate their own expectations concerning the intensity of the second message. In other words, the mere absence of experimenter-induced expectations at time 2 does not negate the likelihood that the subjects created their own expectations, especially since they, as human beings, are frequently in "the business of prediction" (Kelly, 1955) and use repeatable contexts to facilitate that business (see Bateson, 1972).

This oversight on the part of the researchers does not discredit the contribution they made, nor does it completely invalidate their conclusions. On the contrary, it appears that what may have happened is that what Miller and Burgoon themselves assumed to have occurred at time 1 for experimental condition I (expected low intensity but received high intensity) also occurred at time 2 for experimental group III (expected low intensity on the basis of the first message but received moderate but higher-than-expected message intensity). In other words, we can use Miller and Burgoon's explanation of expectancy violation to explain the second message conditions as well as the first. It seems reasonable to assume that when people are prepared for a tough fight but find that their preparation is not needed, their defenses drop and they become more vulnerable to persuasion. They cease to prepare counterarguments, to use Miller and Burgoon's reasoning. Similarly, if individuals prepare to deal with minor aggravation but meet with a barrage of strong arguments countering their position, it is likely that they will mobilize all of their arguments for retaliation, especially, as in experimental condition III, if those counterarguments were already developed in preparation for an earlier battle that never occurred. This perspective implies that there is no need to include even distraction in the explanation of Miller and Burgoon's findings. The explanation for time 1, experimental condition II is the same as that for time 2, experimental condition III (violation of low-intensity message expectation generated counterarguments), and the explanation for time 2, experimental condition II is the same as that for time 1, experimental condition III (violation of high-intensity message expectations generated reduction of defensiveness generated by premessage counterargument preparation).

A violation of expectations that exceeds a person's deviation tolerance threshold for a particular deviator in a particular situation requires an account—an excuse or justification (Reardon-Boynton, 1978), a condition that did not obtain in the Miller and Burgoon study. In experimental condition II at time 1, subject expectations were violated in a negative direction (low intensity expected but high intensity received). In this case, attitude change occurred but was not significantly different from the pretest-posttest control group. The change that did occur can be explained as a function of the subjects' lack of preparation for the high-intensity attack message. The low degree of attitude change is explainable in light of the subjects' development of counterarguments, which probably occurred during the receipt of the message. The attitude change at time 2 occurred despite the violation of expectations (expected a high-intensity message but received a moderate message). In this case, however, the violation was in a positive direction. The subjects in this condition were most likely ready with a strong defense that they did not need. In Reardon-Boynton's terms, the second expectancy violation did not exceed the subjects' deviance-tolerance threshold. The preparation of counterarguments during the first message may have served to inhibit the amount of positive attitude change, but a significant change did appear.

In experimental condition III, time 1, the subjects experienced a positive expectation violation (expected high intensity but received low intensity). As a result, their defenses were not needed. They therefore dropped those defenses, making themselves vulnerable to persuasion. A deviation from expectations had occurred, but in a positive direction. These subjects came to the second message session with expectations for a low-intensity message. Instead they were tricked again, a condition that may have exceeded their tolerance threshold, leading them, in the absence of an account, to call upon the arguments they had prepared prior to the first message. Those counterarguments conjoined with the ones formed during the moderate message created a strong defensive, and thus attitude changed in a negative direction. The only room for a distraction explanation in this description of events is that the defense might have been stronger in experimental condition III, time 2, had the preparation of additional counterarguments not been distracted by the message.

In both experimental conditions II and III, time 2, the subjects experienced a second expectancy violation. In condition II, however, that violation was in a negative direction and thus more irritating. Furthermore, the counterarguments for a high-intensity message had already been prepared prior to the first message. Only in experimental condition III, time 2, was the deviation-tolerance threshold exceeded. Only in that condition were the subjects sufficiently prepared to counterargue strongly, thus producing an obvious negative attitude reversal.

Experimental conditions I and IV can be explained in terms of the natural positive attitude change apparent in all two-message conditions (see Staats, 1968, for message repetition effects), as well as expectancy validation.

One condition does shed some doubt on the explanation just offered. In the two-message, low-intensity control it could be argued that given subjects' expectation that the second message would be low (based on their experience with the first message), they should have become defensive when that expectation was violated in a negative (low-to-moderate) direction. However, two conditions are missing in this case. First, the second message constituted the first expectation violation. Second, that violation was not based on any previous or current comparisons with experimenter-induced expectations. The total violation did not exceed the subjects' deviation-tolerance threshold.

The Miller and Burgoon (1979) study reflects an increasing recognition on the part of social scientists of human subjects' cognitive processes—that is, that subjects do not come to communication contexts without some prior expectations. Researchers should take this into consideration when designing their studies. Miller and Burgoon did just that. They also took great care to rule out competing explanations for the significant differences obtained in their investigation. They looked at interaction effects rather than single-variable monotonic effects. The one thing they did not do was consider that subjects generate their own expectations on the basis of past experience, even in the experimental setting. This may be due to the perspective taken by these two scientists, which reflects a compromise between behaviorism and contextualism, with a slightly greater leaning toward the former. The explanation offered in this text is the product of a stronger subject-cognition orientation. It is interesting to note that both explanations are supported by the same data, yet each could lead to different directions for future research.

MESSAGE VARIABLES

There is little disagreement among persuasion researchers concerning the import of message style and appeals to attitude change. However, there appear to be very few simple answers to the question of what constitutes an effective message. Fear-appeal research is a case in point. While it seems reasonable to assume that fear arousal should increase yielding to persuasive messages, the research in this area does not support this perspective without qualification. Janis and Feshback (1953), for example, found that when fear is strongly aroused and no reassurances are included in the message, the audience is motivated to ignore or minimize the importance of the threat. While much research supports this finding, Leventhal and his associates found that fear-arousing communications do increase attitudinal acceptance when "effective" recommended actions are provided to the subjects as a means of reducing fear. For example, tetanus shots are generally considered more effective as a preventive measure for tetanus than toothbrushing is for dental disease (see Leventhal and Niles, 1964; and Leventhal et al., 1965). Weiss et al. (1963) suggest that the discrepancy among research findings could be attributed to the subjects' initial positions. In the Leventhal et al. (1965) study, the subjects were probably in favor of tetanus shots, but in the Janis and Feshback (1953) study, the subjects might have held an initial position opposing some dental hygiene recommendations. If so, the preferred procedure might have been strengthened by fear rather than what was conveyed in the message.

Many other studies point to the complexity involved in fear appeal research (Miller and Hewgill, 1964; Moltz and Thistlewaite, 1955; Berkowitz and Cottingham, 1960; Singer, 1965; Leventhal and Watts, 1966; Leventhal, 1970). McGuire (1973) suggests that while these conflicting findings are discouraging because they indicate that the answers will not be simple ones, they are encouraging because complexities can serve to generate hypotheses about interaction effects. The Miller and Burgoon (1979) study attests to McGuire's insight. McGuire (1973: 234) points to the two-factor analysis as an example. It suggests that there is a nonmonotonic relationship such that some intermediate level of anxiety is preferable to no anxiety arousal or high anxiety arousal. Furthermore, it appears that the level of anxiety arousal that is most efficacious goes down as message complexity increases and also as the person's chronic anxiety level goes up (see Millman, 1968). Lehmann (1970) and Leventhal (1970), however, have found an even higher-order interaction with self-esteem.

Basically, then, the research on fear appeals indicates that simple answers are not forthcoming. Perhaps this is because fear is a personal matter. That which causes fear for one person may be ignored by another. It may be useful to use fear to enhance the effects of appropriateness or consistency appeals, but only in minimal doses, since distraction or complete rejection results from strong fear appeals.

A second message content variable is style. Bowers (1964) and Bowers and Osborn (1966), for example, have found that metaphorical (as opposed to literal) expressions may enhance persuasive impact (see also McEwen, 1969; Burgoon and Miller, 1971; Burgoon et al., 1978). Intensity of language is another variable frequently associated with receiver reactions to sources. Bostrom et al. (1973) and Mulac (1976) have focused on the effects of obscenity. The former found that female sources using obscenity obtained more attitude change than did their male counterparts. Bradac et al. (1979) describe this finding as "anomalous" in light of the evidence that women use and are also expected to use little obscenity (Kramer, 1974). Also, they explained that Bostrom et al. did not compare the findings for females with a control group. Bradac et al. (1979: 259) therefore conclude that obscenity is inversely related to postcommunication ratings of source competence.

Bradac et al. also reviewed the literature on lexical diversity and verbal immediacy. The former refers to the range of a source's vocabulary, the latter to the degree to which a source associates himself or herself with the message topics. Strong evidence exists to support the inclusion of these variables in persuasion research, since they influence receiver perceptions of the source. However, the authors caution us to consider one disconcerting flaw characteristic of the studies supporting their generalizations. Researchers have rarely operationalized these variables in any precise way relative to the operationalizations of other researchers. This criticism is most applicable to intensity research. The authors (1979: 266) suggest that this failure to agree on operational definitions has three important consequences: "(1) Within levels of a given variable, wide fluctuations may exist from study to study, such that one researcher's 'high' level may be another's 'low' range. (2) Degrees of effect are not amenable to analysis. (3) Effects that are apparently linear may in fact be curvilinear."

Earlier in their paper, Bradac et al. (1979: 257) had mentioned that most of the studies of intensity and lexical diversity are not grounded in theory and so the result has been a "proliferation of unintegrated data." Their integrations are thus a welcome change of approach, but little can be said of these variables with confidence until either agreement on operational definitions or reasons for differences are reached. Furthermore, as Bradac et al. suggest, this research would benefit from the inclusion in the design of context considerations.

Other message style literature and research will be included in later chapters as they relate to interpersonal or noninterpersonal contexts.

A third message content variable is strategy. Specific areas include the treatment of opposition arguments, implicit versus explicit conclusions, order of arguments, and message repetition. In general, it is safe to conclude that the study of any variables in isolation from other contextual variables is likely to result in useless information. Research indicates that ignoring the existence of counterarguments when the audience is intelligent or initially hostile to one's view is counterproductive. Also, if the audience is aware of the opposition arguments, it is better to refute rather than ignore them. In terms of conclusions, some research indicates that explicit conclusions are more effective than implicit ones (Hovland and Mandel, 1952; McGuire, 1964). However, conflicting findings have resulted when the receiver's intelligence level has been taken into consideration.

Argument order has also generated much research effort. Zimbardo and Ebbesen (1970: 21) summarize this research by suggesting the following:

(1) Present one side of the argument when the audience is generally friendly, or when your position is the only one that will be presented, or when you want immediate, though temporary, opinion change.

(2) When opposite views are presented one after the other, the one presented last will probably be more effective. Primacy effect is more predominant when the second side immediately follows the first, while recency effect is more predominant when the opinion measure comes immediately after the second side.

Finally, it appears that message repetition adds to the persuasive impact of a message (Staats, 1968; Stewart, 1964). McGuire (1973: 235) explains that the most impressive finding of the repetition research is that this variable has so little effect. He explains this phenomenon as well as the differential effects when one considers single versus samples of listeners:

An increase in impact usually appears for one or two repetitions but quickly reaches an asymtote beyond which further repetitions have little effect. It may be that with a captive audience comprehension is quickly maximized by the first several repetitions, so there is nothing more to be learned through further repetition. However, when one considers the initial step in the chain of behaviors leading to persuasion, namely being presented with the message in the first place, then repetition may well be efficacious up to a high level when one has a changing audience. In this case, while the effect of repetition on a given listener soon reaches its asymtote, repetitions at different times expose successive samples of listeners to the message.

McGuire's explanation indicates once again that simple, concise generalizations that disregard the context of the communication are of little utility in persuasion research.

A fourth and final message content variable is that of issue salience. Functional perspectives suggest that people are concerned with the usefulness of information. Eagly and Himmelfarb (1978) point out that some people are concerned with maintaining or establishing social relationships with a communicator and that incoming information will therefore be judged on the basis of whether acceptance of it enhances that goal achievement. In short, sometimes the content is secondary to other contextual concerns. When these other concerns are not overriding in their influence, salience of the issue appears to be important to attitude change. Dissonance theory predicts that increasing initial attitude salience increases attitude change, because the counterattitudinal behavior becomes more dissonant. Self-perception theory, on the other hand, predicts that salience of initial attitudes decreases attitude change, because it increases the clarity of internal cues and thereby decreases reliance on external cues. Eagly and Himmelfarb (1978) suggest that current research findings favor dissonance theory.

ATTITUDE SPECIFICITY

The attitude-behavior problem found in research has led some researchers to conclude that an individual might be favorably disposed toward an object, a specific behavior, or a class of behaviors. Fishbein and Ajzen (1975) have developed this position into what may be referred to as the specificity principle. They label behaviors performed at a single point in time "single-act criteria." They give the labels "repeated-observation criteria" to measures of a single behavior assessed at a number of points in time, and "multiple-act criteria" to an index of differing behaviors combined on a single or repeating observation basis. Fishbein and Ajzen consider attitudes toward specific behaviors to be the best predictors of single-act criteria, whereas attitudes toward general tendencies to engage in a specific behavior provide the best predictors of repeated-observation criteria. Finally, multiple-act criteria are better predicted by an equally general attitude than by attitudes toward specific behaviors (see also Lizka, 1974; Weigel et al., 1974).

The specificity principle imposes on the scientist the responsibility to determine what type of index best fits his or her general or specific attitude object. The absence of such a consideration can only lead to continued attitude-behavior discrepancy findings. A number of studies have illustrated the promise such an approach has for attitude research, as well as several means of increasing attitudinal specificity (Eagly and Himmelfarb, 1978: 529).

NORMATIVE INFLUENCES

Research on persuasion has consistently lent support to Donne's statement that "no man is an island unto himself." According to impression-management theory, people manage their communication to preserve positive self-images. Counterattitudinal studies demonstrate how people react when their self-images are threatened by their performance of an unacceptable or inconsistent form of behavior. Those who believe that their behaviors will lead others to perceive them negatively will either provide excuses and justifications for their behaviors or change their attitudes to be more consistent with those behaviors. Schlenker and Riess (1979) have demonstrated that people also try to assume responsibility for actions that lead to beneficial consequences. They suggest that maximal responsibility is sought by the actor when environmental variables decrease the amount of responsibility that can be attributed to that person for proattitudinal actions, especially when the actions and their consequences are important to that individual. In short, if people coincidentally favor a popular side of some issue, they are likely to attempt to convince others that the popular statements reflect their personal attitudes.

EMOTION

The final variable to be discussed in this chapter is emotion. No theory of persuasion would be complete without it, because no human being is complete without emotions. We are not purely cognitive beings, despite our attempts to conceal that fact.

According to Schachter (1964), there are two interacting components in emotion: peripheral physiological arousal and the cognitions associated with such arousal. If there is no cognitive element associated with physiological arousal, people search the environment for arousal explanations. Singer (1966) found that subjects with no ready-made explanations for their arousal could be manipulated into euphoria or anger.

Buck (1976) indicates that the relationship between emotions and cognitions is not yet clear. Much controversy surrounds Schachter's somewhat qualified claim that emotional states are physiologically identical and differentiated only by cognitions about them (see also Plutchik and Ax, 1967; Shapiro and Crider, 1969). Buck, taking a developmental perspective, posits that we learn to interpret our emotions as we attempt to achieve effective interactions with our environment. White (1959) refers to the child's tendency to explore, manipulate, and seek stimulation as a movement toward competence. The drive toward competence moves children away from purely emotional experiences to more reasoned cognitive experiences. According to Buck (1976: 316), the young child's search allows him or her to construct "an inner representation of emotional reality through his experiences with the subjective feelings, verbal labels, positive or negative consequences, and so on, associated with emotional situations."

How these views of emotion fit into a theory of persuasion is our next concern. The theoretical model of persuasion advanced in earlier chapters has a primarily cognitive focus. Perceptions of personal inconsistency, inappropriateness, and ineffectiveness may elicit emotional reactions which facilitate or, as in the case of strong fear appeals, inhibit persuasion. In all three cases the emotions follow the message. In other words, inconsistency, inappropriateness, and ineffectiveness elicit what Buck would term cognitive emotions. They are not pure emotions, such as anger and fear. Buck suggests that the young child may not even experience or be concerned about consistency. As the self-concept develops, we might expect a concomitant concern for consistency. Until then, consistency appeals may be ignored. In terms of the perspective advanced in Chapter 5, such appeals may not elicit any desire in young children to alter their rule repertoires.

It seems reasonable to assume that pure emotional reactions may be used prior to logical appeals to shake the persuadee's confidence in his or her rule structure. As a result, he or she may consider alternative rules. In other words, appeals that elicit less cognitive emotions, such as fear, may set the persuadee on a search for a way to explain and reduce his or her distress. The persuader may explain the distress as due to behavioral inconsistency, inappropriateness, or ineffectiveness. However, emotion alone does not persuade. It may set the stage for or facilitate rule change. Persuasion for adults is a predominantly cognitive activity of rule realignment or reinforcement which benefits from the right amount of emotional arousal.

CONCLUSION

Although the coverage of persuasion variables in this chapter does not exhaust all possibilities, major variables were reviewed. Each of these variables can be viewed as contributing to context versus self-predominance, discussed in Chapter 5. Source credibility, for example, can be used to support an appropriateness appeal, assuming that the source is perceived as an opinion leader for significant others. To the extent that a source is utilized for identification purposes, a consistency appeal may prove more effective.

Message variables can also be manipulated to influence receiver perceptions of the source, as the Bradac et al. (1979) article suggests, or to violate expectations and thereby influence receiver resistance to persuasion (Miller and Burgoon, 1979). Personality information provides some guidance in the determination of persuasive strategy, since it can indirectly indicate the level of self-autonomy allowable in a given context. To the extent that behaviors manifest of personality types are absent, we may assume that context predominates. In such cases, appropriateness appeals.

Each of the variables discussed in this chapter can be used to offset the self-autonomy/context-predominance balance. As mentioned in Chapter 5, this balance is also a function of the noninterpersonal or interpersonal nature of the persuasion context. In the next several chapters we shall look closely at those contexts and their special influence on the operation of the variables we have reviewed.

Chapter 7

INTERPERSONAL PERSUASION

Given the interest interpersonal communication has generated over the past decade, the definition of interpersonal persuasion should be simple to obtain. However, the literature on interpersonal communication indicates that we do not yet have a definition of the widely accepted term *interpersonal*. Miller (1978) has presented a strong case against accepting situational definitions of interpersonal communication. He explains that such definitions are of limited scientific utility. They do not capture the exciting aspects of relationship development. A situation is a static construct directing our attention to socially prescribed roles rather than to the more idiosyncratic rules of interpersonal communication. In other words, to claim that a communication is interpersonal in nature because there are fewer than three persons communicating is a definition that clearly misses the important distinctions between interpersonal and noninterpersonal communication. Instead, any definition of interpersonal communication should focus on the developmental nature of human interaction. It should convey nonstatic, progressive elements of that phenomenon. In short, it should indicate the intrinsic (rule) rather than extrinsic (role) focus of the participants, who create a shared identity rather than relying predominantly on prescribed, prepackaged scripts.

As Miller (1978) points out, all interpersonal communications rely to some extent on extrinsic guidelines. However, the more interpersonal the transaction, the more likely it is that behaviors will be motivated by intrinsic, relationship-generated rules. Miller suggests that we perceive communication types as varying along an interpersonal-noninterpersonal continuum. It follows that, instead of exclusively focusing on the specific situation or context in which a given interaction occurs for its meaning, researchers should also look at the development of that interaction. Is it primarily governed by socially prescribed expectations, or are the interactants predisposed to rely on their own mutually negotiated definitions of what is or is not appropriate? Before a researcher can hope to answer this question, he or she must find some way to identify patterns of interaction indicative of rule or role predominance. These designations would depend on the subjects' and researchers' abilities to separate "owned" from "borrowed" rules. To the extent that "owned" rules predominate, self-autonomy is present in a relationship. Generally, the degree of rule over role predominance is greater in interpersonal communication than in noninterpersonal communication, if only because feedback is typically more available in interpersonal communication and opportunities for explaining slight deviations through verbal or nonverbal aligning actions are therefore available. When few opportunities exist to modify potentially negative attributions, people are more likely to cling to the safety afforded by role prescriptions.

Despite these cautions, it seems nonproductive to rule out the contribution an understanding of situational context can make to the recognition of those interactions guided by intrinsic rules, as opposed to those dependent on extrinsic guidelines. Perhaps what the researcher should be looking at is the extent to which self-autonomy and context influence interactants' choices during the typical episodes of their emerging or declining relationship. Even an intimate couple will often relinquish their personal rule system in situations calling for some degree of decorum on their part. In other words, the situational context often determines whether interactants are free to use the intrinsic rules they have available to them. Thus, while an exclusively situational orientation is dysfunctional to the development of a nonstatic, processual theoretical view of interpersonal communication, it is not productive to remove it from consideration altogether.

With that qualification in mind, Miller's (1978) developmental approach is adopted in this text. The task at hand, then, is to determine what constitutes interpersonal persuasion. As mentioned previously, interpersonal communication is guided by predominantly intrinsic rather than extrinsic rules. Interpersonal communication allows interactants to share rules, modify rules, and create rules in the development of a relationship. To the extent that one person wishes to influence another to accept his or her version of a rule, the potential for persuasion exists. Interpersonal persuasion is an attempt to bring the rules of the other interactant(s) in line with one's own. As such, it is a form of coordinated management of meaning (Pearce, 1976), but its *original* goal is to obtain that coordination without having to relinquish or accommodate the persuader's own rule set. Just as Miller and Burgoon (1973) found it necessary to include the concept of conscious intent in their definition of persuasion so that we might separate it from unintentional influence, this definition of interpersonal persuasion excludes from consideration those forms of coordinated management of meaning that do not have as their goal the alteration of another individual's rule set. For example, the greeting ritual,

Hi, how's it goin'?
Fine, how are things with you?
Fine, thanks.
See ya.
Yep.

is a form of coordinated management of meaning. However, there is little evidence, even if some influence did occur (e.g., "Gee, he's a nice guy"), to support the claim that one actor consciously intended to alter the rule set of the other. In this case, then, interpersonal persuasion did not occur.

Reardon-Boynton (1978) developed a scale to determine the degree to which coordinated management of meaning is obtained through the cooperation of interactants. This coadjuvancy scale, developed to assess children's ability to provide alternative endings for a conversation in which two boys violate the rule of turn-taking three times, distinguishes between coordination achieved by the intrusion of an outside party (arbitration), the yielding of one party to the wishes of the other (acquiescence), and the mutual accommodation of both parties (cooperation). In Chapter 5, similar distinctions were drawn between acquiescence, accommodation, cooperation, and coadjuvancy, with the latter two representing reciprocal persuasion. What this perspective offers is a movement away from unidirectional interpretations of persuasion to bidirectional or multidirectional interpretations. In short, while conscious intent to bring about change must exist on the part of at least one person in order for the activity of persuasion to occur, a person originally perceived as persuadee can also operate as persuader, especially in interpersonal interactions where feedback opportunities occur frequently.

In the next few sections of this chapter we shall look at those interpersonal communication theories that have implications for the study of interpersonal persuasion.

RULES APPROACH

The rules theorist views communication interactants as having expectations, intentions, and the ability to choose from among alternative behaviors. Berger (1979) described this perspective as creating a model of

humans that assumes people prefer rule consensus and agreement. He
suggests that this differs from the model proposed by Miller and Steinberg
(1975), which allows for the possibility that an actor will break the rules
in order to gain rewards. While it is easy to see, especially in terms of
Pearce's (1976) early conceptualizations of rules, why Berger decided that
rule-governed perspectives preclude deviation from rules, it is unlikely that
Pearce (1976), Cushman and Whiting (1972), and others really intended to
do so. Later work by Reardon-Boynton (1978) introduced the concept of
rule deviation into rules theory, a step which brings closer together the
perspective of Miller and Steinberg (1975), who focus on predictability as
the purpose of communication, and the perspective of the rules theorists.

One rules perspective that has received much attention in the field of
communication science is the "coordinated management of meaning"
theory (Pearce, 1976; Cronen and Pearce, 1978). Coordinated management of meaning theorists describe both extrinsic and intrinsic rules as
guides to behavioral selection in communication interactions. Pearce
(1976) contends that people contract with each other to produce particular conversational episodes. Each person assumes that he or she shares with
the other interactant(s) an understanding of what is expected to occur and
an implicit agreement not to violate those expectations. An essential
precondition of coordination of meaning, then, is consensual rules.

Cronen and Pearce (1978) extend the earlier conceptualization of
coordinated management of meaning in their paper, "The Logic of the
Coordinated Mangement of Meaning: An Open Systems Model of Interpersonal Communication." They propose that people attempt to control their
communications to avoid problems much like a system strives to avoid
entropy. Cronen and Pearce describe as "frangible" those conversational
episodes that cannot adjust to variations without crisis. To the extent that
the interactants know a number of ways to conduct the same episode, frangibility is unlikely. Such flexibility is facilitated by the ability of one or
more of the interactants to construe the pattern of the episode. To the
extent that a pattern is discernible, the communicators can interrupt the
natural flow of events and attempt to conduct the episode differently. To
the extent that they are unable to identify the pattern or are not adept at
providing alternative strategies, unwanted repetitive episodes may obtain
(see Cronen et al., 1979).

A classic example of how the structure of conversation can become the
focus of relational communication is provided by the characters George
and Martha in Albee's *Who's Afraid of Virginia Woolf?* Both persons are of

sufficient cognitive complexity to construe the patterns of their repeated episodes. It appears that in an effort to avoid the boredom of repeated content, they challenge each other by continuously violating conversational expectations. In George and Martha's game, the skillful player is the one who can bring the system (conversation) very close to destruction. Playing within the area of greatest frangibility is the most exciting and rewarding aspect of their game. Nick and Honey, the visitors, are obviously used to tamer conversational structures and content. They sit in awe, much as circus spectators who have never been on a tightrope and therefore cannot comprehend how easy tightrope-walking is to the performer, who does it every day. Nick and Honey do not recognize that the seemingly dangerous leans and slips of George and Martha's communications are purposely performed to mesmerize the audience.

The interpersonal skill demonstrated by George and Martha is a function of their ability to climb the abstraction ladder. Unlike most communicators, they can construe the repeatable patterns of their interactions. They are thus in the unusual position of being able to monitor their own behaviors so that the expected is avoided. Their rule violations are such that while the entire relationship is continuously threatened, it is never destroyed. Each comes dangerously close to the deviation-tolerance threshold of his/her spouse, but that is the challenge which makes the game worth playing.

While most of us do not consciously engage in such potentially destructive games, the behavior of these interactants demonstrates how people can gain control of their communication. Since Martha and George are equally adept at performing their game, it is difficult, if not impossible, to name a winner. However, were George and Martha to use the same strategies with their guests, there is little question concerning who would win. Nick and Honey do not possess the ability to climb the abstraction ladder. They are therefore easy prey for George and Martha.

This example illustrates the advantage to be gained from being able to construe the patterns evident in one's conversations. The persuader who knows what to expect from the persuadee can monitor the conversation and, with some additional skill, direct it toward his or her own ends. To borrow from the Miller and Burgoon (1979) study discussed in Chapter 6, persuaders can create expectations in the minds of persuadees that will lead them to prepare counterarguments. If the counterarguments are then rendered useless because of planned expectation violation, the persuadee's defenses will be dropped and the persuader will become vulnerable. While this example is a bit simplistic, it indicates how useful the ability to construe patterns of interaction is to successful persuasion and even to coordinated management of meaning in general.

The question that rules theorists must ask themselves is whether or not models such as the coordinated management of meaning contribute to our understanding of human communication. As vonBertanlannfy (1968: 12) suggests, "a model is a conceptual structure intended to reflect certain aspects of reality [and is] neither exhaustive nor unique." A viable test of the Pearce (1976) and Cronen and Pearce (1978) contributions should determine whether they reflect those aspects of reality the researchers intended them to reflect. The excerpt from *Who's Afraid of Virginia Woolf* suggests that the coordinated management of meaning is intuitively sound. However, as Miller (1978: 178) indicates, in terms of scientific payoffs, "the jury is still out." It is probably true that the jury will be out until rules theorists attempt to specify the scope conditions of their theories (see Reynolds, 1975). Using Bateson's (1972) terminology, what the rules perspective needs is a *frame*. A frame is a premise telling us where the picture ends and the wallpaper begins. To date, rules research has worked its way into many different communication contexts. The demarcation between the picture and the wallpaper is as yet unclear. It may come to pass that attempts to make the concept of rules exhaustive will meet with failure and, as with attitude, an intuitively sound construction of reality will never find the sphere of human activity to which it effectively belongs.

To give rules approaches a fighting chance, then, it is proposed herein that we look to rules for explanations of *primarily* interpersonal forms of communication. Borrowing from Miller (1978), the definition of interpersonal communication will be that form of communication in which predominantly relationship-intrinsic rather than relationship-extrinsic expectations guide interaction. Clearly, Martha and George do not rely on role expectations as a predominant guide to behavior. They have created a relationship that operates on the basis of rules very foreign to those of others. Still, they do use their knowledge of role expectations to manipulate the reactions of their company. Without role expectations (which are actually clusters of rules that have gained widespread acceptance), Nick and Honey would have no basis for comparison, and George and Martha's behavior would not seem deviant. The entire episode would simply be enigmatic.

The point being made here is that rules and roles are not easily separated. The boundaries between them are not definite. A role consists of a set of rules. Some of those rules are clearly central to the role definitions, while others are peripheral. Central rules enjoy the greater degree of consensus among members of a particular social milieu. Even in interpersonal interactions, it is possible for people to use a role to guide rule application. This is a deductive logic approach resulting in predominantly central rule usage. For example, the decision to respond as a professor rather than as a friend to a student's upset response to a grade defines a rule domain. The professor may also take an experimental approach by combining friend and professor rules, thereby reshaping expectations for the relationship. In the next chapter, on persuasion in organizations, this rule-role relationship will be discussed at greater length. It is important for now to explain that role prescriptions are often important to interpersonal interactions, especially initial interactions. As relationships develop, however, greater latitude for self-autonomy exists in the sense of personal rule input. The process of encouraging another party to accept personal rules or create entirely new ones as part of the relationship definition requires persuasion. In short, we could say that rule clusters are more extrinsic (role) to the extent that self is not the predominant author. As indicated in Figure 7.1, movement away from self through relationship, situation, and context represents an extrinsic bias.

As mentioned earlier, it is possible for people to collaborate in the making of roles for their relationship. Role-making involves a self-context-reflexive logic rather than solely inductive or deductive logic. A tracking back and forth between self, relationship, and context occurs in the process of creating a role. To the extent that self is the focal point against which all other elements are measured, flexibility is present and something called a "role" is difficult to identify. This often occurs in interpersonal interactions. Individual rules are identifiable but they appear to have very little interdependence. To the extent that self and nonself elements balance out in the role-making process, a role is usually identifiable and can be used to guide future rule selection. These roles, while made up of rules, discourage change. Context predominates and self-autonomy is submerged in a rigidly defined set of rules.

An example of rigid role prescriptions was described in a recent newspaper account of one of the first Chinese divorce trials open to the public. The husband claimed that his marital problems, including several wife-beatings, were the result of monetary pressures. The wife did not perceive this to be an adequate excuse for such behavior. She expected that she should be treated as an important person in his life, rather than as property—a previously acceptable definition of wives in China. The wife was appealing to rules that she expected be followed in her particular relationship with her husband. The judge, however, decided to base his

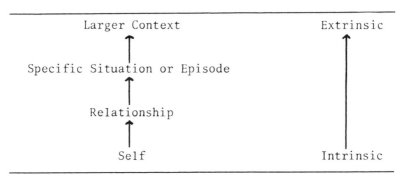

Figure 7.1

decision on traditional role expectations rather than the wife's relational rules. He explained, "The husband is imbued with man's pride. In public a man cannot bow low to his wife. He will not budge an inch from his arguments. In private talks with the judge he can admit his mistakes but, here in public, he cannot do so" (UPI, *Hartford Courant,* February 10, 1980).

This Chinese divorce is an example of what Reardon-Boynton (1978) has referred to as arbitration. Extrinsic rules which may be generated from societal roles are called upon by an outside agent to bring the relationship back to a nonfrangible state. This is not the province of interpersonal persuasion. In interpersonal persuasion the persuader and the persuadee(s) have established a relationship that relies predominantly on rules created during its development. The creation of rules does not exclude the possibility that one person donated an entire set of rules to the relationship. In most relationships, however, the natural order of things is to adjust and readjust rules in the course of development. When rules are not available or a particular episode is new to the individuals involved, they may call on societally prescribed rule sets (roles). The Chinese divorce is an example of this. However, in this example, the additional problem of changing role structures for women in China created a truly enigmatic episode. The judge, in this case, clung to tradition.

For our purposes, then, rules will be considered the stuff of which interpersonal relationships are made. This does not mean that rules are entirely independent of role expectations. Roles are actually commonly accepted rule clusters that are qualified or relinquished in the process of relationship development. In the next chapter, we shall see how rules operate in organizational communication, but the focus will then be on extrinsic rather than intrinsic expectations. The line separating inter-personal communication from noninterpersonal communication may not be accepted for some time. However, this definition constitutes a step toward specifying the scope conditions of a promising theoretical model.

PHENOMENOLOGY

If we plan to investigate interpersonal persuasion in the context of devel-oping relationships that rely on intrinsic rules, where do we start? We could begin by asking the subjects how long they have been together, and then proceed to draw some inferences about their relationship on the basis of that information. This is certainly a commonly accepted procedure. However, in the previous chapters we discussed the problems inherent in allowing experimenters to draw their own inferences about someone else's thought processes (e.g., what constitutes dissonance for one person may not constitute it for another). We also discussed the squeamish response of many scientists to self-report by subjects. A quandary is thus created.

Early in the twentieth century, an approach was developed for under-standing how reality is constituted. The goal of phenomenology has been "to make problematic for study that which everyone else presupposes" (Hawes, 1977: 5). Phenomenologists attempt to render the familiar un-familiar. They are interested in communicators' logics. In a sense, they are looking for rules. However, they attempt to divorce themselves from any epistemological considerations that might inhibit seeing the rules as the actors themselves see them.

While the goal of phenomenology is a welcome response to noncogni-tive, logical positivist procedure, it is fraught with methodological prob-lems. Phenomenology attempts to find the "oozy nature" of reality by observing it from an "uncanny" perspective (putting presuppositions aside) so that the historicality of the phenomenon under study may surface. Communication is viewed as work in progress, the ontological properties of which are to be ascertained without the presuppositions afforded by epistemology. This total denial of epistemological processes in the search for ontological properties of communication poses serious problems. If something is ontological, one can only know that by an epistemological check. Also, if epistemology is to be excluded from phenomenological studies, how will the researcher know whether or not he or she is correct?

Such questions are likely to haunt phenomenological approaches to the study of communication. The purpose behind the approach, however, is not without value. It avoids the pitfalls inherent in assuming too much about one's subjects. It's communication-scholar advocates have made us a bit more cautious about imposing our own versions of reality on our subjects.

INTERPERSONAL PERSUASION:
A RULES APPROACH

At this point, it is obvious that the perspective on interpersonal persuasion to be adopted in this chapter is rules-based. One of the major premises of this approach is that individuals are not driven by external forces to behave in certain ways, but that they *choose* to behave in those ways. Their choices are based on their perceptions of the intrinsic and extrinsic rules operating in a particular context. To the extent that the predominant concern is with intrinsic (relationship) rules, the individuals are engaged in interpersonal rather than noninterpersonal communication. Miller et al. (1977) indicate that this reliance on psychological, rather than cultural and sociological, data in the determination of interpersonal message choices facilitates accuracy. Their perspective suggests that persuaders may use role expectations as a baseline from which the particular persuadee is expected to deviate. That deviation is governed by certain relationship rules and idiosyncratic rules, the latter of which the persuader may be unaware. Although this is not what Miller et al. explicitly state, it seems feasible that despite the predominant reliance on intrinsic rules in interpersonal communication, extrinsic rules may serve as a comparison level. Furthermore, they may be utilized when no relationship rule exists to govern a particular behavioral choice.

For example, if a man and woman have gotten to know each other fairly well in their communication classes but have never dated, we can expect that the first date may pose some difficult choices for each of them. They already have a relationship and some intrinsic rules, but it may be difficult for the man to determine whether or not he should pay for the movies, hold open the car door, hold the woman's coat, and kiss her goodnight. He may find it necessary to rely on role expectations rather than relationship rules until such time as the two work all this out together. If he holds her coat for her and she smiles with obvious admiration and then launches into a ten-minute soliloquy on the positive virtues of chivalrous males, then the young man has been successful and is likely to assign chivalrous rules to that relationship. However, should he then proceed to pay for the movies because he assumes that it is the chivalrous thing to do, only to hear her respond with the statement, "I think that we should each pay for our own ticket. It's really very expensive otherwise," he will have to revise his role-guided behavior.

When persuasion is the goal in interpersonal communication, it may be useful to consider the importance rule maintenance has for a particular individual, since this may serve as a foundation for establishing dissonance. "It's the manly thing to do" is a common interpersonal strategy used by males in comaraderous exchanges and females attempting to convince male friends to alter their behavior. It may be that doing the "male thing" is not as important to the persuadee as doing what is appropriate for the particular relationship, rendering the appeal to this role dysfunctional. If, for example, a male wishes to obtain information concerning the extent of intimacy that two of his friends are experiencing, he may request this information of the male over a few beers. The "male" thing to do might be to divulge such information, but the relationship rule established between the male and female friends may prohibit such disclosure. The male friend's choice of behavior will indicate which rule (extrinsic or intrinsic) has the higher priority in his repertoire. It may also be that the male requesting the information is a close friend and one who can be trusted with private information. In this case, the choice will be based on the intrinsic rules of two relationships as well as the extrinsic guidelines for male comaraderie. The persuadee may find himself justifying the violations of one rule set by appealing to another: "Mary wouldn't want me to discuss this with just anyone, but since you are a good friend, I feel comfortable." Hence, another tactical error obtains as a result of competing rule structures.

INTERPERSONAL PERSUASION STRATEGIES

The fluctuation between role and rule prescriptions characteristic of interpersonal exchanges renders persuasion in this context a complex task. Persuaders always operate on the basis of incomplete information. Their perceptions of a particular interaction or a relationship are never exactly the same as those of the persuadee. Nevertheless, in an effort to simplify the task of predicting what strategies individuals will use to persuade others, a number of taxonomies have been developed. It appears, however, that these taxonomies have created as many problems as they have solved.

Clark and Delia (1969) criticize the business of compliance taxonomy development on the basis of the general lack of attention given to describing the underlying or systematic relationships among strategies. Schenck-Hamlin et al. (1980: 6) suggest that "several unfortunate eventualities arise from this circumstance." They provide three: First, strategy meanings remain abstract and therefore imprecise. Second, since no standard for comparison exists, research on particular strategies cannot be easily compared. Finally, relationships between strategies are infrequently discussed and even then are poorly defined. "As such, they appear more like a listing of elements in a department store catalogue, rather than elements growing out of an organic theory of compliance-gaining."

Schenck-Hamlin et al. attempt to integrate the various compliance strategies by exploring their underlying relationships. As a result, all strategies are classified into three basic types: sanctionative, instructional, and altruistic. Sanctionative strategies are designed to increase the likelihood of the desired response by offering the target rewards or punishments. Instructional strategies provide the target with reasons or justifications for responding in some preferred manner. Altruistic strategies focus on the relationship between the actor and target as a basis for the appeal. The authors then developed a symbolic language for specifying the logic underlying the construction of each compliance-gaining strategy: "From this standpoint the authors are attempting to define the rules associated with forming a compliance-gaining strategy. These are constitutive rules in the sense that they define the form that a particular strategy will take."

The symbolic language of Schenck-Hamlin et al. is too complex to do it justice in this chapter. However, the emphasis in this text on the importance of recognizing the underlying logic of human behavior makes their work particularly relevant. In addition, their approach to defining the underlying logic of persuasive strategies does not ignore the interaction of actor, other, and situation. They define power, a central element of their theory, in terms of the variable, locus of control. To these authors (1980: 22), "locus of control generally refers to the extent to which a sanction, rationale or the target's attraction to the actor is a result of the actions or perception of the actor, target or situation." For example, "in instructional strategies the rationale in explanation is brought about by the actor. Consequently the actor has control of the rationale. However, in direct request the target is responsible for the rationale, since the actor only suggests a direction for the behavior. Finally, altruistic strategies always have the target controlling his/her attraction for the actor" (1980: 21).

While it is possible that another group of researchers not concerned with the locus of control (no power orientation) might find a different logic underlying the various strategies studied by Schenck-Hamlin et al., their symbolic language and accompanying rationale constitute an intuitively intriguing approach to a complex issue.

Furthermore, their logical analysis could, as they suggest, make it possible to determine which strategies can be linked to other strategies if the actor is to remain consistent. Assuming that the authors are correct in this prediction, future logical analysis may increase our ability accurately to map out and compare persuader (or researcher) and persuadee perceptions of the latter's requirements for personal rule consistency. In so doing, the area of greatest threat to accurate explanation and prediction may become less obscure to researchers, since one function of a logic is to make the previously unintelligible comprehensible.

As unconnected as previous compliance strategy studies have been, one taxonomy has received much attention. Schenck-Hamlin et al. (1980) consider it the most comprehensive of those they reviewed. The Marwell and Schmitt (1967) taxonomy, which appears in Table 7.1, focuses on the availability of positive and negative sanctions for what can be categorized as either appropriate or consistent behavior. Of their 16 compliance-gaining techniques, techniques 9-13 appeal to self-image consistency, whereas remainder appeal to the person's need for persuader (1, 2, 5, 7, 8, and 9) or general other (3, 4, 15, and 16) approval.

Miller et al. (1977) extended the work of Marwell and Schmitt by proposing a number of control strategies which can be used in interpersonal and noninterpersonal persuasion. These strategies may be considered means by which one person can convince another to suspend or reject a particular rule. They reduced the Marwell and Schmitt strategies to five factors: I, rewarding activity; II, punishing activity; III, expertise; IV, activation of impersonal commitments; and V, activation of personal commitments.

Miller et al. (1977) used the Marwell and Schmitt taxonomy to determine what strategies are typically used in interpersonal and noninterpersonal situations with long- or short-term consequences. Their findings indicate that some strategies are more appropriate to interpersonal than to noninterpersonal communications. Also, some are used in long-term rather than short-term consequence situations. For example, they found that two strategies, negative esteem and aversive stimulation, are unlikely to be used in interpersonal situations. Long-term consequence situations appear to be

TABLE 7.1   Sixteen Compliance-Gaining Techniques,
with Examples from Family Situations

1. Promise	(If you comply, I will reward you.) "You offer to increase Dick's allowance if he increases his studying."
2. Threat	(If you do not comply, I will punish you.) "You threaten to forbid Dick the use of the car if he does not increase his studying."
3. Expertise (positive)	(If you comply, you will be rewarded because of "the nature of things.") "You point out to Dick that if he gets good grades he will be able to get into a good college and get a good job."
4. Expertise (negative)	(If you do not comply, you will be punished because of "the nature of things.") "You point out to Dick that if he does not get good grades he will not be able to get into a good college or get a good job."
5. Liking	(Actor is friendly and helpful to get target in "good frame of mind" so that he will comply with request.) "You try to be as friendly and pleasant as possible to get Dick in the right frame of mind before asking him to study."
6. Pregiving	(Actor rewards target before requesting compliance.) "You raise Dick's allowance and tell him you now expect him to study."
7. Aversive stimulation	(Actor continuously punishes target, making cessation contingent on compliance.) "You forbid Dick the use of the car and tell him he will not be allowed to drive until he studies more."
8. Debt	(You owe me compliance because of past favors.) "You point out that you have sacrificed and saved to pay for Dick's education and that he owes it to you to get good enough grades to get into a good college."
9. Moral appeal	(You are immoral if you do not comply.) "You tell Dick that it is morally wrong for anyone not to get as good grades as he can and that he should study more."
10. Self-feeling (positive)	(You will feel better about yourself if you comply.) "You tell Dick he will feel proud if he gets himself to study more.
11. Self-feeling (negative)	(You will feel worse about yourself if you do not comply.) "You tell Dick he will feel ashamed if he gets bad grades."
12. Altercasting (positive)	(A person with "good" qualities would comply.) "You tell Dick that since he is a mature and intelligent boy he naturally will want to study more and get good grades."
13. Altercasting (negative)	(Only a person with "bad" qualities would not comply.) "You tell Dick that only someone very childish does not study as he should."
14. Altruism	(I need your compliance very badly, so do it for me.) "You tell Dick that you really want very badly for him to get into a good college and that you wish he should study more as a personal favor to you."

TABLE 7.1   (Continued)

15. Esteem (positive)	(People you value will think better of you if you comply.) "You tell Dick that the whole family will be very proud of him if he gets good grades."
16. Esteem (negative)	(People you value will think worse of you if you do not comply.) "You tell Dick that the whole family will be very disappointed in him if he gets poor grades."

SOURCE: Marwell and Schmitt (1967: 357-358). Reprinted by permission of the American Sociological Association and the authors.

marked by high-probability use of promises, positive altercasting, and altruism, whereas aversive stimulation is unlikely to be used in such situations.

The Miller et al. (1977) study indicates that persuasive strategies are situationally bound. They qualify this conclusion, however, by explaining that, as suggested by attribution theory, people tend to attribute their own action to the situations in which they find themselves, while attributions to others are based on perceptions of personal proclivities and inferences concerning dispositional traits (see also Jones and Nisbett, 1971). Applying this perspective to their own study, Miller et al. (1977: 51) explain,

> It may be, then, that the situational prominence revealed in this study was also a function of respondent orientation. Stated differently, given attribution findings, respondents faced with assessing the likelihood of their own choice of compliance-gaining strategies may have cued to situational differences in answering, responses not reflective of more stable (i.e., across situations) personal tendencies they might normally exhibit in their usual influence attempts. Subsequent research, therefore, will need to parse situational and personal characteristics affecting message choice more carefully.

It may be that the subjects in the Miller et al. study based their message strategy selection on role expectations rather than on relationship rule expectations. As suggested in Chapter 5, perhaps we need studies that look at the personal and situational characteristics affecting message choice as well as studies that look at relationship characteristics which might affect message choice. Miller et al. did examine the effects of relationship type to some extent by indicating whether the consequences were to be long- or short-term. However, we might benefit from breaking this dimension down into more specific categories such as those offered by Fitzpatrick (1977) and applied in the work of Fitzpatrick and Winke (1979).

Fitzpatrick and Winke's (1979) work focused on strategies and tactics used in interpersonal conflicts between same- and opposite-sex persons.

They asked subjects to indicate the nature of their opposite-sex relationship as "married," "engaged," "exclusively involved with this individual," "seriously involved with this individual more than others," or "only casually involved with this individual" (1979: 6). They also asked the subjects to indicate how satisfied they were with both their same- and their opposite-sex relationships. Using Kipnis's Interpersonal Conflict Scale, they asked respondents to estimate how often they used 44 conflict tactics.

One advantage to using this procedure is that asking subjects to consider a particular relationship in which they are presently involved, rather than a fictitious relationship, encourages them to consider rule expectations rather than situationally prescribed role expectations. If the subjects were asked to consider a person with whom they had an ongoing relationship (defined by using the Fitzpatrick and Winke typology) in a particular situation (such as those used in the Miller et al., 1977, study), we would expect to find intrinsic rules operating more frequently than extrinsic rules. To determine the extent to which relationship-intrinsic rules were operating, subjects could be asked to account for their message strategy choice. A content analysis procedure could then be used to determine the ratio of intrinsic to extrinsic rules.

The same data could also provide information relevant to communication competence research. If Weimann (1977: 102) is correct in his definition of the competent communicator as having the ability to "choose among available communicative behaviors in order that he may successfully accomplish his own interpersonal goals during an encounter while maintaining the face and line of his fellow interactants within the constraints of the situation," we would expect to find that subjects whose accounts for strategy choices reflect both their own and the recipient's interpersonal needs and expectations should also be the more competent.

The self-autonomy characteristic of interpersonal contexts renders the development of compliance-strategy context linkages a challenging task. Yet, without such taxonomies and some understanding of the systematic relationships among their components, we are forced to depend on weak foundations for prediction.

The theoretical model advanced in this text proposes that consistency appeals are more effective in interpersonal contexts where behavioral choice is not severely constrained by role expectations. This does not mean that appropriateness and effectiveness appeals are relegated to non-interpersonal contexts only. It does mean, however, that consistency appeals such as Marwell and Schmitt's techniques 9-13 are not likely to be

Initiation Phase	Rule Definition Phase	Rule Confirmation Phase	Strategic Development Phase	Termination Phase

Figure 7.2 Episodic Structure

among the competent communicator's preferred compliance strategies for use in conversations with relatively unfamiliar others, or in contexts where the persuadee must conform (appropriateness) or perform (effectiveness) in ways determined by significant others to retain a valued position. In the former case, the amount of available personal information about a relative stranger is insufficient to generate reliable rule-consistency claims. In the latter case, the persuadee may find personal rule inconsistency tolerable because the situation precludes the opportunity for choice. In such instances, consistency is sacrificed to meet the higher priorities of appropriateness and/or effectiveness.

In the next section, an example of successful unfamiliar-persuadee rule realignment is provided and the reasons for strategy choice explained.

RULE REALIGNMENT IN
INTERPERSONAL PERSUASION

A common assumption of rules theories is that people share expectations for how a particular conversational episode should be enacted. Frentz (1976) tells us that persons engage in five episode phases for which we can assume they have certain expectations. Frentz's episodic structure appears in Figure 7.2.

Some episodes require that we conduct all five phases appearing in Frentz's model. The following discussion is an example:

Jane: Hi, Jim. How are you?   *Initiation*

Jim: Fine.

Jane: I'd like to talk to you for a few
minutes.   *Rule Definition*

Jim: Okay, but make it short. I have to
get to class.   *Rule Confirmation*

Jane: I didn't get the notes from class
yesterday. Do you think I could
borrow yours?   *Strategic Development*

Jim: Sure, no problem.

Jane: I guess I should let you get to class.   *Termination*

Jim: Yeah. I'll call you later.

In conversations with the telephone operator, not all of the phases are necessary. The rules are implied by the purpose of the call, and unless the caller deviates from them, there is little need to confirm their existence. Effective persuasion requires that we recognize the rules operating in the episodes and episode phases in which we are engaged. Structural rules exist to avoid having to deal with superfluous demands. For example, in the following conversation we can see that the rule for appropriate operator-client conversation is shared by both interactants, despite the client's deviant behavior.

Operator: May I help you?

Kathy: Yes, can you tell me what time it is?

Operator: We are not allowed to give the time.

Kathy: Yes, I know, but my electricity went off.

Operator: It is 12:35.

Kathy: Thank you.

Despite her deviation from the consensually shared rule for operator-client communication, the client obtained the desired information. She appealed to another rule, which is that under certain circumstances operator-client communication rules are not binding. The client redefined the superordinate constructs influencing operator rule selection to include "emergency." The explanation, "but my electricity went off," was apparently a sufficient condition for rule 1 violation. It provided an account for the violation of that rule and an antecedent condition for the implementation of rule 2 (the rule for emergencies).

According to Toulmin (1958), the logical form of an argument includes data (evidence), a claim, and a warrant linking the data to the claim. Claims may be accompanied by a qualifier such as "sometimes" or "probably." A qualifier may also have attached to it some exceptions to the rule. Toulmin's model appears in Figure 7.3.

If we were to fit the operator conversation into Toulmin's model, the argument form depicted in Figure 7.4 would obtain. This argument is stated in an unequivocal manner. No qualifiers are included. It is offered as a fait accompli.

SOURCE: Adapted from Toulmin (1958: 103). Reprinted by permission of Cambridge University Press.

Figure 7.3

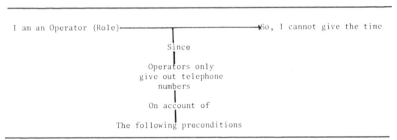

Figure 7.4

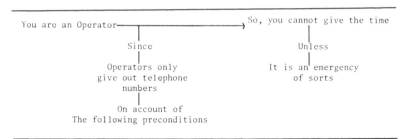

Figure 7.5

Figure 7.5 demonstrates how the client attempted to render the rule in Figure 7.4 inoperative by incorporating an exception to that rule. Essentially the rule depicted in Figure 7.4 remains intact. Only its range of convenience is brought into question. The operator's willingness to provide the time indicates that she considered the rule-exception claim legitimate.

From this example, it is apparent that knowing the rules is a precursor to using them as a means of persuading others. To the extent that an individual knows the rules and can create conditions rendering the strict interpretation of those rules inoperative, he or she can convince others to change their behavior. If he or she can also recognize the rules appropriate to a given role (e.g., operator) and is cognizant of the amount of self-autonomy afforded by that role, the choice of strategy becomes less complex. The client in the operator example could have chosen to appeal to the operator's self-concept rules. She might have said, "Your voice is so pleasant it seems odd that you should refuse to give me the time." This would constitute a personal rule consistency appeal. Given the impersonal nature of operator-client communications, the operator might have resented this personal appeal from a total stranger, or she might have perceived her own personal concerns for consistency an insufficient account for violating company policy. In either situation the client would have lost her case.

As indicated by this example and the work of Miller et al. (1977), certain types of messages will accomplish persuader objectives more efficiently than others. In other words, what constitutes data, a warrant, backing, and an exception will differ across situations. Toulmin (1958) explains that some arguments are field-invariant. This means that they are applicable across a wide range of instances. Some arguments, however, are field-dependent. We can expect to find a predominance of these in interpersonal relations. We can consider part of the definition of the field to be the relationship itself, with its own internal logic consisting of intrinsic rules. The situation interacts with the relationship to render certain rules functional or inoperative.

To the extent that researchers can define the field of a communication as the interactants do, their ability to provide useful predictions is enhanced. Message taxonomies and relationship and situational typologies are useful, but the degree of self-autonomy operating to influence a given interaction can offset predictions based solely on their a priori application. An understanding of the balance of self- and context-orientations experienced by the subjects can assist the researcher in his or her determination of an acceptable level of prediction. According to Kenny (1979), an understanding of 50 percent of human behavior may be accessible through the use of causal models. The rest may be unknowable or only accessible through qualitative analysis. Perhaps what communication scientists need to do is determine how much variance one can reasonably hope to account for in interpersonal as opposed to noninterpersonal contexts. This approach might prevent us from becoming too easily disillusioned with theories that, when tested, do not *always* ensure accurate prediction. Rules theory, for example, has a comparatively high "built-in" error factor because it applies to interpersonal communication, a domain where 50 percent prediction is rather high. Organizational behavior, on the other hand, is largely guided by researcher-accessible role prescriptions that are somewhat more field-invariant than personal rules.

While it is obvious that the above approach needs refinement, it does point us in a direction that may save rules approaches from the scathing indictment that they lack predictive power. This approach is consistent with Heise's acceptance of occasional departures from a traditional causal perspective when describing human beings. He explains that organisms have a tolerance for occasional failures of causality, which indicates that they take a statistical rather than a strictly logical orientation toward their behavior. He adds that a statistical orientation, combined with continuing efforts to define the precise conditions for the existence of a causal relation, "serves strategically as a funnel, bringing awareness of causal relations that are difficult to observe and even those that are in effect only on occasion" (1975: 17). In short the ability to define the conditions under which a causal relation holds refines statistical inferences and prevents premature theory rejection.

This perspective should provide some comfort to those scientists who believe they will have to relinquish all association with causal models if they venture out of the laboratory and into the real context of social interaction. On the contrary, those models will prove quite useful if scientists challenge themselves to discover the underlying logic systems of actors. This will require a closer look at subjects and contexts than presently found in most journal articles.

THE IMPACT OF STYLE

According to Charles Osgood (1960: 293), "any language includes both obligatory and variable features at all levels of analysis, phonemic, morphemic and syntactical." It is certainly not the obligatory features that pose problems for the scientist, but rather those aspects of style that are idiosyncratic. Social scientists have two choices. They can relegate these personal choices made by subjects to error variance, or they can attempt to determine if there are ways to narrow down the portion of style which is personal and not predictable.

Blankenship (1974: 87) suggests that we put aside the view that style is ornament or technique and consider it as "inextricably associated with experience, with substance." She also reminds us that style is clearly related to "choice among the alternatives offered by the language." At times these choices are conscious and at other times unconscious. In all cases, however, they are affected by the contexts in which they occur.

Given this description of style, it is conceivable that, once scientists begin to focus on the subject and his or her context of choice, they may find that similar experiences and ways of categorizing experience (construct systems) lead to choice habits characteristic of the speech community under study. These choice habits may take the form of rule repertoires rather than specific choices. Accurate prediction depends on the researcher's ability to specify those antecedent condition variations impinging on selection from this repertoire.

Recently scientists have begun to devote considerable attention to communicator style (Norton et al., 1975; Norton, 1978; Norton and Pettegrew, 1979; Sypher, 1980). Norton (1978: 99) developed a communicator style measure to investigate "the way one verbally and paraverbally interacts to signal how literal meaning should be taken, interpreted, filtered, or understood." Norton and others (D'Andradde, 1973; Shweder, 1975, 1977) have attempted to determine what constructs or conceptual schema go with what other conceptual schema. They have attempted to uncover patterns of association.

According to Sypher, this procedure taps into raters' feelings about what goes together in the real world. What goes together in the subject's own world might be quite different. Sypher (1980: 5) further argues that "asking respondents to remember how they, or others, communicate without regard to context cannot hope to capture communication behavior which seems for the most part narrowly context dependent." He adds that we must be skeptical of memory-based assessment measures that consistently yield neat clusters, because they typically relate poorly with observations of actual behavior (Newcomb, 1929; Shweder, 1977). This poor relationship is due to the fact that the task demands of experimental settings often pressure subjects to provide inaccurate estimates of actual behavior.

Sypher's (1980) criticism of attempts by scientists to assess style leaves one wondering whether we are then constrained to use only qualitative methods. On the contrary, Norton (1978) has demonstrated that certain dimensions of style do exist. If greater emphasis on context is needed, then future investigations should take this into consideration. Berger (1973), for example, found that across the temporal span of initial interactions, different types of questions dominated. He found that demographic information dominates the first few minutes of interactions, and information dealing with opinions, future plans, and personality occurs later in interactions. Self-autonomy appears to operate at a low level here. Duck (1973) also looked at context influences. He found that different constructs are used more to describe others who are totally unfamiliar than to describe those known for some time. More demographic or role constructs were used to describe strangers, whereas psychological constructs were used to describe well-known persons.

It seems reasonable to assume that Norton's dimensions predominate in novel exchanges where personal style choices are untested. As interactions become more interpersonal, choices are likely to become more idiosyncratic, or guided by a set of relationship-intrinsic rules the identification of which requires reliance on subject report along with observations of patterned interaction (Fisher, 1978; Beach, 1980).

What has been suggested here is that style does interfere with accurate, concise predictions of human communication behavior. However, it may not cloud the issue as much as previously anticipated. As scientists become as adept at identifying intrinsic rules as they now are at recognizing extrinsic rules, that part of style which defies statistical inference may be considerably minimized.

NONVERBAL PERSUASION

A chapter on interpersonal persuasion would not be complete without a discussion of the role of nonverbal behavior. According to Friedman (1979: 5), social scientists have been negligent in their nearly exclusive concern with cognition over emotion:

> Part of this overwhelming concern with cognition in emotion may be due to the fact that emotional reactions are affected by interpretations of the situation. If you do not know that a jellyfish or a dynamite stick is dangerous, you will not be afraid of one. However, it may also be true that the role of cognition is overstated for historical reasons. First, because of a familiarity with cognitive approaches to other aspects of social psychology, cognition may be stressed when examining emotions. Second, cognition may be emphasized because of an underdeveloped methodology with which to study the expressive aspects of emotion. But the idea that the best (or only) way to find out how someone feels is to discover what he or she thinks strictly limits our approach to the emotional side of social life. The notion of nonverbal skill, however, opens up a new road to investigating questions of emotional reaction and expression.

While Friedman's explanation for our "overwhelming concern" with cognition may be accurate, it may also be true that our general disregard for emotional states is due more to the low value our society ascribes to emotional reactions. People spend most of their daily lives in structured environments where emotional reactions are treated as reflections of weakness and as dysfunctional to productivity. We prefer to think of ourselves as rational, not emotional. The truth is that we are emotional and that cognitions and emotions are intrinsically related. Buck (1975: 7) explains:

> The impact of the affective stimuli is felt at both a cognitive and a physiological level. On the cognitive level, the individual understands and interprets the stimuli on the basis of his past experience and present social role. On the physiological level, his nervous and endocrine systems work to adapt the body to the changed circumstances created by the affective stimuli. The cognitive and physiological responses interact with one another: the subjective experience of one's physiological reaction is an important source of information for the cognitive interpretation of the situation, and that cognitive interpretation itself may come to require bodily adaptation.

There is even some evidence to support the belief that when a person cannot cognitively comprehend the experience of another human, he or she can emotionally experience it. For example, people can experience a "sympathetic induction of emotion" (McDougall, 1908) in which they feel the emotions they perceive in others. Whether thought precedes or succeeds sympathy is very difficult to determine. Friedman's (1979: 8) definition supports the latter interpretation: "Broadly construed, sympathy refers to the instinctually based ability of people immediately to experience the emotions of others." In this way Friedman differentiates *compassion* (the synonym for the common usage of the term *sympathy*) from *sympathy*, which he, following Darwin (1965), views as the basis for intimacy.

Given these important links between emotion, cognition, and behavior, it seems implausible that persuasion could occur in any face-to-face situation without some involvement of nonverbal communication. It is part of the perceived reality of both persuader and persuadee.

Perhaps one area of investigation that truly illustrates the importance of nonverbal communication to social interaction is the study of gender effects in decoding and encoding nonverbal behavior. An extensive review of nonverbal decoding literature by Judith Hall (1978: 854) indicates a female advantage (unaffected by age), with the qualification that it "is not, however, a large difference."

Rosenthal and DePaulo (1979) examined literature on sex differences in social interaction and concluded that while women are superior to men in detecting intended, controllable nonverbal cues, they lose this ability as the cues become more revealing of true feelings: "As women mature, those who tend to focus on the positive or 'good' in the nonverbal cues of others may tend to become less accurate decoders of nonverbal cues and more especially so as these nonverbal cues become less intended, less controllable, or more leaky" (1979: 97). Thus, while women are superior to males in their decoding of clear, nondeceptive behavior, they lose this advantage as ambivalence and deception increase. It appears that women interpret these cues as the deceiver wants them to be interpreted, suggesting that females are more interpersonally accommodating than males.

NONVERBAL BEHAVIOR AND DECEPTION

The widespread acceptance of deception in our society (discussed in Chapter 3) is another reason for considering the influence of nonverbal behavior on social interaction important to persuasion study. Buck's (1980) study of the facial feedback hypothesis suggests that we have been lying so long with our faces that we have come to "disregard our own facial feedback as a reliable source of information to some extent" (1980: 820). He explains further that people may be able to discriminate between the internal cues associated with spontaneous facial expressions and those associated with intentional facial expressions. It would appear, then, that at least we have trained ourselves to avoid being victims of our own deception.

NONVERBAL BEHAVIOR AND
CONSCIOUS INTENT

The definition of persuasion adopted in this text specifies that conscious intent must be present for the activity of persuasion to occur. This separation of persuasion from influence has several implications for the study of nonverbal persuasion. For example, if a nonverbal behavior is unintentional, it may be possible to support the claim that it is inappropriate or inconsistent, but the likelihood of that claim bringing about a change in rule choice is minimal. An individual may in future situations attempt to control that inadvertent behavior, but short of that little change can be expected.

The greatest contribution of nonverbal study to persuasion resides in the area of conscious encoding on the part of the persuader, and both conscious and nonconscious decoding by the persuadee. This does not mean that the persuasion activity cannot be influenced by unintentional nonverbal behavior. On the contrary, the communication apprehension literature stands as strong evidence for the far-reaching impact a relatively uncontrolled behavior pattern can have on educational, career, and social success (McCrosky and Richmond, 1977; Daly, 1979; Burgoon on "unwillingness to communicate," 1976). However, this text emphasizes human ability to alter the constructs and rules of others intentionally, and so renders some types of nonverbal research more pertinent than others.

The study of touch offers some intriguing possibilities for nonverbal persuasion research. Reardon and Carilli (1979: 11) report that touch is a "predominantly female privilege throughout life but a male privilege at only one stage of life—youth." Could this mean that males are likely to be less persuasible on subjects that are emotion-laden? Certainly evidence exists to support the idea that males are not rewarded for behavior that suggests a level of sensitivity commonly reserved for female communication.

Whether this intentional perspective excludes neurophysiological studies (see Andersen et al., 1979) from nonverbal persuasion study is not yet clear, since this is a relatively recent area of investigation. Sex differences in brain-hemisphere integration, for example, may have some untested implications for future research on the encoding of persuasive messages.

If Ekman and Friesen (1974b) are accurate in their designation of face movements as more controlled than any other body movements, this type of research may prove beneficial to achieving a greater understanding of the role of nonverbal behavior in the encoding and decoding of persuasive messages. For example, we might ask, If an inappropriate or inconsistent verbal remark is accompanied by an appropriate or consistent nonverbal behavior, what influence does this have on the decoding of that multichannel message?

We could go on and on, including some research domains and excluding others, to derive a clear-cut picture of what nonverbal persuasion entails. Such behavior might be premature, since nonverbal behavior has only recently been granted the recognition it deserves as an important aspect of human communication. For now let it suffice to say that the discovery of its importance to the study of human persuasion is not too distant and long overdue.

CONCLUSION

Of the three persuasion contexts examined in this text—interpersonal, organizational, and mass media—interpersonal offers the greatest opportunity for self-autonomy and reciprocal persuasion. Interpersonal interactions are characterized by a predominance of relationship-intrinsic rules to which each interactant can consistently contribute. Feedback opportunities are immediate and generally frequent when compared to organization and mass media contexts. Individuals are more willing to operate in ways that deviate from role prescriptions. They realize that the resultant undesirable attributions others may formulate about them may be qualified or dismissed by the addition of aligning actions that justify or excuse questionable behavior. The "self" is thereby accorded the opportunity to serve as a generative mechanism of behavior (see Cushman et al., 1980).

Since interpersonal interactions offer opportunities to become more familiar with the rules of fellow interactants, inconsistency appeals (personal rule focus) can be used with greater confidence. If the self were not a viable generative mechanism of behavioral choice in such contexts, appeals to personal rule inconsistencies would be of little use in persuading an actor to change. Appeals to superordinate construct accuracy or the appropriateness of particular actions would prove more effective. Since personal rules are typically valued and accessible in interpersonal interactions, rather than submerged in the context predominance characteristic of some organizational and most mass media communications, the likelihood of inconsistency appeal success is comparatively higher.

The compliance strategy taxonomies introduced in this text reflect the varied weights self, other, and context impose on the selection of behavior. Researchers can use their understanding of these weights to predict strategy selection. The Marwell and Schmitt (1967) compliance-gaining techniques include appeals to satisfactions with self (e.g., "You will feel better about yourself if you comply"), to pressure from others ("People will think better of you if you comply"), and to specific-situation or larger-context conditions ("If you comply you will be rewarded because of 'the nature of things' "). To date, most compliance strategy taxonomies have been exclusively derived from researcher expectations rather than from actual observations of respondents in specific situations. The extent of correspondence between "saying" and "doing" is, as a result, still unclear (see Miller and Burgoon, 1978). Nevertheless, these taxonomies reflect the influence personal and situational variables can have on message choice.

Nonverbal persuasion was described in this chapter as an area of study worthy of more attention. Nonverbal behaviors often reflect affective responses to phenomena, a sorely neglected but extremely important aspect of human communication and persuasion. Perhaps our preference for a cognitive model of human behavior has led us to ignore the emotions that influence the selection and reception of compliance messages. Moreover, this influence should be an important consideration in the study of persuasion in both interpersonal and noninterpersonal contexts.

In the next two chapters we shall look at persuasion in increasingly noninterpersonal contexts, where opportunities for reciprocal persuasion are limited by a number of conditions that foster context predominance at the expense of self-autonomy.

Chapter 8

PERSUASION IN ORGANIZATIONS

Earlier in this text, the balance of context-predominance and self-auton-omy was described as having a substantial influence on reciprocal per-suasion. Chapter 7 emphasized the relatively high potential for self-auton-omy characteristic of interpersonal contexts. In this chapter, we will look at the organizational context, which, as indicated by its name alone, is generally less conducive to self-autonomy than interpersonal contexts. As Farace et al. (1978: 271) explain, "the function of the process of organiza-tion is the reduction of variability in human behavior. Organizations render the collective behavior and the outcomes of many individuals predictable." Farace et al. (1978) add that the predictability of human behavior is accomplished through communication. Like Kelly (1955), they see prediction as the business of human communication. For these au-thors, "communication is effective when the outcome of a message event can be accurately predicted. To the extent that prediction is incorrect, then the communication involved is ineffective" (1978: 273-274).

The alignment of communication with prediction was a popular per-spective during the 1970s. Recently, however, articles have evidenced an increasing discontent with this fieldwide myopia. Even Farace et al. mention that within organizations high levels of certainty can be as dysfunctional as low levels. It follows that communication may create optimal levels of certainty and uncertainty.

We may find in coming years that our emphasis on certainty as the preferred goal of communication provides an excellent example of what Kurt Lewin referred to as the "law of the hammer." In our desire to make human behavior predictable so that we may consider our study of it a scientific enterprise, we have imposed our methodological preferences on our subjects without recognizing the disservice we have perpetrated on them and ourselves. There appears to be little reason to assume that humans generally prefer uncertainty over certainty, but there is good reason to believe that their preferences are variable and responsive to the context in which they find themselves. This variability is what makes the study of human communication so interesting. It makes us "social" scientists. As such we are not in the business of "right" answers; we are in the business of accurate explanations and useful predictions. To the extent that manifestations of self-autonomy are perceived as threatening to a relationship, we can expect to see a general preference for communication that facilitates prediction. Conversely, to the extent that self-autonomy can function to improve a relationship or guarantee its maintenance, communication that teases its users away from the quiescence of high predictability may be of greater utility.

It is time for us to feel sufficiently confident as scientists to let our subject matter shape our methodology rather than attempt to "fulfill an a priori methodology" (Harre, 1977). Dean Hewes (1978) has demonstrated the deleterious effects such methodological commitments can have on interpersonal communication theory. There is every reason to believe, however, that organizational and mass media theory have been equally affected. With this caution in mind, this chapter will introduce a persuasion-oriented perspective on organizational communication that borrows from perspectives varying in their commitment to viewing communication as functioning exclusively to increase prediction. This will be accomplished by addressing two questions: (1) How much self-autonomy can organizations afford to tolerate and/or encourage? (2) What is the relationship between self-autonomy, persuasion, and prediction?

THREE MODELS OF ORGANIZATIONAL
GOAL INTEGRATION

Organizations enter into relationships with their employees characterized by varying levels of goal integration. High goal integration exists when an organization creates conditions that allow its members to meet both organizational and personal objectives. It follows that to the extent goal integration is valued by an organization, self-autonomy will be valued. Moreover, to the extent that self-autonomy is encouraged, persuasion is likely to be reciprocal. Individuals will influence the organization and vice versa.

The Exchange Model

Barrett (1977) proposed the existence of three models of organization-employee interaction. The first of these models he called the exchange model. Organizations operating according to this model provide incentives to employees to increase productivity. They exchange money and social outlets for work. Barrett explains that this is an extrinsic reward model characterized by very little goal integration. What the organization does for the employee makes no direct contribution to it, and what the employee does for the organization makes no direct contribution to him or her. In the terms introduced in this text, the type of persuasion manifest in such climates is acquiescence. The employee relinquishes his or her personal rules in favor of the organizational rules for at least the eight-hour work day. He or she experiences little encouragement to question the status quo. Any attempts to change the goals of the organization are not welcome; a relationship of mutual tolerance with unidirectional persuasion obtains. Certainty is valued over creativity and self-autonomy is submerged in context-predominance.

In organizations using this model, the employees may engage in what McKelvey (1969) calls passive idealism or passive cynicism. Merton (1957) describes passivity as a preference to change one's expectations of the organization rather than vice versa. Idealism is characterized by positive sentiments toward the organization and a sense of control over one's career advancement. Cynicism is characterized by negative sentiments toward the organization and a belief that it controls career advancement.

If personal rules are important to an individual, having to relinquish them even for forty hours a week can create cognitive inconsistency unless the employee engages in some form of rationalization. If the organization operating under the exchange model were to offer some hope for employee participation in the shaping of organization rules, such rationalization might be unnecessary. It does not. Therefore employees are likely to justify their personal rule relinquishment by strongly disliking the organization but reasoning that the job provides the money they need to enjoy their weekends. This is an example of passive cynicism. Another possible rationalization takes the form of feeling very loyal to the organization. The incentives may be interpreted as indications that promotion is possible if the employee wishes to work. This is passive idealism.

The Socialization Model

The second organizational model introduced by Barrett is the socialization model. Organizations following this model operate from the premise that people can be persuaded to value activities that help the organization achieve its objectives. Departing a bit from Barrett's perspective, we may interpret this to mean that employees are expected to relinquish or revise those personal rules that are incompatible with the organizational rules. The persuasion characteristics of this model, then, are acquiescence and accommodation. Persuasion, as in the case of the exchange model, is primarily unidirectional. The organization is the persuader, the employee the persuadee. This does not mean that employee acquiescence and accommodation is devoid of the potential to persuade superiors that he or she is concerned about the organization and therefore worthy of promotion. On the contrary, research indicates that the extent of communication influence is usually related to perceived homophily (Byrne, 1969; Rogers and Shoemaker, 1971; Alpert and Anderson, 1973; Falcione et al., 1977). Thus, if an employee wishes to be promoted, the emulation of superiors loyal to the organization's objectives is likely to be of some assistance.

Barrett explains that the socialization model involves leadership by example. The superior who stresses the importance of organizational objectives, and with conviction calls for them to be pursued with diligence, can accelerate the socialization process. To the extent that superiors are successful at encouraging employees' private acceptance of organizational rules, they are likely to create conditions conducive to peer socialization. In this case peers also persuade each other to adopt organizational rules and so employee socialization becomes a vertical (superior-subordinate) and horizontal (peer-peer) process.

Reardon-Boynton and Fairhurst (1978) attempted to identify the rules operative in a military organization characterized by a socialization perspective in dealing with officers. The subjects in this study were Navy submariners of four ranks: ensign, lieutenant j.g., lieutenant, and lieutenant commander. Reardon-Boynton and Fairhurst were interested in determining which message types these officers would use in responding to a subordinate's, a peer's, or a superior officer's request for some time on an extremely busy day. They assumed that consensus on the type of response in each condition would indicate the operation of an implicit rule provided by the formal context. As they expected, these officers demonstrated greater rule conformity when responding to superiors and subordinates (the latter were students at the submarine school who were there to learn and get the attention that would make them good naval officers). In the peer condition, the officers felt comfortable calling upon their own rule structures to guide their behavior rather than any guidelines provided by the organization. It appears that the military organization accepts greater self-autonomy in peer communications, manifested in wider variations in response choice.

The Reardon-Boynton and Fairhurst (1978) study indicates that, at least in formal organizations, rules exist to guide behavioral choice. However, the focus on rules to some extent obscures the difference between roles and rules. The use of rank as a variable does account for role to a certain extent, but just how much that contributes to the behavioral choice is not clear. In short, a question that has rarely, if ever, been addressed in organizational research is the extent to which roles and rules interpenetrate to influence behavioral repertoire development and behavior selection from that repertoire.

The term *interpenetrate* is used here in a manner similar to Cronen and Pearce's (1978) treatment of it. They contend that to the extent two persons' rule sets interpenetrate (in the sense of being of "good fit"), coordinated management of meaning is facilitated. It seems likely then that role and rule expectations can also interpenetrate in the job context, to facilitate or inhibit job satisfaction. For example, if people's personal rules conflict with the role expectations their companies have for them, problems are likely to arise. Most people alter their rule sets to at least some extent to accommodate the job demands. The extent of that alteration defines the degree of role-rule interpenetration.

Some organizations facilitate the rule accommodation phase through training sessions and other, less formal reminders of the importance of conformity. Persuasion here involves selling the idea that the job comes first and personal considerations second. This may initially cause some cognitive dissonance, but the existence of rewards for a choice well made can "sweeten the pot." If a person's reaction to dissonance is to deny its existence, then he or she may relinquish the personal rule set entirely, rendering him or her an "organizational man." This is probably not as typical as less extensive forms of rule accommodation.

Self-attribution literature lends support to this conceptualization of the gradual reduction of personal rules in favor of role expectations. When employees see themselves behaving in ways consistent with job expectations, they may decide that such behavior is reflective of their own rules rather than those given by the company. To the extent that an individual does this, little demarcation exists between the self he knows on the job and the self he knows in other contexts. Perfect role and rule interpenetration is thus obtained and this individual becomes very predictable, and, furthermore, vulnerable to persuasion by those who know the messages that will create in his or her mind the perception of inappropriateness or ineffectiveness.

Although most individuals do not totally sacrifice their rule sets for the good of the organization, it is true that employees like to know what is expected of them. Role ambiguity (Hamner and Tosi, 1974; Miles, 1975; Locke, 1968) and role conflict (Gross et al., 1958; Kahn et al., 1964; Tosi, 1971; Schuler, 1975; Reardon et al., 1980) literature and research indicate that job satisfaction depends on both knowing what others expect (role ambiguity) and agreement among those others (role conflict).

Reardon et al. (1980) proposed a theoretical model of rule invalidation, a condition exacerbated by role ambiguity and role conflict. They contend that a new job creates an uncertain situation in which old rule sets may prove inappropriate. They explain that people use their construct systems to interpret the new environment and determine appropriate rules on the basis of that information. If the construct systems and/or rule sets are incompatible with the novel context in which the employee finds himself or herself, new constructs and new rules may have to be generated. This task is facilitated by a clear understanding of what is expected.

People who do not know what is expected of them are vulnerable to persuasion, since they have no baseline for comparison of information input. Also, such people have not established what Reardon et al. (1980) describe as the rule invalidation threshold. People who have been at a particular job for some time establish comfortable sets of rules. The invalidation of those rules requires more evidence than the invalidation of newly developed rules. In Toulmin's terms, the data, warrant, and backing used to create rule-role discrepancy must be substantial when low levels of both role ambiguity and role conflict exist and toleration thresholds are well established. Under such conditions, people are relatively certain of what is expected. Convincing them that role or rule discrepancy exists is no easy task. It follows from this discussion of rule and role expectations that one means of determining how effective a campaign to increase employee motivation might be is, first, to determine the extent to which employees perceive their personal rules and occupational roles to be compatible. The second step would be to close that rule-role gap through (a) the provision of accounts for its existence (e.g., to get the job done right we sometimes have to put personal preferences aside); (b) increase incentives for role-consistent behavior; or (c) develop a program of workshops and seminars in which rule and role differences are diminished through employer role-expectation accommodation to employee personal rule expectations. More attention will be given to the relationship of roles and rules later in this chapter. For now, it is important to recognize their relationship as growing increasingly close as organizational socialization succeeds.

On the surface, this socialization of employees to conform with company policy appears quite useful. After all, a degree of certainty is valued in organizations, the very existence of which discourages self-autonomy. However, Alpert and Anderson (1973) caution that too much similarity can be dysfunctional to organization objectives. They consider certain dissimilarities to augment persuasion and so they introduce the concept "optimal dissimilarity" or "optimal total heterophily."

This preference for some dissimilarity over total homophily suggests that organizations that encourage only acquiescence and accommodation characteristic of the exchange and socialization models may actually inhibit progress. Perhaps these models are best utilized at some, but not all, levels of the organizational hierarchy. Organizations must locate their own balance of flexibility and rigidity. They must discover the optimal level of employee self-autonomy they can or must allow in order to function efficiently. The dilemma is one of balancing rigidity with flexibility to encourage innovation, an objective that the concept of organization discourages (Thompson, 1967).

The conclusion to be drawn here about the socialization model is that it is very useful for establishing the homogeneity organizations typically prize, but it can, if taken to an extreme, mitigate against innovation. The nurturance of certainty, and thereby prediction, is not always in the best interest of the organization. Instead, organizations might encourage high levels of communication competence so that they may deal constructively with uncertainty. Farace et al. (1978: 287) describe competence skills as relating to "the employee's understanding of the communication rules of the organization, and his or her ability to work with (and around) the rules." They add that "competent individuals know how to 'cut the red tape'."

The Accommodation Model

The third model introduced by Barrett steps beyond the unidirectional persuasion perspective of the two previous models to give employees some say in the shaping of organizational rules and goals. This is the accommodation model. The organization adopting this model operates as follows: "The needs and motives of the individual are taken as a given, and the organization is structured and operated in such a way that the pursuit of organizational objectives will be intrinsically rewarding and will provide for the simultaneous pursuit of the individual's existing goals" (Barrett, 1977: 11).

This model encourages greater self-autonomy than the other models and thus creates a climate conducive to cooperation and coadjuvancy. Since the employees are included in much of the problem-solving, objective-setting, and decision-making activities of the organization, reciprocal rule revision (cooperative persuasion) and the generation of mutually satisfying new rules (coadjuvancy) are overtly encouraged.

It is difficult to imagine an efficient organization operating under this model at all levels at all times. However, it is possible for organizations to be responsive to the personal needs of their employees. Herzberg (1966) advocated designing job roles to meet individual needs. And Argyris (1964) suggested the use of personality theory in the determination of job design. This high-level goal integration, while encouraging some uncertainty, discourages stagnation. The apparent risk here is that uncertainty generates communication (Huber et al., 1975) and thus increases the potential for conflict (Huseman et al., 1977). However, Weick (1969) suggests that uncertainty provides members with the motivation to engage in organizing behaviors. It appears that people tend toward certainty when confronted with high levels of uncertainty, and move to maximize uncertainty when too much certainty exists (Danowski, 1975). This perspective suggests that those large, conglomerate organizations that encourage management by confrontation between top-level executives from each subsidiary may actually generate organizing behavior through fostering conflict uncertainty.

Barrett's (1977: 98-99) research indicates that the goal integration found in socializing and accommodating organizations generates positive results:

> Organizational units that rank high in goal integration also tend to rank high with regard to the amount of communication that occurs within them, the amount of influence exercised over the unit's activities by all levels of employees within the unit, the adequacy of coordination within the unit and between it and other units, and the number of innovative ideas that are generated for solving work problems. In addition, individuals who rank high in the extent to which they see their personal goals as being integrated with the

organization's objectives also tend to rank high in their motivation to come to work and work hard, in their satisfaction with the organization and their job in it, and in their feelings of loyalty to the organization and commitment to its success.

The research findings discussed above have some far-reaching implications for the development of organizational incentive programs and training. For example, if it is true that low levels of uncertainty and complete allegiance to a company's objectives, or what McKelvey (1969) refers to as "crusading idealism," are dysfunctional to creativity, then organizations that attempt to make the job both the core and the fruit of employee life may be doing themselves a disservice. In the mid 1950s, Robert Dubin (1956) addressed this issue. From his work he concluded that attempts to center primary human relationships in work are at odds with social reality. He points to Weber's (1947) position that impersonality and efficiency can exist together, provided there are other places in society where the primary social relations can be experienced. This suggests that organizations might spend less time attempting to persuade employees to become full-time participants in the "company team" and instead support community affairs and the nonwork activities of its employees. This, Dubin (1956: 141) suggests, might be a "more significant way to enhance attachment of employees to their company."

In terms of training, organizations relying on innovation should train their employees to deal constructively with uncertainty and the large amounts of communication it generates. Agyris (1962) considers interpersonal competence the best communication predictor of organizational success. Yet, many upper-level managers are not trained to deal with out-of-role behavior. For example, several managers with whom I have communicated indicate that they discourage any display of emotions. This preference for "rational" behavior may actually result from an inability to deal with emotions. Certainly our organizations cannot function efficiently if employees are encouraged to scream and cry at will, but such extreme emotional outbursts are usually the result of continually refusing to accept one's emotions as a natural and profoundly positive indication of being human.

The organization has long been the province of men, and men in our society are expected to suppress emotions on the job—a fact probably responsible, in part, for the longer life span of females. Some organizations have begun to respond to the emotional needs of their employees by employing counselors, but few companies actually train their employees to accept emotions as a natural way for humans to signal the existence of a problem, rather than as a threat to organizational efficiency. More is lost in a blanket refusal to address the realities of human emotion than is lost in the small amount of time it would take to train managers to deal effectively with emotionality. If McGuire (1973: 744) is correct in his belief that "we notice any aspect (or dimension) of ourselves to the extent that our characteristic on that dimension is pecular in our social mileau," it is likely that employees who perceive their own emotions as "peculiar" in the job environment will spend much precious time attending to and controlling them. If he or she were free to accept them and allowed and even assisted in dealing with them, productivity might increase.

Limited research directly supports the perspective that emotions should be dealt with directly to avoid lapses in productivity, but the emergence of female executives who were probably not trained from birth to consider emotions a sign of their waning femininity may open this avenue to future investigation. Research indicates that female leaders stress interpersonal relations, are more receptive to the ideas of others, and encourage effort more than their male counterparts (Baird and Bradley, 1979). Some managers have seen female sensitivity as an advantage on which to capitalize. Marion Woods (1975) found that male managers are discovering that women have a unique sensitivity capable of being put to good use with important clients. Whether sensitivity and other "feminine" characteristics are actually exclusive to women, whether male-female differences are innate, immutable, or merely the residue of social learning (Mischel, 1974), and whether these differences can be put to use in organizations is still unclear. However, considering that the number of women entering the work force continues to increase, and that organizations are likely to find themselves dealing with them as clients or employees, we cannot afford to devote too much more time to research that only tells us that male managers have difficulty communicating with females. It should come as no surprise that they do. Questions organizational researchers can answer for managers are, How can the qualities that are uniquely male or female be utilized by the organization to achieve its objectives? How can the organization assist males and females in dealing with the stereotypes that encroach on their potential productivity?

ROLES AND RULES:
THE PROCESS OF CHANGE

In the previous section of this chapter, three models of organizational influence, varying in amount of potential self-autonomy and level of reciprocity in persuasion, were introduced. Throughout that discussion the "organization" was treated as an "out there somewhere" entity. The boundaries between employees and the organization itself were not clearly defined. The omission was one of intention rather than oversight. As Starbuck (1976: 1071) tells us, the term *organization* "implies the conjunction of several related but imperfectly correlated phenomena." The shape and boundaries of organizations vary according to which phenomena one wishes to observe. Any specification of boundaries is necessarily an arbitrary invention of the perceiver. Starbuck (1976: 1071) provides a useful metaphor:

> An organization displays some of the properties of a cloud or magnetic field. When one is far enough inside it, he can see its characteristics and effects all about him; and when one is far enough outside it, he can see that it comprises a distinctive section of social space. But as he approaches the boundary, the boundary fades into ambiguity and becomes only a region of gradual transition that extends from the organization's central core far out into the surrounding space. One can sometimes say "Now I am inside" or "Now I am outside," but he can never confidently say "This is the boundary."

Similarly, roles people assume within the organization are without clear boundaries. The employee may be able to say, "This is clearly inside" or "This is clearly outside" when referring to his or her role expectations, but it is unlikely that any clear boundaries can be specified. This is because roles, like organizations, cannot be identified by the presence of a single phenomenon. They, too, are the result of a conjunction between "related but imperfectly correlated phenomena." Furthermore, as Graen (1976) points out, they are not "fixed" but changing—a condition, he adds, accelerated in recent years by the transient nature of our society.

Even if we cannot identify role boundaries, much research attention has been given to identifying the phenomena that constitute a role. This side-door approach has generated a number of studies, the results of which indicate that organization members themselves often experience great difficulty defining their roles. The difficulty arises because the individual controls only a portion of that definition.

When attempting to imbue a role with meaning, the organization member is likely to experience at least one of three problems, involving agreement, ambiguity, and/or overload. Graen (1976) describes *agreement* as the extent to which superiors, peers, and self share the same role expectations. To the extent that differences exist, the member experiences role conflict. *Ambiguity* refers to the amount and quality of feedback provided to the member concerning his or her in-role or out-of-role behavior. Finally, *overload* refers to the problem of dealing with too much information or consistent demands for change. People have limited capacities to acquire new information. If situations overwhelm the organizational member's limits, he or she may avoid those situations in the future. Moreover, as Reardon et al. (1980) point out, new employees need time to generate new rules when role expectations are unfamiliar. They require time to integrate their old rules with those provided them by new peers and superiors. This perspective on roles suggests that early bureaucratic models of organizational roles must be rejected. These models were based on the assumption that there is "one best way" of performing a function. The result was a fixed role model prescribing the a priori, inflexible designing of a role without regard for employee differences. Graen (1976) considers this fixed model responsible for much employee dissatisfaction and high turnover rates. He points to a series of studies by Ford (1969), which led to an AT&T policy change making roles more flexible. The result was a marked reduction in turnover rates.

The exchange model introduced earlier in this chapter describes that situation wherein an employee is expected to "fill a role" rather than assist in its creation and change. The socialization model allows for somewhat more employee input, but only the accommodation model treats role as a product of reciprocal communication and persuasion.

Graen (1976) suggests that interpersonal models of role development are, in the general case, more accurate than fixed models. Kahn et al. (1964) proposed such a model. They described the organizational member as interdependent with other members in his or her "role set." They explained that the role set shapes the focal person's behavior through communication. Katz and Kahn (1966) proposed an interpersonal role-making model. According to this model, a leader conveys expectations to the member through a number of different channels. The member receives and interprets these messages. The leader determines the success of his or her communication by observing the member's role behavior.

Graen, while recognizing the value of the Katz and Kahn model, criticizes its neglect of the negotiation capabilities of the organization member. The member may do more than reject the leader's opinion; he or she may attempt to modify the leader's expectations. Graen refers to this reciprocal exchange of expectations as the "role-making" process.

Role-making is not a solitary activity. A role is shaped and molded by (1) organizational or situational demands, (2) social or role set demands, and (3) personal or personality demands. These three sources of pressure are comparable to context, social, and personal rules. To the extent that discrepancies exist between them, the role is not fixed but flexible. The employee must decide which source of pressure to accommodate and which to ignore. To the extent that the choices favoring personal rules do not lead to punishment or expulsion, we may assume that self-autonomy is an acceptable in-role behavior. As mentioned earlier in this chapter, such independence renders the cooperation and coadjuvancy form of persuasion more frequent than acquiescence and accommodation.

Since absolute self-autonomy is seldom the norm, employees are usually confronted with the task of integrating the role expectations of two or more pressure sources. Graen (1976: 1213) suggests that employees' choices depend on (1) the perceived value of the role consequences, and (2) the probability that striving for a given rating (e.g., winner, hired hand, loser) will lead to being so rated. To the extent that the employee is consequent-oriented, these two considerations are likely to govern his or her choices.

The role-making process does not, however, end with any particular set of choices or the attainment of some goal. The daily process of social and context rule opposition and integration guarantees continual role modification. To the extent that the employee provides the organization with unexpected positive rewards through extrarole behaviors, he or she will accrue idiosyncracy credits that can be used to bargain for greater self-autonomy. To the extent that the role itself then becomes identified with high levels of independence, the employee has successfully altered the rules that previously defined the role. In this sense, he or she has persuaded the organization to change.

ROLES AND COUNTERATTITUDINAL ADVOCACY

Often, people are hired to perform jobs or "fill" roles that conflict with some of their personal rules. They accept the job because they need the money or experience and thereby place themselves in a potentially uncomfortable state of rule-role discrepancy. According to counterattitudinal advocacy literature, however, it seems reasonable to assume that, given sufficient opportunity to enact the personal rule-discrepant role, the employee may persuade himself or herself that the extent of discrepancy is minimal or nonexistent.

Counterattitudinal research indicates that when people are offered a justification for performing in some dissonance-producing way, the potential for attitude change is decreased. In such cases, it is possible for employees to justify their personal rule-discrepant behavior by reasoning that they need the money. Similarly, if an individual perceives that he or she had no real choice but to take on the rule-discrepant role, another justification renders change unlikely (Miller and Burgoon, 1973).

Assume for the moment, however, that our employee, Mr. P, is a person who does not really need a higher salary, nor does his organization require that he accept the promotion that would place him in a rule-role discrepant position. Assume also that Mr. P accepts the promotion because he believes that another opportunity may not come for a while. Money was not a factor and he was free to choose. Dissonance is the likely result. All that is missing now to fit this situation to the "early" dissonance interpretation is effort. If Mr. P takes the new role seriously and attempts to do his new job exceptionally well, he is more likely to convince himself that his choice was the right one. As Miller and Burgoon (1973: 63) explain,

> for a persuader to employ counterattitudinal advocacy effectively, he must induce the persuadee to encode, or irrevocably commit himself to encode, a belief-discrepant message. Additionally, however, the persuader must concern himself with other factors associated with the situation. He must seek to provide barely enough justification to induce the persuadee to comply with his request. He must strive to structure the environment so as to provide the persuadee with a high level of perceived choice. And finally, the task must be demanding enough to ensure a fair amount of energy expenditure by the persuadee.

"Later" dissonance interpretations refute the idea that dissonance results from mere inconsistency between private and public assent, but hold that counterattitudinal advocacy effectiveness relies on the presence of the perception by the actor that his or her behavior will result in aversive consequences. For example, Mr. P's acceptance of the new role might result in other persons losing their jobs, or Mr. P himself might face the wrath of his family when they discover that the job requires extensive travel. Unless Mr. P is a rather insensitive person, in which case dissonance may not be a common experience for him anyway, his acceptance of the new role will cause him discomfort unless he can convince himself that it was the best choice. Miller and Burgoon (1973) consider the distinction between "early" and "later" interpretations of dissonancy a "theoretical enigma" with some practical implications for persuaders.

Bodaken et al. (1979) have offered a somewhat enigma-reducing, alternative interpretation of counterattitudinal advocacy that may have utility for managers interested in persuading employees to assume roles conflicting with their rules. Borrowing from Berger (1972), Bodaken et al. posit that role involvement, self-perceived role-enactment competence, and amount of role information influence the extent of change resulting from counterattitudinal advocacy. Since Bodaken et al. used students as subjects, some caution is warranted in deriving implications for organizational contexts from their findings. However, each of the variables manipulated by Bodaken et al. can be observed or assessed by manager interview of employees. In this sense, then, the Bodaken et al. study may have some practical application.

Bodaken et al. hypothesized the existence of a positive relationship between amount of task-relevant information and self-perceived role-enactment competence. They also hypothesized positive relationships between preenactment perceptions of competence and postperformance evaluation. Furthermore, they considered self-perceived role-enactment competence to be positively related to reported attitude change.

The results of two studies conducted by these researchers provided little justification for considering task-relevant information a useful predictor of self-perceived role-enactment competence and thus an important variable in the counterattitudinal change process. Not to be easily dissuaded, Bodaken and his colleagues reformulated "information" as message intensity, and found a positive relationship between message intensity and both self-perceived role-enactment competence and postencoding attitude change. They concluded (1979: 212) that "the disappointment in failing to confirm Berger's original information theorizing is offset by concluding that the information proposition can be reformulated in terms of the message intensity."

While it may have been a bit of a conceptual and methodological leap to reformulate "information" as "message intensity" instead of merely considering message intensity a variable distinct from information, these researchers produced some intriguing results. In applying their model to organizational persuasion (an equivalent "leap"), we may consider message intensity in written messages to operate much like effort in physical role enactment. If a manager, wishing to persuade a reluctant employee to accept a role, encourages him or her to try the role for a while and give it his or her best effort, self-persuasion may result. Given the Bodaken et al. findings supporting the hypothesized relationship between self-perceived role-enactment competence and postenactment evaluation, and given the finding that attitude change is a function of this relationship, the manager could also work on increasing the employee's own predictions of his or her role-enactment competence during the trial period. Bodaken et al. caution that any discrepancy between self-perceived role-enactment competence and evaluation could result in very little attitude change. Hence, the manager who wishes to try this persuasion technique must be fairly confident that the employee will do well in the role during a trial period (often characterized by role ambiguity and role conflict) before embarking on this trail.

The Berger (1972) model and subsequent research by Bodaken et al. (1979) serve as indirect support for the utility counterattitudinal research may have for organizational persuasion, despite the "mediational murk" that supposedly surrounded such research in the past (Rosenberg, 1968).

THE ORGANIZATIONAL ENVIRONMENT

Previous sections of this chapter have focused on the internal workings of organizations. The organization was viewed as the environment for individual members. Increasingly over the last several years, social scientists have come to think of the organization as having an environment consisting of "the totality of physical and social factors external to a system's boundary that are directly taken into consideration in the decision-making behavior of individuals in the system" (Rogers and Agarwala-Rogers, 1976: 61). This essentially means that organizations receive from outside their own boundaries information that influences policy-making activities. In turn, the organizations provide other organizations, such as the mass media, with information concerning their internal workings. A relationship is thereby established between organization and environment.

Much of the information on mass persuasion to be discussed in the next chapter is relevant to this aspect of organizational persuasion. It is at this level that persuasion becomes highly noninterpersonal, a characteristic having strong implications for message strategy selection. Perhaps nowhere is self-autonomy more submerged by context-predominance than in the public relations business. Here the organization member clearly represents the organization to the public. The public relations representative is what Rogers and Agarwala-Rogers refer to as a "bridge," an individual who, via a communication dyad, connects his or her group to another group. Sometimes organizations prefer to contract with public relations firms to serve as liaisons between the organization and the environment. Both bridges and liaisons occupy extremely important positions, since they can function as expediters or bottlenecks in information flow between the organization and its environment. The need to represent the organization without underrepresenting the self in ways which would lead to loss of credibility makes this job an intriguing focus for persuasion study.

CONCLUSION

No single chapter on persuasion in organizations can adequately cover this extensive area of study. An attempt has been made in this chapter to focus on the interrelationships of roles and rules as they function to influence the selection of persuasion strategies. Roles, like organizations, do not have clear boundaries. They are consistently influenced by the persons who claim them. Some roles afford greater personal input, whereas others, such as that of the public relations representative, require a delicate balance of role and rule influences on behavioral selection.

To the extent that people perceive discrepancies between their role prescriptions and personal rules, discomfort is likely. If this condition is exacerbated by role ambiguity and role conflict from other sources, job dissatisfaction will result, unless new rules reflecting an integration of personal and organizational objectives are generated.

The perspective on internal organizational persuasion offered in this chapter suggests that while interpersonal persuasion occurs in organizations, the strong influence of context makes the use of intrinsic rules less frequent than the use of extrinsic rules in business-related interactions. Roles thus become very important, and therefore appeals to appropriate in-role behavior are often more effective than appeals to inconsistency. To the extent that an organization prefers goal integration, personal rule and organizational role expectations are considered equally important. In such cases, the persuader must determine whether personal rule inconsistency appeals are as potentially effective in eliciting behavior change as appeals to appropriateness or effectiveness.

Finally, the organization was described as having an environment that influences its policy-making activities. Individuals serving as bridges and liaisons between the organization and its environment facilitate or inhibit accurate information flow. In the next chapter, on mass media, some of the strategies useful to organization-external persuasion will be discussed.

Chapter 9

PERSUASION AND THE MASS MEDIA

It is obvious from the discussions in previous chapters that all forms of communication influence and even shape who we are as well as what we wish to be. The media, however, are our most pervasive forms of communication. For this reason they have been the target of much criticism, both deserved and exaggerated. Common complaints are that the media do not reflect our lives accurately, that they degrade the taste of the masses, and that they encourage people to do things they would otherwise not consider.

Newcomb (1979b) suggests that this negativism, toward television in particular, has restricted the development of a critical climate. Very few careful descriptions of television programs exist. Instead, most serious commentaries focus on the audience and thus deny television properties of its own. Furthermore, television is usually condemned for what it is not rather than for what it is, or, Newcomb adds, for what it might become. Television is therefore perceived as an intruder in our culture.

According to Newcomb, the result of the unquestioned negativism and fear is a mass audience that has little of the respect for television that it has for books. Because there is little if any disagreement among audience members concerning the negative attributes of television, there is little if any need to develop counterarguments. The mass audience, then, is an uncritical audience and as such is left at the mercy of those who are willing to manipulate it.

Researchers have done little to contradict this negativism. They, like the mass audience to which they belong, have already passed sentence on television. Certainly, there are studies that indicate that television can make positive contributions, but assumed negativism predominates in this arena too. It would appear, then, that when it comes to television personkind has shirked its responsibility through an uncritical acceptance. What we need are critiques of the cultural or contextual milieu of television. Perhaps, like books, television is to become a repository of cultural heritage, whether respected or abhorred. In any event it is necessary that we attempt to integrate mass communication theory and research in a fashion that will facilitate the active analysis of television. Its popularity alone supports this proposition. For all the negativism, television is one of the most popular communication mediums ever experienced by our culture.

THE MASS AUDIENCE

John Corner (1979) explains that social science has, in the past few years, become more theoretically anxious and self-critical than it was in the postwar phase of expansion and institutionalization. He contends that this theoretical uncertainty has developed because of "a shift in the focus of research from specific social phenomena to the methods and conceptual vocabulary through which the researcher both 'knows' and systematically explores such phenomena" (1979: 26). One concept that has come under scrutiny as a result of this shift has been "mass." This concept has been accused of being misleading and pernicuous because it implies that the audience is an "undifferentiated, inert aggregate, and thus ignores the varied and specific forms of social interaction" (1979: 27). Corner summarizes these criticisms as follows:

(1) The concept unquestioningly inherits the notions concerning large-scale, homogeneous groupings from the mass society theorists.
(2) In doing so it also and necessarily assumes that the masses are "inherently stupid, unstable, easily influenced."
(3) It limits communication studies to "a few specialized areas like broadcasting and the cinema and what it miscalls popular literature."

Corner contends that these criticisms are addressed to the weakest meaning of "mass," and he is convinced that this weak meaning has not "overtaken us or prevented our attending to variation and complexity" (1979: 28). He points to the "uses and gratifications" approach as one which, while maintaining "mass" in its formulations, has stressed the activity of audience members rather than their passivity.

The most cogent of Corner's arguments is his interpretation of the adjective *mass* as applying to the communication system rather than to the audience. He explains that "such a usage importantly differentiates 'mass communication' from 'mass culture,' a notion which is harder to defend in terms of a specifiable process." Gerbner's (1967) definition of mass communication encompasses this perspective: "Mass communication is the technologically and institutionally based mass production and distribution of the most broadly shared continuous flow of public messages in industrial societies." Mass communication, from this perspective, is a communication system that conveys messages to individuals who negotiate their meanings within a complex of social and interpersonal relationships (Corner, 1979: 30). It is what Corner refers to as the "paradox" between mass communication's often individualized mode of reception and its vast productive and distributive networks which will serve as the focus of discussion in subsequent sections of this chapter.

THE CHALLENGE OF
MASS COMMUNICATION

In Chapter 7, interpersonal and noninterpersonal communication were differentiated on the basis of whether intrinsic or extrinsic rules were the primary force governing behavioral choice. As Corner (1979) indicates, however, the mass media audience consists of individuals who negotiate meanings just as interpersonal communication interactants do. The primary difference is that the mass audience members have what Schramm and Roberts (1972: 392) refer to as a greater "latitude of interpretation and response":

> Characteristics of the mass communication situation, such as the receiver's freedom from many of the social constraints which operate in interpersonal communication, greatly attenuated feedback, and lack of opportunity to tailor messages for specific people allow any individual receiver a good deal more latitude of interpretation and response than he has when speaking face-to-face with friend, colleague or acquaintance.

Goffman (1967) considers every face-to-face interaction a situation that places the interactants in jeopardy. They risk losing "face." Each time we open our mouths to speak with others we risk possible rejection of our message and/or ourselves. Because of this, most of us pay very close attention to the image we are conveying and protect ourselves from undesirable attributions by using disclaimers, aligning actions, accounts, and so forth, to lessen the impact and thus the impression imparted by our message. We choose our behavioral responses with the understanding that they will not pass unnoticed or uninterpreted.

Mass media, on the other hand, infrequently require of us immediate responses that are visible to our significant others. Behavior can be postponed. Advertising, for example, may not create a need or generate a response for weeks after the initial message. The demands that media place on us, then, are much less immediate. Also, if we do not like what we are reading or viewing, termination of our interaction with most media can occur without anyone being the wiser. In this sense there is more choice involved in our relationships with media than in our interpersonal relationships. It is gauche, at best, to walk away from a conversation. An account, such as "I have to run. My meeting is in five minutes," is usually required. This perspective stands in opposition to the argument that media shape us without providing us a means of escape. Even in our interactions with media we are choice makers, and one does not need "fifty ways" to leave a media relationship. Merely walking away often suffices.

Despite this apparent freedom to leave the media relationships we have established, it appears that most of us prefer to remain in those relationships. Functional theories, such as uses and gratifications, suggest that we do so to meet a variety of needs. Mass media can provide company to the lonely, vicarious pleasure to the overworked, compliments to the person with a low self-image, otherwise unobtainable knowledge to the curious, and simple entertainment. They are less demanding than most of our friends and colleagues and are more easily accessible. Is it any wonder, then, that so many people rely on the media? On the contrary, one might wonder how they ever tear themselves away.

Michael Novak (1977: 41) suggests that television is "the molder of the soul's geography." He explains that it builds incrementally a psychic structure of expectations. If this is true, the lack of a demand for immediate response from the audience does not in any way indicate that it is not being influenced. The influence may be just as far-reaching as that of interpersonal communication, although the effects may not become obvious for some time. While it is true that interpersonal communication episodes, if repeated over and over, have the potential to shape the attitudes and behaviors of interactants, the reciprocal nature of such interactions requires that the participants verbally or nonverbally commit themselves to some position in relationship to the subject at hand. As discussed in Chapter 7, when people are opposed to a certain perspective and realize that they may be required to make some statement, they will create counterarguments. What of the media participants, who know that they will not be required to respond in any overt manner? They are the uncritical participants. They are therefore the most vulnerable to persuasion.

Novak (1977) contends that television speeds up the rhythm of attention, thereby training the viewer to expect a certain fast-paced, multiple-logic activity in his or her interactions. Watt and Krull (1976) have demonstrated that the form or structure of media messages can have serious effects on the aggressive levels of adolescents. Their research indicates that "one could predict as accurately the aggressive levels of adolescents by considering only the form of the programming which they view as by considering the degree of violence in the programming which they view" (1976: 107).

In terms of our relationship expectations, Novak (1977) holds that television portrayals of interpersonal relationships only "whet the appetite," in contrast to what real-world interactions provide, because television cannot tap certain depths of experience. As a result, it gives us a superficial perspective of human emotion. Furthermore, Novak explains, television does not represent the nation in terms of accents, cultural patterns, and so on. It is thus a biased medium.

This bias, Novak adds, is exacerbated by the fact that television, as an industry, is run by intellectuals. As such, it represents the "educated class's fantasies about the fantasies of the population" (1977: 50). To attract the attention of the population, these intellectuals celebrate two mythic strains in American character: the lawless and the irreverent. Novak suggests that this consistent celebration of the transgressing of inhibitions could actually lead to the collapse of inhibitions.

Before joining Novak in his indictment of television, let us take a few moments to consider Leo Rosten's (1977) perspective on this issue. Rosten suggests that we look not only at the medium as the source of evil, but at the masses as well. He explains that the deficiencies of the mass media are a function, in part at least, of the deficiencies of the masses. While it may be true that the media do not create an unlimited number of plots to entertain us, life itself has a limited number of plots. In terms of the lack of fresh talent, Rosten (1977: 5) states that talent is scarce. He adds, "Our land has produced few-first rate minds, and of those with first-rate brains, fewer have imagination; of those with brains and imagination, fewer still possess judgment."

Concerning the lack of first-quality material, Rosten (1977: 6) replies, "To edit is to judge, to judge is, inevitably, to reward some and disappoint others." It is important to remember, Rosten implies, that the aesthetic level of the mass media is not geared to the tastes of the intellectual. As adverse to admitting it as the intellectual is, he or she is not a member of the masses. There is, Rosten explains, an "inevitable gap" between the common and the superior. The intellectuals, guilt-ridden by the awareness that they are not members of the masses, do themselves a great disservice because they dismiss those attributes of character that set them apart and make intellectualism possible.

Thus, while it may be true that mass media, and television in particular, could improve stylistically and respond to the needs of the population they serve, it must be remembered that they are money-making enterprises selling what the people want. This perspective implies that media are only half the reason for any problems they appear to create. The audiences that buy or view them are the other half.

In the next section, we shall look at the most popular models of television effects and their contributions to the negativism described by Newcomb.

MODELS OF TELEVISION INFLUENCE

Newcomb (1979) may be accurate in his contention that the negativism surrounding television has restricted the development of a critical climate, but the inescapable fact that mass communication research is characterized by a very low level of theoretical integration may also deserve some blame. McQuail (1979) suggests that this obvious neglect of theory is due to the demands placed on researchers for quick answers. He explains that research on the effects of television has been stimulated mainly by policy concerns. Broadcasters, educators, parents, and others have sought evidence to justify actions to protect "defenseless" audiences such as children. Theoretical integration has been sorely neglected.

McQuail also tells us that legislators, parents, teachers, and other interested parties regard themselves as experts able to see for themselves the influence of television and other media on the audience members. Under these circumstances, the scientist is reduced to a technician or fact producer. To please the self-appointed experts, he or she is often forced to work within a theoretical framework simple enough for the lay "expert" to comprehend.

Finally, television has the dubious honor of being one of the only social influence processes that appear to lend themselves neatly to cause-effect explanations. Attempts to explain the effects of family, friends, school, or other interpersonal aspects of the socialization process are complicated by the realization that such experiences are personal and highly variable. Television, on the other hand, is viewed simultaneously by people across the country. It is thus one of the few sources of common experience and is often naively assumed to be interpreted in the same manner by all those who share in the experience. It has been difficult for those in a rush for answers to realize that people develop relationships with television characters in much the same way that they develop interpersonal relationships. The television character constitutes only one of two sources of relationship definition. In their attempts to identify the common source, researchers have often neglected the relationship. As McQuail (1976: 347) explains,

> the world of what happens between sender and receiver is too often regarded by the empirical researcher as terra incognita, dealt with mainly in terms of type of effect and conditions of content and viewer characteristics associated with such effects.

McQuail holds that there is no need for this vagueness. He adds that we do know enough to account for the effect processes we observe. We can get at the "why" of effects. A first step in this process is to recognize the difference between *effect* and *influence*. The latter refers to the intentional exertion of power over others, while the former merely refers to reaction or response of audience members. Since this book is about persuasion, the primary focus will be on the intentional exertion of power.

McQuail describes four models of influence: information-processing, conditioning or associational, functional, and relational. The relational model focuses on the relationship between the sender and receiver of the message. This model is the most generally useful for explaining the effects of television on the "defenseless" as well as on more "prepared" audiences.

McQuail places considerable emphasis on the role of power in the relationship between sender and receiver. He explains that while the concept of power has restricted applications in mass communication, since the material rewards, physical force, and other motivational factors operative in interpersonal contexts are not available, its influence is not seriously attenuated. McQuail (1976: 353) indicates that the essential point concerning power is that "the would-be sender of influence must have some 'assets' relevant to the needs of the receiver, while the latter must actively co-operate if the influence is to succeed." The first segment of this definition of power reflects the functional view of influence. As you may recall from Chapter 4, functional theories explain attitude change as a "function" of personal needs. Instrumental, ego-defensive, value-expressive, and knowledge were the four functions discussed by Katz (1960). Certainly, having something that someone else wants or needs can be considered a position of power. However, it is the second part of McQuail's definition that separates the relational view from the functional view of influence. The sender and receiver must cooperate in this power relationship if influence is to succeed. People can and often do reject power. There must be sufficient motivation to cooperate. It is in the unveiling of this motivation to cooperate that the "why" of television effects lies.

Kelman's (1961) social influence perspective provides a rationalization for audience cooperation with the media. He suggests that there are three basic processes of influence: compliance, identification, and internalization. Compliance occurs when an individual accepts influence from another person or group because he or she hopes to obtain a favorable reaction from the other. Kelman explains that this person may be interested in attaining certain specific rewards or in avoiding some type of punishment. The particular behavior is not adopted because the individual believes in it, but rather because its adoption is instrumental in the production of some satisfying social effect.

Identification occurs when an individual adopts a particular behavior because it is associated with a satisfying self-defining relationship to the other person or group. In this way the individual defines his or her own role in the relationship in terms of the role of the other person(s). Pearce (1976) describes four modes of negotiation used in interpersonal communication, which reflect Kelman's notion that an individual will adopt a particular behavior in order to participate in a relationship. Pearce's four modes of negotiation are invocation, ingratiation, creating shared experiences, and metacommunication. He describes these as means whereby coordinated management of meaning is attained. Like Kelman, Pearce assumes that the individual participates in a role relationship with another not necessarily because of some belief in the particular role content but because he or she wishes to meet the expectations of the other. This assures the continuation of his or her relationship with the other person or group. Unlike compliance, however, identification does involve both private and public acceptance of the role.

Kelman's third process of social influence is internalization. This occurs when an individual accepts influence because the behavior is congruent with his or her value system. Unlike compliance and identification, internalization occurs when the content of the behavior is rewarding. The behavior is adopted because it is seen as somehow integrated with the individual's particular orientation with regard to his or her world.

Kelman's perspective is introduced here because it is possible to construe mass media influence as a function of the types of relationships people establish with media. Often the media attempt to define the relationship or at least set the parameters for its development. For example, some advertising has as its primary goal the compliance of its target audience. According to Kelman's social influence typology, the advertiser should attempt to link the product with the social needs of the persuadee. If, instead, the advertiser wishes to convince the persuadee that participation in successful relationships with, for example, the opposite sex involves the use of a particular perfume, then identification is the goal. The acceptance of this product is seen as a prerequisite for the persuadee's adoption of a preferred role. If the advertiser has a product that can be seen as value-supportive, or can demonstrate that the absence of this product somehow conflicts with the persuadee's orientation toward his or her environment, then internalization is possible. Kelman considers credibility of the change agent a necessary element in internalization. If the product is endorsed by someone whom the persuadee perceives as possessing a similar value system, internalization is facilitated. The credible source revises the persuadee's conception of a particular means-end relationship by suggesting that the endorsed product will lead to the desired end, or at least function to increase its likelihood.

Kelman's (1961) summary of the distinctions between the three processes appears in Table 9.1. This table suggests that persuasion depends on the ability of the persuader to create (1) conditions that bring into question the persuadee's perceptions of what is socially rewarding, what constitutes a satisfying relationship role definition, or the means whereby he or she is adhering to a particular value, and (2) acceptable methods to solve this problem.

Kelman's model provides guidelines for the creation of appropriateness and consistency appeals. His social influence typology is actually quite consistent with the perspective on persuasion introduced in Chapter 5 of this text. For example, Kelman's "basis for the importance of the induction" is, in the terms used in this text, the persuadee's constructs, which together elicit an orientation that is primarily situation-, role-, or self-focused. Kelman does not discuss the rules such orientations generate, but his emphasis on antecedents, consequents, and behavioral choices implies their existence.

TABLE 9.1   Summary of the Distinctions Between the Three Processes

Antecedents	Compliance	Identification	Internalization
1. Basis for the importance of the induction	Concern with social effect of behavior	Concern with social anchorage of behavior	Concern with value congruence of behavior
2. Source of power of the influence agent	Means control	Attractiveness	Credibility
3. Manner of achieving prepotency of the induced response	Limitation of choice behavior	Delineation of role requirements	Reorganization of mean-end framework
Consequents:			
1. Conditions of performance of induced response	Surveillance by influencing agent	Salience of relationship to agent	Relevance of values to issue
2. Conditions of change and extinction of induced response	Changed perception of conditions for social rewards	Changed perception of conditions for satisfying self-defining relationships	Changed perception of conditions for values maximation
3. Type of behavior system in which induced response is embedded	External demands of a specific setting	Expectations defining a specific role	Person's value system

SOURCE: Kelman (1961: 67). Reprinted by permission of Elsevier North Holland, Inc. Copyright 1961 by The Trustees of Columbia University.

Kelman recognized that certain conditions render appeals to context or role prescriptions potentially more effective than appeals to personal values. The conditions for change in Table 9.1 suggest that, should the persuader's goal be internalization (self-orientation) rather than compliance (context- or other-orientation), he or she must create means-end inconsistency in terms of the persuadee's values (or rules) rather than in terms of his or her desire for social approval.

Also consistent with the perspective in this text, Kelman's model implies the need for some familiarity with the persuadees and their environments. For example, even if the persuadee is under surveillance by others, compliance may not obtain. Also, if the persuader refers to role relationships that are not salient or values irrelevant to the persuadee, identification and internalization will not occur.

The Kelman model is a relational model of influence. It does not appear to be power-oriented. However, McQuail's (1979) definition of power as having some "assets" relevant to the receiver is implied in the model. It is the task of the persuader to convince the persuadee that some product or behavior will meet needs for social approval, social relationship anchorage, or value congruence. In this sense, a power relationship can be said to exist between the persuader and the persuadee. Mass media create this type of relationship with their audiences. Advertisements provide the receiver information for facilitating social acceptance. Program content can teach people how to play roles that will allow them to participate in satisfying relationships with others. The news can teach people not only what to value, but also when and how to shift those values to make them congruent with those of significant others.

Cartwright (1971) introduced a perspective on mass persuasion which, like Kelman's, focuses on the antecedent conditions and desired consequences perceived by the persuadee. Cartwright's approach constitutes one of the few attempts to understand what happens psychologically when someone attempts to influence the behavior of another person—the "why" of effect. Cartwright suggests that influence requires a chain of processes that are both complex and interrelated, but which in broad terms may be characterized as (1) creating a particular cognitive structure, (2) creating a particular motivational structure, and (3) creating a particular behavioral (action) structure (1971: 429). These processes are comparable to the antecedent conditions, desired consequences, and behavioral repertoire of the rule model.

According to Cartwright (1971), personal needs provide energy for behavior and contribute to the establishment of goals in a person's cognitive structure. These goals are achieved by appropriate choices from the individual's behavioral repertoire. Cartwright describes this relationship between goals and behavior as one the mass media can use for persuasion by showing that a behavior can bring about the desired goal. The role of mass media then becomes one of modifying or creating needs as well as providing the means by which those goals may be attained:

> It follows from these general observations about the nature of human motivations that efforts to influence the behavior of another person must attempt either to modify needs (and goals) or to change the person's motivational structure as to which activities lead to which goals. This means that a person can be induced to do voluntarily something that he would otherwise not do only if a need can

be established for which this action is a goal or if the action can be made to be seen as a path to an existing goal. Little is known at the present time about the establishment of needs, but it appears unlikely that any single campaign via the mass media can actually establish new needs [Cartwright, 1971: 438].

Although Cartwright does not specify inconsistency production as the means whereby goals and/or the ways of attaining them can be changed, he does suggest that a given action will be accepted as a path to a goal if it fits into the person's larger cognitive structure, or what was described in Chapter 2 as individual's constitutive and regulative rules. If the persuader can demonstrate that the persuadee's typical behavior just does not "fit" with the expectations society has for him or her (appropriateness) or with some other more important personal rule (consistency), persuasion is facilitated. The next step is to convince the persuadee to adopt the persuader's proposal.

On this issue Cartwright provides some rules of thumb: The greater the number of goals attainable by one path, the more likely it is that a person will take that path. Second, the more specifically defined the path of action to a goal, the more likely it is that the particular motivational structure that would lead to the goal will gain control of behavior. Third, the more specifically a path of action is located in time, the more likely it is that the motivational structure will gain control of behavior. Finally, one way to set into action a motivational structure that has lain dormant is to place the persuadee in a position where he or she must decide whether to accept or reject the persuader's proposal.

Kelman, Cartwright, McQuail, and others have suggested that we consider mass communications media as partners in a relationship with individual receivers whose cognitive structures and motivations differ. This perspective places part of the responsibility for influence on the audience members. It shifts us away from the negativism that Newcomb considers dysfunctional to the development of critical viewing. It suggests that while media may have the power to "shape our soul," as Novak suggests, they do so only if we perceive that what they propose "fits" our cognitive and motivational structures. This does not mean that media cannot create needs. On the contrary, they probably do so quite often. However, they do so only if we choose to participate in relationships with them. In the succeeding sections of this chapter we shall look closely at our relationships with advertisements and programs and why they have the potential to influence our everyday behavioral choices.

ADVERTISING:
THE BLATANT PERSUASION

As indicated previously, it is somewhat unduly pessimistic to view ourselves as the unwitting pawns of mass media. However, just as the interpersonally competent individual has "the edge" when attempting to influence others, certainly advertisers, whose entire careers are devoted to determining what we value, have an advantage. They study our rule systems and develop messages that will convince us that what we desire can be obtained by purchasing the products they advertise. When our rules and values do not provide a path for such persuasion, they create for us what LaPiere (1954) refers to as *fugitive* values. This term refers to the high priority or desirability we give to objects or behaviors because of their newness. Just as a disc jockey can make a song a hit by choosing to replay it frequently, advertisers can convince us that some behavior is valued by society merely because we are repeatedly exposed to it in the context of a "fun" commercial. Nietzke (1977) suggests that Americans are obsessed with fun, that they need to have it or to experience it vicariously. Advertisers know this and realize that the association between a product and fun in the minds of audience members can create a market where no market previously existed. It is not necessary for advertisers to state explicitly, "If you want to be appreciated by gorgeous members of the opposite sex, use this product." Instead they create for the audience an "array of cues" (Cox, 1962). These cues refer to price, color, scent, the opinions of others, and so on. The consumer is expected to use these cues as a basis for making judgments about the product. In this way the mass media create contexts for us and then tell us how to respond appropriately.

Cox (1962) has shown that the information value of a cue is a function (but not a simple function) of the predictive and confidence values assigned to the cue by the consumer. The predictive value of a cue is a measure of the probability with which that cue seems associated with (i.e., predicts) a specific product attribute. For example, if a consumer can be convinced that a particular car has high-quality internal components, he or she will most likely believe that there is a high probability the car is of good quality. This cue, then, has high predictive value. Confidence value is a measure of how certain the consumer is that the cue is what it appears to be. For example, even if consumers realize that high-quality internal components are indicative of a good quality automobile, if they are unable to determine to their satisfaction that the automobile actually has such good-quality components, the confidence value of the cue is likely to be low.

Cox's perspective on how people evaluate products is consistent with interpersonal communication studies indicating that people will use the "best" information available to them when formulating impressions of others. Cox explains that perceiving information value as a function of two different and independent dimensions not only indicates that it is not a simple additive or multiplicative function of predictive value, but that often highly predictive value information will not be used, merely because the consumer has low confidence in it. On the other hand, low value information (in terms of prediction) may be overutilized because its confidence value is high. Eagly et al. (1980) conducted a study in which one group of subjects was given information only about the sex of an individual, while another group was given information about both the sex and the job position of the individual. The group receiving only sex information used that information to judge the individual, but the group that had what one would assume to be higher predictive and confidence value information ceased to use sex information. It appears that sex does function as a status characteristic because in real life it correlates with status. It therefore has sufficient predictive and confidence value to be used as a status cue unless higher value information is available.

It seems feasible to assume that similar cognitive functions occur when an individual is attempting to judge a product instead of another individual. Persuaders must determine what constitutes high predictive and confidence value cues for their target groups, given the particular product.

Cox (1962: 421) suggests that the marketer's ability to change the image of a product or brand depends on how well he or she uses two main strategies: "He may alter the characteristics of dominant cues, and/or he may alter the information value of the cues in the array in order to make some cues more (or less) dominant or to alter the nature of cue-attributed associations. To the extent that he can (a) identify dominant cues, and (b) specify the factors which will alter the information of a cue, his job will be that much easier, and his efforts that much more effective."

Cox focuses on an approach to persuasion similar to that introduced in Chapter 4: demonstrating the inaccuracy of superordinate constructs. For example, altering the dominance of cues in the array is actually fiddling with the consumers' construct systems. If, as Cox points out, the consumer interested in purchasing a high-quality fidelity speaker for a new stereo system still considers size of the speaker to be the dominant cue, the persuader must determine which approach might alter that antiquated cue hierarchy. He or she might decide to appeal to the "common knowl-edge" that "good things come in small packages" or demonstrate that technology has advanced to that point where smaller calculators are even more efficient than their larger predecessors, and so the same is now true of speakers. In essence, the persuader must show the consumer that his or her present construct system for the evaluation of speakers is inaccurate. Once the persuader has successfully convinced the potential buyer of the superior predictive value of factors other than size, it becomes neccessary to increase the confidence value of those cues by comparing speakers that lack what the persuader considers dominant cues with those speakers possessing those attributes. If the persuader then recognizes that the desired consequences of the consumer are good sound and fair deal, he or she can imply or explain that buying the less expensive brand would constitute the application of an inappropriate rule, given the new con-structs and these desired consequences.

This does not appear difficult until one considers that, in contrast to the one-on-one sale of a product, the mass media disseminate information to large audiences whose members may be at different points in the process of influence. What is meant here by the process of influence is similar to what marketers refer to as the hierarchy-of-effects model. Advertising messages, for example, can influence one or more of several response stages. The typical sequence is awareness, comprehension, convic-tion, and action (Ray, 1973). Ray suggests that these stages can be subsumed under one of three major levels: cognitive, affective, and cona-tive. He contends that the important question is whether cognitive pre-cedes affective and conative, or some alternative formulation is appro-priate. Ray points out that there is sufficient evidence in marketing research to indicate that learning or cognitive response is often not a measurable precedent to either affect (evaluation) or conation (behavior). Similarly, as discussed in Chapter 4, the affective-conation (attitude-behav-ior) relationship has received much criticism over the past forty years of attitude research.

Ray suggests that, in lieu of discarding this hierarchy-of-effects model altogether, we consider the possibility that all marketing situations can fit one of three response orders: (1) the learning hierarchy: cognitive-affec-tive-conative; (2) the dissonance-attribution hierarchy: conative-affec-tive-cognitive; and (3) the low-involvement hierarchy: cognitive-cona-tive-affective.

Ray indicates that the learning hierarchy occurs when the audience is involved in the topic of the campaign and when there are clear differences between alternatives. He suggests that diffusion of innovation research provides the best illustration of this type of situation. Exceptions to this order, which often occur because of varying availability of the mass media, demonstrate behavior change prior to affective or cognitive changes. These situations are explained by the dissonance-attribution hierarchy. This hierarchy assumes that a choice from among undifferentiated alternatives is made through some nonmass media source, followed by attitude and cognitive responses to that choice. Finally, the low-involvement hierarchy is based on the notion of almost unlimited effect on the cognitive variable because audience members either do not care or are not involved. In such situations there is very little perceptual defense against advertising messages, and so, after much repetition of the message, the advertiser can alter the conative and later the affective responses of the audience members (see also Krugman, 1965).

It is often difficult for advertisers to determine which hierarchy level best reflects a particular audience. The amount of interpersonal interaction with respect to a particular type of product prior to a new message about that product is often impossible to determine. In such cases, the best bet is to assume that the relationship between the product and the buyer is practically nonexistent. All levels must then be considered. Awareness, comprehension, conviction, and action must be addressed in such advertisements. Once the product has received sufficient exposure and been a focus of conviction, action is feasible. This is similar to those interpersonal episodes in which past interactions serve as the rule-definition and rule-confirmation phases. Once a product has developed a relationship with its buyers, much of the effort that once went into the definition of the relationship can go into the continuation of it.

In the next section of this chapter we shall look at the relationships advertisers attempt to develop with children, and the steps that have been taken by the Federal Communication Commission and other groups to prevent the advertiser from becoming the powerful member of that relationship.

CHILDREN AND ADVERTISING

Much research attention has been given to children's perceptions of television advertising. Children constitute the most "defenseless" of the uncritical audiences that participate in a media relationship with television. The natural propensity for parents and educators to protect children from harm has made the question concerning just how much power television has over children a very important one.

In terms of advertising, two of the major questions being asked by researchers are whether children can separate program content from commercial content, and whether they realize that commercials are attempts to persuade them to buy particular products. In 1974 the Federal Communication Commission determined that all licensees must ensure that a clear separation be maintained between program content and commercial messages. This requirement identifies television as a substantial contributor to the child's conceptualization of reality. However, just how prepared children are to distinguish between those messages whose sole purpose is to shape their perceptions and those intended to inform or entertain has not been determined. To protect children from the possibility that advertisers might take "unfair advantage" of them, the FCC has recommended the implementation of methods that facilitate the child's ability at least to separate persuasive content from program content.

The FCC has suggested that commercials be "clustered" at the beginnings or ends of programs. This is one method of compensating for the young child's egocentric or private thought processes, which are characterized by an absence of reflexivity or criticism of his or her own thinking. Imprisoned by limited, nonreflextive processes, the child must rely on outside sources to provide separations, integrations, and critiques of new information that will, through the processes of assimilation and accommodation, become part of his or her conceptualization of the "real" world (Piaget, 1962; Kohlberg, 1966, 1969).

Unlike other audiences addressed by the mass media, children do not bring to the relationship the cognitive capacities necessary to recognize subtle persuasion, nor do they possess past experiences that would caution them against accepting, without question, attempts to influence their behavior. In terms of Cox's (1962) predictive and confidence value criteria, children are learning what to value and, should their favorite television character tell them that a toy possesses attributes they have learned are important, their confidence in that cue will be enhanced. Unable to construe their relationship with the television episodically (behavior-pattern identification), young children are incapable of recognizing where they are being led.

The controversy over what the advertiser is doing to children has frequently taken on the appearance of a monkey-in-the-middle game, in which the responsibility for children's responses to advertising is passed back and forth between parents and advertisers. Considerable concern has been expressed by consumer advocates and social-policy decision makers about the effects of advertising on family relations (Robertson, 1979). Of primary concern is the potential strain that may be imposed on parent-child relations due to consistent consumption requests. Many advertisers respond to this negativism by suggesting that advertising can provide positive interaction between parent and child, since it represents an opportunity for consumer learning. The low level of parental concern about children's commercials reported in several recent studies (Bauer and Greyser, 1968; Atkin, 1975a; Feldman et al., 1977) suggests that even if this opportunity exists, parents are not likely to take advantage of it. Robertson (1979) contends that what appears to be parents' abdication of responsibility for the mediation and regulation of child viewing may be explained by the pressure parents may feel to not interfere with other socialization objectives met by television viewing.

Low parental concern about advertising does not mean that parents are not offended or upset by it. Feldman et al. (1977), for example, found little relationship between parental dissatisfaction with commercials and parental monitoring of children's television-viewing. It appears that parents are aware that commercials increase parent-child conflict and that commercials may persuade children to want things they do not need (Culley et al., 1976). These two problems can be explained in terms of the regulative rule model. If a child learns to expect certain behaviors from parents as a result of watching television commercials, to the extent that those expectations are violated, family conflict potential is increased. The following model depicts the rule violation children may be perceiving when parents refuse to buy something they want:

ANTECEDENT CONDITIONS: Mothers and fathers love their children.

DESIRED CONSEQUENCES: Mothers and fathers want their children to be happy.

BEHAVIORAL CHOICE: Because my mother and father love me and want me to be happy, they will buy what I want.

Although the National Association of Broadcasters Code prohibits directing children through commercials to purchase a product or service or ask their parents or other adults to buy the product or service for them, advertisers can still succeed in conveying this message implicitly. When Johnny hugs his mother and tells her that she is the greatest mom in the whole world because she bought the product he and his friends wanted, the implication is that great moms conform to their children's expectations in the purchase of items. The child whose parent refuses to conform to such expectations may begin to believe that her mother or father does not wish to make her happy or, even worse, that they do not love her. Both advertisers and parents recognize that this logic can be created and nurtured in the mind of the child and thus place annoying pressure on the parent to purchase what the child wants. Perhaps the best way for parents to combat this pressure is to help the child revise his or her logic as follows:

ANTECEDENT CONDITIONS: Mothers and fathers love their children.

DESIRED CONSEQUENCES: Mothers and fathers want their children to be happy.

BEHAVIORAL CHOICE: Because my mother and father love me and want me to be happy, they will buy me what I need and things that are good for me.

Research is needed which focuses on the effects of parental attempts to revise television-generated modes of logic. In essence, parents could be trained to inoculate their children against persuasive messages that have the potential to influence family life negatively. If parents thought that they could succeed in monitoring the influence television has on their children's perceptions of parental concern, they might be more willing to make the attempt.

It is likely that the battle over the potentially negative effects of advertising on children will go on for some time. The extent of child disappointment in not receiving advertised products (Robertson and Rossiter, 1977; Sheikh and Moleski, 1977; Atkin, 1975a; Greenberg and Gorn, 1978), influence of product-choice strategies used by children (Wartella et al., 1979), developmental stages of consumer information-processing (see Wackman and Ward, 1976; Brown, 1976; Robertson and Rossiter, 1977; Capon and Kuhn, 1978; Wartella et al., 1979), and form complexity as a factor in attention to commercials (see Wartella and Ettema, 1974; Watt and Krull, 1976; McEwen et al., 1977) are only a few of the issues that have captivated researchers over the past few years. While many of the findings may have contributed to the negativism Newcomb(1979) views as an inhibitor to critical viewing, they have also contributed to our understanding of the unique relationship between children and the mass media.

ADVERTISING AND THE
PORTRAYAL OF MINORITIES

Few mass media experts would disagree with the position that television has influenced the values of this country. The extent of that influence, however, is difficult to determine. Loevinger (1979) introduced a theory of mass communication that places some limitations on the potential influence of mass media. His reflective-projective theory postulates that mass communications are best understood as "mirrors of society that reflect an ambiguous image in which each observer projects or sees his own vision of himself and society" (1979: 252). Recognizing the diversity among audience members, program producers have often settled for creating homogenized versions of Americans. The result is an extensive mosaic of inaccurate reflections of society which many persons begin to believe is the real world. As Cummings (1979: 78) has explained, "Hollywood has provided us with cultural fantasies and reinforcing reveries; the icons of our age, creating and defining ourselves for us, are celluloid chimeras which, like those incredible walking-talking-wetting dolls, come closer and closer to being the real thing."

Cummings believes that distinguishing between illusion and reality has become increasingly difficult because of the mass media's influence on our perceptions. He adds that cultural ambiguity increases individual anxiety because, while persons may know more, they are less sure of that knowledge. As a consequence, the critics, commentators, and media personalities in general become the interpreters of complex reality for the befuddled spectator.

Most people are aware that this ambiguity discussed by Cummings is very apparent in sex-role stereotypes. Sex-role stereotypes impose limitations on behavioral choices. When these stereotypes undergo changes, people become unsure about which behaviors are masculine and which are feminine. If Cummings is accurate, then we should expect to find these confused individuals looking to the mass media for some behavioral guidelines. For women, those guidelines are likely to reflect some noncomplimentary messages. The first major message is that women are not as important to society as men. This message is conveyed implicitly through the low percentage of women, as opposed to men, appearing in television advertisements. This consistent imbalance is a symbolic annihilation of women, because their role is trivialized (Tuchman, 1978).

Absence is not the only mode of symbolic annihilation experienced by women in the media. Gerbner (1978) postulates the existence of three main tactics used in television to resist the changing status of women: discrediting, isolating, and undercutting. Discrediting is manifested in the selection of the most bizarre or provocative aspects of the threatening movement as the primary focus for television coverage. For example, Gerbner points to television's focus on supposedly "typical women's libbers," who are seen as hostile, aggressive, unappreciative of men, and unwilling to listen to reason.

The second form of resistance is isolation. The tactic here is to segregate women, to put them "in their place," such as the kitchen or the bathroom. Toilet paper commercials are an excellent example of this type of tactic. Men appear to care very little about the type of toilet paper they use, whereas women often appear to spend their days worrying about the potential embarrassment involved in selecting the wrong roll.

Undercutting is what Gerbner (1978: 48) describes as "basically the tactic of terror." The "institutionalization of rape" or the treatment of it as a "normal crime" is one form of undercutting the changing image of women. A second form is seen in the acceptance of pornography as a "liberating force" rather than as a mode of exploitation. Advertising is frequently a culprit here. Sometimes the insult is conveyed by subliminal messages, messages sufficiently subtle to be deniable if advertisers were asked to justify their inclusion in the ad. Most advertising pornography is more obvious. However, our society has become accustomed to seeing partially nude women trapsing across the television screen.

The rules being conveyed to the "befuddled" spectator are ones that perpetuate condescending behavior toward women. For instance, women appear to be totally incapable of experiencing the camaraderie so characteristic of men in beer commercials. Conflict literature indicates that women are more competitive toward each other than they are toward males (Frost and Wilmot, 1978). They have never learned to disguise their competitive emotions with the verbal battles characteristic of male camaraderie. Television does much to feed this damaging image. The only time we see a woman competing in advertisements is when she wishes to have her husband's shirts designated as the cleanest or her home as smelling better than the homes of other women. The back-slapping verbal dueling of males appears to allow no place for a woman unless she is the subject of the exchange. The male has cornered the market on this type of humor.

Gerbner (1978) paints a dismal picture for the future concerning changes in these negative depictions of women on television. Until the structure of social relations between the two sexes becomes intolerably insulting to women, it is likely that advertisers will continue to portray women in insipid roles. Since very few women appear to be sufficiently incensed by their trivialization in media advertising, advertisers are at liberty to perpetuate images that should have met their demise years ago. The desired consequences of a clean toilet bowl, a soft toilet tissue, and shirts without spots separate the women from the men, whose desired consequences are usually focused on issues of insurance, liquor, sports, and other "more important" matters. Until advertising begins to respond to the inconsistencies between the media reflection of what women consider important and their real interests, people will continue to derive behavioral guidelines from distorted images of women.

Women are certainly not the only segment of our population unfairly portrayed on the television screen. The elderly are consistently devalued as consumers by their underrepresentation in commercials (Gantz et al., 1980). Damaging as this problem is, underrepresentation is not nearly as damaging as the one-dimensional, undeveloped character images of the elderly. Korzenny and Neuendorf (1980) provide support for the positive role television can play in enhancing the self-images of elderly persons. They, like women, are attempting to accommodate their rule systems to changing societal expectations for elderly persons. Certainly, negative stereotypes linger and are perpetuated by a youth-oriented mass media, but as their increasing numbers become too obvious to ignore, the elderly are beginning to emerge as an important segment of our society. If, however, the elderly look to the mass media for guidance concerning appropriate behavior, they are likely to experience the same devaluation that women experience through the mass media.

Another segment of society suffering the effects of underrepresentation in the media are minority groups such as blacks and hispanics. Research in this area has focused on the effects of symbolic annihilation on the minority child. Comstock and Cobbey (1979) explain that all children share general needs for information. However, they perceive the minority child's relationship with the television as somewhat special. They conclude that what sets minority children apart is their relative isolation from other sources for the satisfaction of information needs. They add (1979: 110), "This circumstance arises in part from their ethnicity, but more from the socioeconomic disadvantage that is frequently associated with minority status. Thus the evidence suggests that minority children share with children of lower socioeconomic status generally a particular reliance on television—because it brings information that is not otherwise readily available."

The special dependency relationship between ethnic minority children and television defines this mass medium as the creator and disseminator of societal expectations for these youngsters. To the extent that those images consistently viewed by children are distortions of reality, their rule repertoires will be insufficient to meet their needs in the real world. This does not mean that the only source of influence for the minority child is the television, but it certainly appears to be a primary source.

The emphasis given to television advertising as an important source of role information has excluded from discussion the less obvious forms of persuasion prevalent in television. In the next section we shall look at how television programs contribute to our social expectations for self and others.

THE TELEVISION PROGRAM AS A
SOURCE OF PERSUASION

In previous sections of this chapter the mass audience was described as a collection of individuals who, while sharing many rules, differ in their perceptions of events. Emphasis was placed on the relationships these audience members establish with the mass media. It was suggested that we recognize that individuals, perhaps even more so than in interpersonal relationships, can choose to participate in episodes of reciprocal influence with the media. There is no need to apologize or account for one's rudeness toward a mass medium.

Despite this perspective on mass media as selected participants in our everyday communications, it could be argued that some media allow for greater choice than others. For example, a book is a private medium. Television, on the other hand, is a public medium that many of us view in the company of others. Frequently people find themselves viewing programs they have not truly chosen, but to continue the interpersonal interactions with family and/or peers, they participate in the media event.

Television advertising and program content can be separated in much the same fashion. It is probably safe to assume that few persons select the programs they view on the basis of what advertisements they can expect to experience. However, their interactions with advertisements are usually the result of having selected a given program. In this sense there is more choice involved in program-viewing than in advertisement-viewing. We can conclude that the program viewer is comparatively more responsible for his or her media relationship than is the advertisement viewer. When program viewers flip the dial to a particular program, they are indicating some preference for a particular type of relationship.

What does this perspective mean in terms of television criticism? It means that despite the abundance of journal and magazine articles pronouncing the negativism toward television that Newcomb (1978) finds unhealthy, television program relationships are more a product of choice than most other relationships in individuals' daily lives. Viewers' complaints about the sex and violence that they "must" be exposed to are little more than a sour-grapes philosophy if they continue to participate in these supposedly unpleasant interactions. The television viewer is a willing persuadee who has found a subject for condemnation and whose negative opinions will bring little disagreement from fellow viewers, who also define themselves as unwilling participants in a relationship where divorce is out of the question.

Be this as it may, the prevalent perspective is still one describing the television viewer as a victim of much that is evil in our society. Victims are those with an excuse for passivity. Their mental set does not predispose them to search for a way out. Vandenberg and Watt (1977-1978) provide some support for this perspective. Their survey of Connecticut television viewers indicates that despite high subject preference for audience-member and industry, rather than government, regulation of sex and violence in programming, few parents monitor the viewing patterns of children. Vandenberg and Watt found that almost half of the children under 18 had no time restrictions on viewing, and almost two-thirds had no content restrictions.

Our perceptions of ourselves as victims of mass communications media has allowed us to relinquish our right to choose our media relationships. Our behavior fits Ray's (1973) low-involvement model. Because we either do not care or are not involved in the media relationship choice, almost unlimited effect on the cognitive variable is afforded. Little perceptual defense exists and so, after much repetition of the same themes, the programmer can alter the conative and later the affective responses to sex and violence. They become a fact of life.

The high tolerance for mass media biases indicates that people do not seek to resolve minor inconsistencies with any predictable regularity. Viewers who complain frequently about the content of the programs they watch but refuse to do anything about it might be convinced that their behavior and desired consequences are inconsistent. However, unless they can also be convinced that there is something they can do about this inconsistency and that it constitutes a problem of greater magnitude than they previously imagined, the inconsistency is likely to remain unchallenged. This is the anatomy of the negativism Newcomb (1978) perceived as a roadblock to developing an effective critical attitude toward television.

The general malaise characteristic of the television viewer places viewers in the position of contributing less to the media relationship definition than programs and advertising contribute. They are thus relegated to a position of little power in McQuail's (1979) terms. They are consistently the persuadees, rarely the persuaders. They have defined themselves and, as the Atkin (1975b). Feldman et al. (1977), and Vandenberg and Watt (1977-1978) studies indicate, their children, as victims in a potentially damaging relationship.

CONCLUSION

Jay Jackson (1966) refers to that condition in which persons agree about some sentiment toward a person or object (high consensus) but few sanctions exist to encourage or discourage relevant action (low intensity) one of *vacuous consensus*. This characterizes the general negativism toward television that Newcomb describes as responsible for our lack of concerted effort to bring about positive changes. This societywide malaise is the result of a victimization myth that immobilizes us further. A victim is someone who has an excuse for passivity. By defining ourselves as such, we have given up the self-autonomy we could elicit in defining our relationships with television and mass media in general.

Moreover, our general acceptance of deception in media, and particularly in advertising, reflects a set of superordinate constructs that we pass from generation to generation (Wolf and Hexamer, 1980). The effects of this mental set are reflected in the prevalence of sexual, age, and ethnic stereotypes pervading mass media messages.

If the possibility exists that mass media "shape the soul's geography" or even contribute to it, then children should be encouraged by schools and parents to take responsibility for their media relationships. Miller and Burgoon (1979) have clearly demonstrated that people prepare counterarguments when they expect intensely persuasive messages. Without such expectations message recipients are more vulnerable, since the self-autonomy that often serves to check and balance "borrowed rules" in interpersonal exchanges is absent.

The main point is not that mass media messages are without virtue. On the contrary, they have contributed greatly to our education. Even advertising, generally viewed as the most overt form of mass media persuasion, has opened our eyes to products that have made life more comfortable. What is needed is greater persuadee responsibility in media relationships. Without it, some mass media messages will continue to enjoy undeserved credibility.

Besides describing mass media relationships, this chapter has also introduced models of mass persuasion which support or extend the perspective advanced in this text. Kelman's model suggests the use of persuasion strategies paralleling the accuracy, appropriateness, consistency, and effectiveness appeals described in Chapter 2. While appropriateness is the most commonly used marketing appeal, Kelman's perspective does not preclude the use of accuracy, consistency, and effectiveness in mass media persuasive messages.

This chapter completes the context focus evidenced in Chapters 7 and 8. In subsequent chapters, past persuasion research designs will be examined and future research alternatives reflecting a context orientation will be considered.

Chapter 10

TWO METHODOLOGICAL TRADITIONS

Gail Theus Fairhurst

*Previous chapters have focused on past and recent persuasion
theory and research with particular emphasis on the drawing
of implications for interpersonal, organizational, and mass media
contexts. It is appropriate at this time to shift our focus a bit to the
methods we have used to study persuasion and how they have
influenced both the research questions we have asked and the conclusions we have drawn.*

*In this chapter, Gail Theus Fairhurst focuses on the advantages and
disadvantages of popular persuasion research methods. Her con-
densed coverage of this extensive area provides both an important
overview and the type of critique Seibold (1979) considers imperative to the healthy development of a domain of study. Fairhurst's
examination of two methodological traditions also sets the stage
for the following chapter, which will consider methodological alternatives consistent with the theoretical model advanced in this text.*

Craftsmen will often spend countless hours caring for their tools, making
sure they are in working order so that the craft is shaped by those tools
rather than destroyed by them. Likewise, the tools a researcher employs
affect the quality of the research, either allowing confidence in the test of
the theory or leaving uncertainty about whether the results are due to the
methods used or the phenomenon's true behavior.

The subject of this chapter is methodology. Specifically, we will take
up two methodological traditions in persuasion research. The first of these
involves attitude measurement. Historically, the terms *persuasion* and

---

AUTHOR'S NOTE: The author wishes to thank William Snavely, Cynthia Berryman-
Fink, Kathleen Reardon, and William Schenck-Hamlin for their helpful comments on
manuscript versions of this chapter.

attitude change have been almost interchangeable because investigators have ignored other kinds of persuasion effects (e.g., on social norms). The preoccupation with the concept of attitude led to both intensive and sophisticated measurement attempts. We shall be reviewing some of those in the early parts of this chapter.

The second methodological tradition concerns the experiment as the major source of information about persuasion. In the past, many investigators felt the experiment was ideally suited to the study of persuasion. Subjects who were easily accessible (like students) could be brought together to listen passively to a source deliver a persuasive message under controlled experimental conditions. The effects of the persuasive message were then assessed in terms of the direction and the degree of attitude change. As we shall see, however, this once-popular way to ask questions about persuasion may have contributed to a decline in persuasion research in the 1970s.

There are a host of methodological issues that this chapter will not cover. However, we can compile past research in communication and other fields to give the reader a sense of where we have been methodologically and what methodological concerns we have today as a result of our history.

ATTITUDE MEASUREMENT

When investigating phenomena, researchers are constantly working on two levels, the conceptual and the operational. At the conceptual level, the researcher seeks definition and meaning for the phenomenon. At the operational level, measurement of the phenomenon in concrete terms is the central concern. The theories advanced in earlier chapters of this text have in one form or another located relationships among phenomena at the conceptual level. As research and research methods have become more sophisticated, there has been a greater awareness of the theorizing that also takes place at the operational level. At this level, researchers theorize about data.

A theory of data speculates on the nature of the information used to infer given phenomena. Thus, a theory of data is really a theory within a theory: a theory of measurement within a theory of social behavior, like persuasion. Since information can come in many forms, a theory of data is crucial. For example, a researcher can measure an attitude with either of the following statements: (1) "Please state your attitude toward issue x."

((2) Please answer either 'strongly agree,' 'agree,' 'undecided,' 'disagree,' or 'strongly disagree,' depending upon how you feel about the following statement on issue x." Both statements are designed to elicit an attitude, but both can yield substantially different, even contradictory, kinds of information. Could both statements elicit the same attitude? Is one way of measuring an attitude better than the others? Why is this so?

The answers to these questions and others like them constitute a theory of data. Just as the necessity of a good theory of persuasion is established by its ability to explain a given persuasive phenomenon, so too a theory of data explains why the measurement instrument captures the essence of that phenomenon. Just as a good theory of persuasion can predict future instances, a good theory of data can state the kinds of influences likely to affect a certain measuring device.

Theories about the behavior of phenomena and theories of data are so intertwined that they are tested concomitantly. As Ericsson and Simon (1980) suggest, theories of data are present, valid or not, whenever researchers treat their data as veridical. These authors further state that the expansion of theories to include a theory of measurement instruments is commonplace in physics. For example, experiments that entail weighing objects require very basic theories of pan balance, at the very least. The same is true for research that employs verbal reports of any kind. Attitude research and measurement are no exceptions. In this section of the chapter we shall discuss standard attitude scaling techniques, each of which constitutes a "theory of data." They are all multiitem instruments measuring a person's affective responses to or evaluations of a given attitude object. While two of the procedures (those of Thurstone and Guttman) are not widely used today, they remain important contributions.

Following the discussion of these standardized instruments, we shall take up a second class of indicators. They are really a potpourri of other available scaling procedures, ranging from intentions and beliefs to physiological responses.

Standard Attitude-Scaling

Thurstone's method of equal appearing intervals. Among the first to introduce metric scaling into attitude measurement was L. L. Thurstone (1929). Thurstone scaling orders a set of belief statements along a psychological continuum with respect to the adjudged degree of an attribute each statement possesses. Since Thurstone assumed that different statements reflect different degrees of favorableness or unfavorableness with respect

TABLE 10.1   Thurstone Scale: Attitudes Toward Bussing

Scale Value		Statement
Least favorable	.8	A. No one should be forced to go to a school they do not wish to attend because of bussing.
	1.6	B. Federal laws and court decisions should not force bussing on a community.
	2.4	C. State governments should have the right to decide if bussing is needed in their state and how it should be handled.
	3.2	D. City finances should be considered when recommending bussing policies.
Most favorable	4.0	E. Bussing should be implemented through concerted community action.

to a given attitude object, a person's response to those items was expected to be indicative of his or her attitude. Thurstone proposed a number of ways whereby the location of an item along an evaluative dimension could be determined through assignment of a scale value. A detailed account of all of Thurstone's psychological scaling methods can be found in Edwards (1957).

The most widely used of Thurstone's scaling procedures was the method of equal appearing intervals. In this method, first outlined by Thurstone and Chave (1929), not only were attitude statements ordered along a favorableness-unfavorableness dimension, but the ordering appeared to reflect equal distances between statements.

Each of approximately twenty statements are assigned a scale value by a judging procedure to be explained below. A person's attitude is then determined by asking that person to check those items with which he or she agrees. Since the items are independent of one another, acceptance of any one item does not suggest acceptance of any others. A person's attitude is reflected numerically in the mean of the items that were checked. An abbreviated version of a Thurstone scaling using equal appearing intervals is given in Table 10.1.

Equal appearing intervals are arrived at through a judging procedure employing a separate sample of subjects who usually have some knowledge of the topic. Each of several attitude statements are printed on separate cards. Subjects are asked to sort all nonambiguous statements into eleven piles, which are arrayed in front of them. The extremes of the eleven categories and the middle category are defined for subjects as extremely unfavorable, extremely favorable, and neutral, respectively. Subjects are asked to consider all intermediate categories as equidistant from adjacent categories. Note than an estimate of the *favorableness* of a statement with respect to an attitude object is different from an estimate of *agreement* with a statement. In the construction of a scale, judges are asked only for their estimates of the amount of *favorableness* a statement possesses with respect to an attitude object.

Returning to the previous example in Table 10.1, the statement, "No one should be forced to go to a school he or she does not wish to attend because of bussing," indicates an extremely unfavorable attitude toward bussing and therefore belongs in the first category (A).

Two important numerical values result from the judges' sort of the statements into eleven categories. The first is the scale value for each attitude statement, which is the median or mean of the distribution of judgments for that statement. The second is the degree to which subjects agreed on the placement of an item in a given category. Using these values as a criterion, investigators strive for between 20 and 22 attitude statements that have relatively equidistant scale values as well as high interjudge agreement. If two or more statements have the same scale values, the one with the highest interjudge agreement is retained in the final scale.

A necessary assumption of this method of equal appearing intervals requires that a judge's estimate of the degree of favorableness be independent of one's attitude (i.e., degree of agreement) toward the attitude object. Any relationship between scale values and individual attitudes confounds the interpretation of any attitude score derived from scale values. This assumption has been called into question, although available empirical evidence suggests it is justified in most cases.

Likert's method of summated ratings. The method of summated ratings developed by Likert (1932) is easier to construct than a Thurstone scale because it does not require the use of judges. Instead, Likert assumed that a researcher could render a priori judgments regarding whether or not a large pool of items is favorable or unfavorable to an attitude object. Once classified, the statements are then given to a group of subjects who indicate their degree of agreement with the statement. Five response alternatives are permitted (strongly agree, agree, undecided, disagree, and strongly disagree). An individual's ratings of each belief statement are summed to produce a single, representative score; hence the term *summated ratings*. The following is an example of a Likert scale item:

A. The sale of pornographic material is responsible for violent crimes
   . against women in our society.

	Rating Value
a. Strongly Agree	1
b. Agree	2
c. Undecided	3
d. Disagree	4
e. Strongly Disagree	5

As with any scale construction, some means must be used to determine the worthiness of a statement for the scale. Likert employed the criterion of internal consistency. Essentially, this criterion states that the more favorable a person's attitude is, the more likely he or she will endorse favorable attitude statements as well as reject unfavorable statements. An item analysis of the attitude scores permits a test of this criterion for each attitude statement. There are different kinds of item analyses. The one originally employed by Likert is quite simple.

First, a frequency distribution of attitude scores is compiled. Second, the 25 percent of the subjects with the highest scores and the 25 percent of the subjects with the lowest scores are selected for further analysis. It is assumed that both groups are somewhat homogeneous with regard to their respective attitudes. Finally, individual attitude statements are judged according to how well they discriminate between high and low groups. (The average score for an item for the high group is tested against the average score for that item for the low group.) Statistical tests are performed to measure the degree of difference. Attitude statements can then be ordered by their discriminating ability. More recent item analyses employ correlational techniques and computers to determine internal consistency.

Whichever form of item analysis is used—and one must be used in order to qualify as a Likert scale—the goal in summated ratings is a set of 20-25 belief statements that adequately differentiate between the high and low groups. The entire sample's attitude scores can then be recomputed only on those statements deemed acceptable by the item analysis, or a new sample may be brought in to respond to the items.

In order to justify adding the ratings for each belief statement to arrive at an attitude score, Likert assumed that each belief statement is a (linear) function of the same attitude dimension. Consequently, the attitude items all must be highly intercorrelated as well as correlated with a common attribute.

Unlike a Thurstone scale, the interpretation of an attitude score cannot be made independent of the distribution of scores for a given group. Also in contrast to Thurstone, no assumption is made about the relative distances between scale values. The distance between "strongly disagree" and "disagree" may be larger or smaller than the distance between "disagree" and "undecided." Consequently, no precise estimate can be made of how far apart people are—only their relative ordering with respect to an attitude object.

Guttman's scalogram analysis. A Guttman (1944) scale cumulatively orders a set of belief statements along a unidimensional scale. A rather simplistic example should serve to convey the logic of this scale. If a person has enough money to purchase a $10 item, you know immediately that he or she has enough money to purchase a $5 item or a $2 item. In a Guttman scale, also called a cumulative scale, if a person endorses a favorable statement with respect to a given attitude object, you know he or she also endorses a less favorable statement. The cumulative properties of the scale assure that those statements less difficult to accept will be endorsed on the basis of knowing the most difficult item a person will accept.

Let us assume we have a 5-item scale like the one in Table 10.2. Guttman assesses the unidimensionality of the scale by examining the pattern of endorsement of the 5 items. For a perfect Guttman scale, individuals will have one of the following five response patterns or "scale types":

	Responses Endorsed				
Scale Type	A	B	C	D	E
0	No	No	No	No	No
1	Yes	No	No	No	No
2	Yes	Yes	No	No	No
3	Yes	Yes	Yes	No	No
4	Yes	Yes	Yes	Yes	No
5	Yes	Yes	Yes	Yes	Yes

TABLE 10.2   Guttman Scale: Attitudes Toward Quotas

Degree of Acceptability	Statement
Least difficult to accept	A. Professional school opportunities should be provided for minorities.
	B. Money should be set aside to aid the implemention of professional school opportunities for minorities.
	C. Professional schools should actively recruit minorities for professional schools.
	D. Professional schools should set goals every year with respect to the number of minorities they plan to recruit.
Most difficult to accept	E. Mandatory quota systems should be employed to force professional school opportunities for minorities.

Notice, I said for a "perfect" Guttman scale (i.e., one that is cumulative and unidimensional). In practice, however, inconsistent endorsements are often made. For example, an individual might endorse statements A, B, and D, but not C. This is considered to be a response error because, unlike a perfect Guttman scale, knowing the most difficult statements a person will accept does not presume knowledge of the statements less difficult to accept. Specifically, we would be incorrect in predicting that this subject endorses statement C, even though the more difficult-to-accept statement D was endorsed. The error in this example could be the result of measurement error, which is the usual assumption, or it could indicate a deviation from unidimensionality.

The worthiness of a scale is assessed by counting the number of errors or changes needed to make a response pattern consistent with one of Guttman's scale types and then summing across all subjects. Guttman then uses the coefficient of reproducibility to assess how close a given scale is to a Guttman scale. The coefficient of R is:

$$R = 1 - \frac{\text{number of errors}}{\text{total number of responses}}$$

where total number of responses = sample size $\times$ number of items

Guttman suggested an R value ⩾ .85 is an indication that the attribute is "scalable."

The attitude scores (i.e., the closest scale type to a response pattern) of approximately 100 individuals are used to analyze a scale. Items are either deleted or rearranged until a minimum number of errors is achieved. Unlike Likert and Thurstone scaling, where the scales are constructed from a large pool of items, Guttman scaling is chiefly concerned with testing the assumption that a set of items are unidimensional and cumulative. As such, Guttman scaling is not really a method for scale construction (Edwards, 1957).

Once a suitable scale has been achieved and subjects have indicated their degree of agreement with the responses, individuals may be ordered unambiguously on the attitude scale.

Osgood's semantic differential. The semantic differential is one of the most widely used measures of attitude today, although it was introduced as a measurement of meaning (Osgood et al., 1957). Osgood argued, however, that a person's attitude toward some object is tantamount to the evaluative meanings a person holds for that object. Basic to this method is the assumption that the meaning of a word or concept can be represented in a hypothetical semantic space of an unknown number of dimensions.

The procedure is actually very simple. A concept is evaluated on a large number of bipolar adjectival scales with seven categories and a mid-point of neutrality. For example, the word *feminist* is measured by one's ratings on the following set of semantic scales in Table 10.3.

The responses to the bipolar scales, which Osgood took as indications of belief strength, are then subjected to a factor analysis. The purpose of the factor analysis is to discover the underlying dimensions along which concepts may vary. Osgood's own research, which went beyond the measurement of attitude objects, consistently yielded three dimensions or factors. They were evaluation (e.g., good-bad, pleasant-unpleasant), potency (e.g., strong-weak, large-small), and activity (e.g., active-passive, busy-idle).

An attitude scale can be developed by subjecting a set of bipolar scales to a factor analysis and retaining those scales which have high loadings on the evaluative dimension. The alternative to this is to select scales which other investigators have found to load on the evaluative dimension. Researchers should be warned of this latter alternative, because the evaluative factor structure can change from one subject population to another, from one concept to another, and from one factoring method to another. Cronkhite (1976) had ten different subpopulations rate nine different

TABLE 10.3 Semantic Differential: Attitudes Toward the Term Feminist

	"feminist"						
good ____	____	____	____	____	____	____	bad
unpleasant ____	____	____	____	____	____	____	pleasant
rewarding ____	____	____	____	____	____	____	punishing

concepts on 39 evaluative semantic differential scales plus the "strong-weak" (potency) and "fast-slow" (activity) scales. Among his findings, factor structures and representative scales differed dramatically among concepts. For example, the fast-slow scale, typically representative of Osgood's activity dimension, loaded on the evaluative dimension for the concept "freedom." Cronkhite (1976: 321) explains:

> [I]t does help to know that the ratings were done in the late 1960's when "freedom" was either a God-term or a dirty word, depending upon who was using it. Further, the real discriminator between "good" and "bad" freedom at that time was the issue of speed. The "fast-slow" scale probably is so clearly evaluative in this case because it reflects the rater's reactions to the slogan "Freedom Now!"

This is a good example of the contextual dependency of some semantic differential scales. Osgood terms these *concept-scale interactions.* Rater-scale interactions occur when differences in evaluative factor structures stem from using different subpopulations. While Cronkhite and others have found this effect to be less pronounced than concept-scale inter-actions, rater-scale interactions can combine with concept-scale inter-actions to produce concept-rater combinations, which are also capable of altering the factor structure.

Finally, while it is not our goal to communicate the specifics of factor analysis, it is enough to say that there are different ways of determining the solutions for factors. Not all solutions will produce the same evaluative factor structure.

However suitable scales are found, most semantic differential measures of attitude contain 5-10 evaluative scales interspersed with a few potency and activity scales. Subjects are then asked to rate a concept on each scale, of which the endpoints are +3 and −3, corresponding to the positive and negative poles of the scale. An attitude score is computed by summing the responses to the evaluative scales.

Discussion of the methods. The four methods of attitude measurement just outlined all arrive at a single numerical score based on a subject's response to a set of belief statements with respect to a given object. These multiitem and unidimensional methods differ in the assumptions they make about the nature of the test items and the type of information yielded about attitudes.

For example, Thurstone's method requires the use of judges while the other methods do not. Tittle and Hill (1967) note that to the extent the judges are biased and lack sufficient consensus, scale values will be distorted. They further point out that the judging procedure introduces a number of perceptual variables (e.g., assimilation and contrast effects), the effects of which have not been fully explored. Therein lies the basis for measurement error.

The response characteristics of Guttman scale items are different from the rest, in that Guttman scale has cumulative properties that limit the range of response patterns. Acceptance of a favorable item implies acceptance of less favorable items. Contrast that with Thurstone or Likert items, where any number of response patterns can occur. Sherif and Sherif's (1967) work on latitudes of acceptance and rejection does not support Guttman's assumption. They found that highly involved subjects will support extremely favorable statements and reject mildly favorable statements.

Finally, there are some differences, albeit not major, in the reliability and validity of the above methods. Tittle and Hill (1967) found Likert's method of summated ratings to be the superior of the four. In their study of personal participation in student political activity, Likert's measure was found to be the best predictor and to have the highest reliability. Thurstone's method was the poorest predictor and the least reliable. Likert's scale was found to differ substantially from Thurstone in its ability to incorporate attitude intensity in its final score as well as in the number of self-referent items (i.e., those containing "I" and "me") in the measuring instrument. While the semantic differential demonstrated high reliability, the tendency to adopt a response set toward the "favorable" and "unfavorable" sides of the continuum resulted in low predictive validity. A response set results whenever subjects pay little attention to the content of the adjectival pairs and respond in a manner consistent with one or the other side of the continuum.

For further information on scale comparability, the reader is referred to Tittle and Hill (1967) and Edwards (1957).

Other Scaling Techniques

Physiological measures. In contrast to the self-report techniques of standard attitude scaling, another effective indicator of attitude is the involuntary physiological responses of individuals to attitude stimuli. The most popular of the physiological measures of arousal is the Galvanic Skin Response Test (GSR), which takes readings on pupil dilation, heart rate, electrical skin resistance, and so on.

Although some researchers have established that there are differences in GSRs when comparing individuals with different attitudes toward some object (Westie and DeFleur, 1959), the physiological indicants of attitude have one weakness. As general measures of arousal they cannot indicate the direction of arousal. That is, it is impossible to tell whether the arousal state indicates a positive or a negative attitude. Thus, these measures do not truly capture the evaluative nature of attitudes because the directional nature remains unspecified (Fishbein and Ajzen, 1975).

Cognitive measures. Some investigators have tried to reduce attitudes to belief statements of the form, "Object X is good (bad, ugly, true, false, and so on)." Instead of locating an individual directly along an evaluative dimension, a subject is located along a probability dimension. For example, a subject might be asked to provide a subjective probability estimate of the statement, "Redheads are hot tempered." Attitudes are assumed to correlate with the connotative value of the belief statement. Hunter et al. (1976) argue this is because beliefs play a role in the determination of the affective value of a message. For example, the statement, "Redheads are hot tempered," is only a negative message for those who dislike hot-tempered people. Also, both beliefs and attitudes can be influenced by the same message. Thus, negatively portraying redheads in a given message will shape beliefs about redheads.

Edwards (1957) takes it as a given that there will be inconsistencies in the belief systems of those with like attitudes. These inconsistencies stem from the fact that beliefs vary in their degree of association with a given attitude. Thus, inferences of a person's attitude can be made only as long as the belief statements selected for measurement are sufficiently correlated with the underlying attitude.

Behavioral measures. The behavioral indicants of attitude can be subdivided into two categories. The first involves the recording of consistently performed choice behavior, like voting or church attendance. On the whole, these are rather crude indicators. A major drawback to taking these behaviors as symptomatic of an attitude is that there is a host of other factors besides attitudes which could result in the same behavior. For

TABLE 10.4   Behavioral Differential: Attitudes Toward a "Feminist"

		A feminist					
would	___	___	___	___	___	___	___would not
		admire the ideas of this person.					
would	___	___	___	___	___	___	___would not
		ask for help from this person.					
would	___	___	___	___	___	___	___would not
		attempt a social relationship with this person.					

example, regular church attendance may be less indicative of one's attitude toward religion than of mere force of habit. Consistently voting Democratic in elections may be less indicative of one's political attitudes than of subscription to a group norm that reinforces such voting behavior. If such behaviors are to be established as valid measures of attitude, all extraneous influences must be strictly controlled.

The second behavioral indicator of attitudes involves intention, such that a favorable intention should elicit a favorable behavior. In 1925, Bogardus developed a measure of social distance between a respondent and various ethnic groups (e.g., German, Greek, Japanese). The scale consisted of 7 rank-ordered (in terms of social distance) intention statements with respect to a given group. The most positive intention statement asked whether the respondent would marry into a group, while the most negative asked whether the respondent would have an ethnic member expelled from the country. (Note that Bogardus developed a Guttman scale.) A social distance score was computed by summing the number of intentions for which negative or excluding responses were given. Presumably, a person's behavior with respect to the group under scrutiny would follow from his or her intention statements.

Triandis (1964) developed the behavioral differential, a generalized instrument measuring the behavioral intentions of respondents toward any person or group. At first glance, the scale looks a little like the semantic differential, with the exception that the intention statements are the bipolar ends of the scale and the nature of the behavior to be substantiated is stated below. The person or concept to be judged is placed at the top of the scale. Table 10.4 provides an example. Respondents are asked to place a mark on the scales which indicate the likelihood of their behavior with respect to the stimulus person.

While Fishbein and Ajzen (1975; Ajzen and Fishbein, 1969, 1973) have given perhaps the most systematic attention to the concept of intention, they break from previous thinking by not treating intention as a behavioral manifestation of an attitude. Instead, they treat intention as the outcome of both attitudinal and normative influences where no necessary relation is held to exist between one's attitude and any given intention. For further details, see Fishbein and Ajzen (1975).

Summary

In the previous discussion we reviewed and analyzed techniques for attitude measurement, giving specific attention to the standard attitude-scaling techniques of Thurstone, Guttman, Likert, and Osgood. We also discussed behavioral, physiological, and cognitive indicators of attitudes. In the next section we shall not entirely abandon attitude measurement, but we shall consider it in the context of the experimental procedures used to study persuasion.

The experiment is the second methodological tradition of which the student of persuasion should be aware. Recently, there has been some controversy over the frequent use of experimental methods to study persuasion. We shall be examining the role of such methods with an eye to the past and future of persuasion research.

THE EXPERIMENT

As stated earlier, the experiment has been the major source of information about persuasion and attitude change. When you think of the word *experiment*, no doubt some kind of testing procedure comes to mind. Most experts, however, attempt to define *experiment* more formally. For example, Underwood and Shaughnessy (1975: 9) define an experiment as "a procedure in which at least two different treatments are applied to subjects and the differential influence (if any) on behavior is measured."

One of the reasons why experimentation has been the most frequent methodological choice among researchers is that persuasion and attitude change in the traditional sense are easily studied in a laboratory environment. If we examine several characteristics of the typical experiment, we can see both the advantages and disadvantages involved in this choice.

The first such characteristic involves the *sample* assembled by the experimenter. College students have been employed most frequently because of their availability to the experimenter. While researchers may humorously acknowledge that more is known about the college sophomore than about any other segment of our society, it is quite a serious matter. As mentioned earlier in the text, the generalizability of results from college-populated studies to the general population is questionable. College students are usually more intelligent and more discerning of experimental influence attempts. In addition, they are often a captive audience motivated by reasons other than those that are best for the research effort (e.g., money or course credit).

A second characteristic of the typical experiment is the persuasive *message* the experimenter has constructed. The message requests the receivers to change their attitudes and deals with a topic that is not ego-involving for the subjects. Ego-involving topics are more resistant to change because prior defenses and previously acquired information act to refute incoming information. Not only is the topic not ego-involving and the advocated position different from that of the receiver, but the message is relatively short in duration and can be administered to a large group in one experimental session. When one considers the fact that most persuasion experiments are one-shot influence attempts, measurable effects are only possible with attitudes that are extremely susceptible to change (Hovland, 1959). However, even if non-ego-involving topics are used, they often do not have measurable consequences in the typical one-shot persuasion experiment.

Exposure to the persuasive message is a third characteristic of the typical persuasion experiment. Subjects are asked to attend to the persuasive message once any initial testing is completed. No reciprocal exchange between source and receiver is requested; quite often this is precluded because source messages are often tape-recorded or in written form. Perhaps the most distinguishing characteristic of traditional persuasion research is the use of the public speaking or mass media format in the transmission of persuasive messages. Interpersonal persuasion is ignored and assumed to operate largely on a public speaking model. This is quite an inferential leap in light of the differences between the two settings. In public speaking situations, the direction of influence is one-way; many listeners are requested to listen passively to the influence attempt. In interpersonal settings, the direction of influence is two-way, with source-receiver roles exchanged often by fewer people in reciprocal influence attempts.

The experimental *environment* is a fourth characteristic of the typical persuasion experiment. The tape-recorded or written form of source messages mentioned in the previous paragraph is a control an experimenter applies so that no other source characteristic has an opportunity to emerge differentially across treatments, and thus constitute a rival explanation for whatever effect surfaces. There are many other actions an experimenter might take to control the environment of the subjects. The environment is thereby contrived and devoid of the competing influences that would accompany persuasion in a more natural setting (e.g., peer influence, distraction, and the like). In fact, the experimenter seeks to control or effectively neutralize any influence that could prevent causal inferences concerning the manipulated variable. These controls range from exerting (1) *physical* control over some influences (for example, making sure all treatment messages are approximately the same word length so that no group unintentionally receives more information than another, or selecting a room free from disturbance) to (2) *selective* control over some influences by randomly assigning a subject to a treatment or control group (random assignment functions to make the experimental groups comparable prior to treatment) to (3) *statistical* control over some influences by incorporating them into the design of the experiment (Kennedy, 1978). Sometimes after pretesting, there are differences in the experimental groups that could persist after exposure to a persuasive message and surface in posttesting. This is not uncommon, because there is a host of factors which could affect the experimental outcome that a researcher cannot completely control (e.g., background factors, abilities). Chiefly through multivariate statistics, an experimenter will statistically remove the influence of pretesting differences so that the effects of a persuasive message and the manipulated variables on attitude change can be observed unambiguously.

Finally, *testing* is a fifth characteristic of the typical persuasion experiment. Subjects will usually be tested prior to the experiment for their existing attitudes, levels of knowledge, personality traits, and so on, in whatever areas the experimenter deems relevant. After listening to a persuasive message, subjects are requested to record their responses to the experimental induction. That can take two forms. First, the experimenter may want to check on the effectiveness of the manipulation or persuasive message. For example, if source credibility was manipulated, the experimenter may want to see to what extent sources were differentially evaluated. Sometimes researchers will check to see if subjects understood the message. Second, some measure of attitude will be employed. Attitude change has been the predominant persuasive effect experimenters have sought to measure. Even in the face of evidence to the contrary, the attitude construct has been considered the most important instigator of behavior. If a pretest was administered, the same content items used to measure attitude in the pretest will be used in the posttest. A change score is derived from the difference between "before" and "after" responses.

Unfortunately, the measurement of attitude in the experimental environment has often been done on the basis of expediency and intuition. "Quick and dirty" single-item response measures and/or indices with presumed validity and reliability have been the norm. Rarely did investigators take advantage of the standard attitude-scaling techniques, which were far more time-consuming to develop. When they were used, they were often used incorrectly (as when semantic differential scales were borrowed from other investigations and applied to a different study, with little concern for concept or rater-scale interactions).

Not all phenomena lend themselves to study by experimentation. For example, many small-group phenomena that require a history in order to surface are not easily handled in a laboratory. However, the accessible sample, the easily administered treatment, the easily manipulated environment, the readily measured effects, and a willingness to accept a narrowly defined view of persuasion manifested in the public speaking/mass media model made the experiment the number-one source of information about persuasion and attitude change.

Now that we have acquainted ourselves with some of the distinguishing features of traditional persuasion research, it should be helpful to see some examples. Unlike the research reviewed in other chapters, the following examples will focus on the methods and procedures used in the conduct of experiments. The attention to these details should reveal both the advantages and disadvantages surrounding experimentation as a way of asking questions about persuasion.

The first research example deals with source credibility, an area which ushered the field of speech communication into the social and behavioral sciences. The second research example deals with message information quantity and previously acquired information, an area which has been given some recent attention in speech communication journals.

Much can be learned by keeping a critical but constructive eye to the experimental process. Of course, it is always easier to be in the critic's role. When you encounter a criticism in the upcoming pages, ask yourself to what extent has the experimental method been incorrectly applied, improper conceptualization of the persuasive process occurred, or some combination of both. We shall return to this point at the end of this chapter.

Source Credibility

Source credibility has been one of the most frequently studied variables in the field of speech communication. Its popularity is most apparent in persuasion research. This is easily understood because sources which are perceived as more credible should be more influential than less credible sources. While this may appear rather obvious, investigators have sought to explore the precise conditions under which a highly credible source will prompt attitude change as well as an indication of the magnitude of the effect.

Unfortunately, source credibility is one variable plagued by "definitional overload" (Baxter, 1975). Beginning with Aristotle some 2300 years ago, the construct has been associated with perceptions of competence, intelligence, character, sincerity, believability, trustworthiness, dynamism, importance, prestige, status, reputation, and the list goes on and on. With conceptual definitions ranging from very general source attributions to very specific ones, it is critical that we know how a researcher is defining the construct.

The link between source credibility and persuasion was the subject of early speech communication research. In these studies, the same persuasive message was administered to all experimental groups while the level of source credibility varied across groups. If subjects were asked to assess the level of credibility, it was done as a check on the manipulation. Of paramount interest is the degree of attitude change found for the different levels of credibility. Haiman (1949) and Hovland and Weiss (1951) report experiments that are typical.

Haiman exposed three college audiences to a speech on national compulsory health insurance. Each audience heard from a different source. Audience X's source was Eugene Dennis, Secretary General of the Communist Party of America; audience Y's source was Dr. Thomas Parran, Surgeon General of the United States; and audience Z's source was an anonymous college sophomore from Northwestern University.

The experimental procedure was very simple. First, subjects were asked to indicate their opinion on Woodward's shift of opinion ballot. Second, they were exposed to the introductions of the sources. Third, they listened to the taped speech. Fourth, they marked their "after-speech" opinions (more sure, less sure, change to yes, change to no, or no change). Finally, they were asked to assess the speaker's reputation and competence on a 9-point rating scale.

The credibility assessment of reputation and competence was significantly higher for Parran than it was for Dennis or the college sophomore. (Actually, the college sophomore could not be assessed for reputation because he was unnamed.) On the shift of opinion ballot, Dr. Parran obtained a significantly greater shift of opinion than the other two sources. No significant differences existed between Dennis and the college sophomore.

In further analyzing the shift of opinion ballots, Haiman found that there was a significantly greater proportion of persons in audience Y (Parran) making favorable shifts of opinion than in the other two audiences. There was also a significantly smaller proportion of persons in audience Y remaining unchanged in opinion than in the other two audiences. Haiman concluded that the prestige of the speaker influences the effectiveness of the persuasive influence attempts.

Hovland and Weiss (1951) defined source credibility in terms of trustworthiness. The basic design of their study was also very simple. Approximately one week before receiving a persuasive message, subjects (undergraduate history students at Yale University) were pretested for their attitudes and an assessment of the trustworthiness of various sources. Identical persuasive messages were then presented to two groups, one with a trustworthy source associated with it, and one with an untrustworthy source associated with it. Immediately after reading the persuasive message and some four weeks later, subjects were requested to fill out a second questionnaire to measure opinion change.

Unlike Haiman's study, Hovland and Weiss avoided possible confounds due to the selection of a given topic by using four different topics. High and low credibility sources were associated with each topic. Pretesting revealed large differences in the evaluation of high and low credibility sources. Table 10.5 reveals the four topics, the eight sources, three of which are unnamed, and the percentage rating a source as trustworthy.

In addition to four topics and eight sources, Hovland and Weiss constructed an affirmative and negative version of each arguement, each with a strustworthy and untrustworthy source associated with it. Thus, there were 24 combinations of topic, version, and source, with each subject receiving only one combination.

Before looking at the amount of opinion change Hovland and Weiss reported, the experimental procedure they used to disassociate the pretesting from the experimental message and posttesting should be examined.

The pretest came to subjects as a general opinion survey conducted by a "National Opinion Survey Council." Several questions, including those pertaining to the four topics, were included. So as not to bias the responses to the messages, a guest lecturer was brought into the history class students were taking to mask the purpose of the experiment. The

TABLE 10.5   Credibility of Sources

Topic	Source	Percentage Rating Source Trustworthy
Antihistamines	New England Journal of Biology and Medicine	94.7
	Magazine A (monthly pictorial magazine	5.9
Atomic submarines	Robert J. Oppenheimer	93.7
	Pravada	1.3
Steel shortage	Bulletin of National Resources Planning Board	80.9
	Writer A ("rightist" newspaper columnist)	17.0
Future of movies	Fortune	89.2
	Writer B (gossip columnist)	21.2

guest lecturer stated that he was invited to discuss the psychology of communication. He informed students that he needed some "live data" from the class before he could discuss his subject matter. He then requested them to read several newspaper and magazine articles followed by a questionnaire. The posttest differed in format from the pretest, although the content items related to the four topics remained the same, so that a change score could be computed from before and after responses. The second posttest, administered one month after the first, was essentially the same.

Did the high credibility source elicit greater opinion change than the low credibility source? Table 10.6 shows the net change for trustworthy and untrustworthy sources for each of the four topics, as well as the average net change for all four topics given the different sources. The average difference was 14.1 percent. The likelihood that this difference was caused by chance is only 3 times in 100, or .03. Thus, this difference appears believable, allowing Hovland and Weiss to assert that trustworthy sources will affect greater attitude change than untrustworthy sources. The reader is referred to Hovland and Weiss for the results of other tests they conducted in this investigation.

Haiman's and Hovland and Weiss's research bears many of the earmarks of traditional persuasion research. Both employed a college sample, both used non-ego-involving topics, and both employed a public speaking/mass media model. In addition, no other persuasive outcome besides attitude

TABLE 10.6   Source Credibility and Opinion Change

Issue	Trustworthy Source	Untrustworthy Source	Net Attitude Source
Atomic submarines	36.0	0.6	35.4
Antihistamines	25.5	11.1	23.4
Steel shortage	18.2	7.4	10.8
Future of movies	12.9	17.2	-3.3
	22.5	8.4	14.1

change was assessed, and single-item response formats were used to measure source credibility.

As mentioned earlier, Hovland and Weiss wisely included four different topics rather than just one, as Haiman did. We therefore have an opportunity to assess directly whether the effect holds across topics. As Table 10.6 demonstrates, the magnitude of the effect is not constant across topics. To begin with, the effect holds for only three out of four topics, because in the last topic the untrustworthy source was more persuasive! Further, even for the three topics where the effect holds, it is evident that some topics are more prone to change than others when source credibility is considered.

In reanalyzing Hovland and Weiss's data, Zimbardo and Ebbesen (1970) found that the 14.1 percent difference in opinion change scores resulted from a 78.2 percent difference in trustworthiness scores. Recall that the 14.1 percent difference was found to be statistically significant (only 3 times in 100 could this effect occur by chance). While this effect has theoretical significance, Zimbardo and Ebbesen are quite correct in raising questions of its practical significance. Outside the laboratory, persons are rarely exposed to extremes in source credibility attributions. Thus, could any demonstrable effect on attitude change surface among sources slightly or even moderately differing in ethos? Probably not. Haiman's research provides some indirect support for this. Recall that the Communist party member and the college sophomore were not significantly different from one another on the competence dimension. Although Haiman did not report data, presumably these two sources would differ slightly in their level of credibility, because of their diverse natures. Assuming at least a small difference in credibility, it is interesting to note that there was no difference in the amount of opinion shift between groups.

While Haiman measured credibility in terms of two dimensions, competence and reputation, Hovland and Weiss treated source credibility undimensionally. Recall that they interpreted credibility to mean "trustworthy" and measured the construct on a single five-point scale with endpoints "trustworthy" and "untrustworthy." The single unidimensional rating scale was not an uncommon measurement technique in the early investigations of source credibility. Unfortunately, it became rather quickly outdated. Even though researchers like Hoveland and Weiss suspected the multidimensionality of the credibility construct, they continued to use a undimensional conceptualization and rating scale. All too often, researchers excell in experimental methods and procedures and are weaker in conceptualization and measurement of their variables. Any experiment, regardless of its procedures, is seriously compromised without this concern.

In speech communication, researchers spent much of their energy trying to discover the dimensionality or the determinants of the credibility construct (Berlo et al., 1970; McCroskey, 1966). In these studies, the basic procedure was very simple. Subjects (usually college students) were introduced to a number of sources possessing either high, moderate, or low credibility. They were then requested to complete a number of scales thought relevant to credibility assessment. For example, McCroskey (1966) used a combination of Likert items and semantic differentials. Berlo et al. (1970) used semantic differentials only, which was the norm. The scales were then subjected to a factor analysis that reduced the scales to a set of common dimensions.

While several investigators established the multidimensionality of the credibility construct, few could agree on the number, kind, and significance of the dimensions. For example, McCroskey's factor analysis produced an authoritativeness and character factor structure. Berlo et al. found three factors, safety, qualification, and dynamism.

The extent to which factor structures vary from one investigation to another is known as the factor invariance issue. Baxter (1975) makes the point that when scales from other investigations are applied uncritically and in an a priori fashion to another investigation, the factor invariance issue is virtually ignored. In other words, that one study uncovered three factors labled A, B, and C, does not necessarily follow that another study with different sources, a different sample, and different testing conditions will yield the same factors. This is especially relevant if semantic differentials are used, because of the likelihood of concept and rater-scale interactions.

We have strayed just a bit from our discussion of experimentation, but only to demonstrate that the measurement issue is inextricably tied to all other experimental procedures. Without correct construct conceptualization and measurement, the experiment is seriously compromised. The controversy surrounding the measurement of source credibility suggests that we must be cautious in interpreting the results of the countless investigations where source credibility has been used as either an independent or a dependent variable. Specific attention must be given to how credibility was conceptualized and measured, because different conceptions of the dimensionality, uncritical application of another's scales, or inattention to the analysis can preclude comparability across experiments.

Message Information Quantity and Previously Held Information

In a variety of studies, persuasion effects were demonstrated once sources of resistance to persuasion were controlled or effectively neutralized. One such source of resistance is the amount of information a receiver has acquired prior to treatment with a persuasive message. Because previously acquired information is already assimilated into a person's belief system, subsequent reception of the same information has reduced impact. Like many persuasive phenomena, no one theoretical approach can claim to have satisfactorily answered the questions surrounding the notion that information must be new to be effective.

McCroskey (1969) was among the first in speech communication to examine the effects of prior familiarity with information. This interest stemmed from a more general interest in the effects of evidence on persuasive communication. For example, McCroskey designed an experiment to test the effects of three variables on attitude change: evidence, prior familiarity with the evidence, and initial credibility. Initial level of credibility was included in the study because in previous research, evidence was found to be unnecessary to produce attitude change when the source is initially perceived as highly credible. Evidence was useful, however, in producing attitude change when the source was low to moderate in credibility.

Consequently, McCroskey hypothesized that evidence will increase attitude change and credibility only in the conditions including low credibility and no prior familiarity with the evidence. McCroskey manipulated two levels of credibility (high and low) and two levels of evidence (evidence and no evidence). Prior familiarity was manipulated by unobtrusively exposing one-half of the subjects to the evidence prior to exposure to the experimental speeches containing the same evidence. The topic of the speech was federal control of education. It was selected because it was assumed that subjects (college students) were unfamiliar with the evidence. After all subjects were pretested and one-half of them exposed to the evidence, all subjects listened to the experimental speeches. A posttest to measure change in attitude and source credibility was then given. The data supported McCroskey's hypothesis. Only subjects in the low credibility and low familiarity conditions experienced attitude change and a change in source credibility. McCroskey concluded information must be new to be effective.

Not unlike McCroskey, examining evidence and source credibility, Lashbrook et al. (1977) investigated the variables message information quantity and source credibility. Instead of using a merely uninformed audience, Lashbrook et al. used an exclusively apathetic (as opposed to neutral) audience whose prior knowledge and motivation to accrue knowledge were low. Once again, it was assumed prior knowledge would prompt resistance to attitude change. For apathetic audiences, they hypothesized that attitude change should be a linear function of the information received, assuming that credibility information and message quantity information could be summed. However, like McCroskey, they posited one qualification to their hypothesis. They argued that there was a limit on the amount of information that could be processed. This resulted in predictions of high message information levels and high credibility sources, producing an overload or highly redundant condition with little or no belief change. Thus, an inverted U relationship between levels of message information and attitude change was posited.

Lashbrook et al. first had to determine which subjects were apathetic with respect to a given issue. Program ARISTOTLE, an audience analysis computer program, was developed for just such a purpose. The authors manipulated two levels of credibility and three levels of message quantity. Message quantity was operationalized as the number of unique subissues judged relevant to the topic of revenue-sharing at the county government level. Thus, the high message information levels contained 16 subissues, the moderate information levels contained 8 subissues, and the low information level contained 4. The same 4 issues were included in the 8-issue message, and the same 8 issues were included in the 16-issue message. The issues in the 4-issue message were identified by Program ARISTOTLE as especially suitable for an apathetic audience. The 16-issue message and the high credible source was considered the information overload condition.

Some fifteen weeks after the collection of pretest data to identify the topic and the apathetics, the experimental treatment was administered. It consisted of several things: (1) a cover story for the experiment, (2) a source credibility induction followed by a check on this manipulation, (3) one of three persuasive messages (containing either 16, 8, or 4 issues on the topic), and (4) a posttest whose chief purpose was to measure attitude change.

A major advantage to the Lashbrook et al. study was the use of five independent control groups whose purpose was to test for the influence of variables external to the experiment. For example, to make sure attitudes did not change during the fifteen-week period between the pretest and the treatment, a group of subjects was tested for attitude change some three weeks after the pretest, a second group was tested six weeks after the pretest, and a third group was tested nine weeks after the pretest. There was no evidence of attitude change.

For the highly credible source, the inverted U relationship between message information quantity and attitude change was supported. However, this relationship was not supported for the low credibility source. Lashbrook et al. speculate that due to the filtering effects of low credibility, more information may be needed to produce attitude change than for high credibility sources.

Danes et al. (1978) proposed the accumulated information ratio to account for the inhibiting effects of previously held information. Attitude change is directly proportional to the amount of information in a message (message mass) and inversely proportional to the amount of previously held information (prior mass). Danes et al. prepared two messages, one involving the nuclear production of electricity and another involving USSR military strength. The college student sample received a treatment package containing (1) a pretest involving belief and prior information scales, (2) one of two persuasive messages where subjects were requested to read and underline the important parts of the article, and (3) a posttest containing the same belief and information scales used in the pretest.

This is the first study where prior information was actually measured and allowed to vary. It was operationalized as a joint index involving a self-report of the amount of information a subject perceived he or she possessed on the topic, as well as a frequency count of the number of times a topic had been heard in various settings (e.g., media, books, friends).

Danes et al. hypothesized that the accumulated information ratio is superior to those models that see belief change as merely a function of the amount of change requested with or without taking into account the degree of extremity and certainty in one's beliefs. Support was found for the superiority of the ratio, although the relative superiority of the model seemed topic-specific. There was a great deal more belief change for the nuclear message over the military message.

The research on the effects of message information quantity and previously accumulated information also bears many of the earmarks of traditional persuasion research. The samples were composed of college students, the topics were not ego-involving, and attitude change was the chief persuasive outcome. Additionally, other types of messages besides persuasive arguments were ignored (e.g., news reports, government documents), other channels besides written stimulus materials were not considered (e.g., interprersonal channels), and other types of decisions besides those that require a psychological commitment immediately after receiving the information were not requested (e.g., protracted decision-making periods). Lin (1971) and others argue that it is false to assume that different types of messages, different channels, and different time-based decision periods will produce the same effects.

Added to this are the extremes of message quantity investigators must go to in order to establish a particular effect. Some experimental tests of these variables have kept the amount of previously acquired information controlled and low, while administering large amounts of information to subjects in the stimulus. For example, Lashbrook et al. provided 16 subissues concerning the topic of revenue-sharing in the high information condition to an apathetic audience with little motivation or information. This is atypical of the information accumulation conditions in natural settings, where the levels of accumulated information are not controlled or are low but ever-increasing and subject to factors that inhibit memory. Further, large amounts of information are typically not received at any one point in time, but gradually, over time, thereby working to decrease the correlative effect established in the laboratory. Once again, investigators are forced to create a set of highly contrived conditions not likely to be found outside the laboratory to demonstrate the existence of an effect.

Finally, problems in variable operationalization surface when accumulated information is allowed to vary. Danes et al. operationalized prior information on a number of subjective knowledge scales (know a lot/know a little, aware/not aware, knowledgeable/not knowledgeable) as distinguished from objective knowledge assessment. Their reasoning seemed justifiable in that misinformed subjects would be classified as lacking information, even though incorrect information still provides resistance to persuasive attempts. Unfortunately, subjective knowledge scales are self-reports of knowledge, and all the many problems with self-report data are present. Chief among these problems is the social desirability factor. Subjects are unlikely to report low levels of information for some topics for fear of appearing stupid. There is also some question as to whether subjects can correctly assess the amount of information they have accumulated. Some people chronically overestimate their level of knowledge on certain topics, while experts in some fields would underestimate their knowledge level.

Conclusion

We have just presented several examples of traditional persuasion research in the areas of source credibility and message information quantity. In our discussion of each study, we tried to focus specifically on the experimental process, with a particular emphasis on the problems that can arise. It is hoped that this critical focus has not prevented us from giving a fair portrayal of each research effort.

The problems that surfaced in the source credibility and message quantity research examples were similar. For example, both sets of examples used a college-based sample and both experienced some measurement problems. There were, however, three more important problem similarities. First, both employed a public speaking or mass media model, excluding interpersonal persuasion. Second, both used messages dealing with issues that were not ego-involving. Third, both ignored persuasive outcomes other than attitude change. These three problem similarities are important to our assessment of persuasion theory and the frequent use of experimental methods. Recall that earlier we asked you to consider whether the problems in the research examples were the result of an incorrect use of the experimental method, weak conceptualizing of the persuasion process, or some combination of both. What conclusions have you drawn? What implications exist for future persuasion research?

It appears that there has been an overreliance on experimental methods to study persuasion. However, the problems in traditional persuasion research are chiefly the result of too narrowly defining the persuasion process. When researchers ignored interpersonal persuasion (and the reciprocal nature of the influence process), ego-involving issues, and effects other than attitudes, these were conceptual—not methodological—

decisions. They were decisions limiting the questions that could be asked about persuasion, which in turn precipitated the decline of persuasion research.

Thus we really cannot fault experimental methods. Their overuse was more a symptom than a cause of the problem. Indeed, the research examples presented here, and much of traditional persuasion research in general, are well-run experiments defensible by today's standards. Miller and Burgoon (1978) concur: "The problem lies not with the quality of the individual studies, but rather with the impoverished conceptual foundation imposed by the traditional view of persuasion."

Thus, the experiment can remain an important source of information about persuasion, but an even more central question remains: Is there hope for persuasion research? That is the subject of the next chapter.

Chapter 11

SOME FUTURE METHODOLOGICAL

CONSIDERATIONS

In this text a new perspective on persuasion has been introduced that does not deny the value of "older" views. On the contrary, much early twentieth-century work in persuasion articulated a perspective on persuasion that afforded greater prediction than had previously been known. The substantial progress made serves as a foundation for the theoretical model advanced in this text.

Kuhn describes the obligation of new theory as involving changes which impinge on the areas of special competence that a bevy of researchers have given a lifetime to develop. It is impossible to deny the value of their contributions without denying in some way the value of their own existence. Resistance is thus inevitable and necessary. It compels researchers to find reasons why they can or cannot accept prior theory and requires that they familiarize themselves with the constructs and rules of their mentors, so that knowledge becomes a process of accretion rather than sporadic replacements. In fact, it is likely that no great idea ever existed which, if put into print, would not require at least one footnote.

The dependency of present theory on the past is what led Kuhn (1975: 7) to propose that "a new theory, however special its range of application, is seldom or never just an increment to what is already known. Its assimilation requires the reconstruction of prior theory and the reevaluation of prior fact, an intrinsically revolutionary process that is seldom completed by a single man and never overnight."

This process view of theoretical development implies that to each change there is a season, a time when the scientific community is ready to consider alternatives. Now is such a time for persuasion. The embers of prior battles are still exuding smoke, but the front is quiet and most soldiers have gone on to other wars. As indicated in Chapter 1, researchers are calling for a new perspective on persuasion, not so much out of a nostalgic preoccupation with history, but because of what Miller and Burgoon (1978: 45) describe as "the inexorable pervasiveness of the persuasion process."

If persons were not responsible for their actions, then persuasion would merely consist of revising the antecedent conditions of the behavior in question to include those conditions known necessarily to lead to the preferred behavior. As responsible agents of their behaviors, aware that their choices will be used by others to formulate impressions, people interpret antecedent conditions and look ahead to behavioral consequences before choosing a particular course of action. It is therefore virtually impossible to create a set of antecedent conditions that will inevitably lead to the selection of the preferred behavior. Instead, the persuader must identify the persuadee's logic for the application of a particular rule. Then he or she must demonstrate that the prerequisites for the application of that rule are present, whereas the prerequisites for alternative rules are absent. Given their awareness of responsibility and the need to be appreciated by significant others, people make choices on the basis of underlying logics composed of "owned" and "borrowed" rules. Each behavioral choice is considered thoroughly logical to the actor if it is perceived by him or her as consistent with his or her personal rules, appropriate according to the expectations of relevant others, and an effective means to the attainment of a desired consequent. If a persuader can convince the actor that one of these prerequisites to assessing a behavior as logical is missing, the chances of altering that behavior are enhanced.

Prevailing models of persuasion have not adequately addressed the influence of people's logics on their behavior. Dray (1963) attempted to describe human behavior as characteristically rational. However, his definition of rationality was not sufficiently "rigorous" to direct future scientific investigations. To him all that was necessary to define a behavior as rational was to show that it made good sense from the agent's own point of view.

While Dray's perspective placed Hempel's (1942) concept of necessary cause in question, it erred in the direction of giving the agent too much credit for the sensibility of his or her actions. People need the approval of self and others and therefore they rarely behave in purely rational ways. Rationality is not unidimensional. As indicated in previous chapters, people often violate one rule to accommodate another. They can and do act inappropriately on occasion to avoid being inconsistent or ineffective. They behave irrationally in one sense to be rational in another sense.

A conceptualization of behavior consistent with the perspective advanced in this text is that people do attempt to behave in ways that make sense to themselves and others. The sensible nature of a behavior, however, is not inherent in the action, the actor, or the context. It is found in their interrelationship. If the context is predominant, as in formal organizations, the self is submerged as a generative mechanism and personal rule consistency may be sacrificed for behavioral appropriateness. In those situations where self-autonomy is valued, personal rules are of greater import than context rules to behavioral selection. In such cases, the personal rules are used to determine what is rational. Often, as in cults, and even in the typical viewer-television relationship, people relinquish the self-autonomy they could exercise in behavioral choice and follow a set of "borrowed" rules. In extreme cases, the self fails to check and balance extrinsic rules and the individual becomes vulnerable to those who make the rules.

Given this perspective on self-autonomy and context predominance, blind following of charismatic leaders and total commitment to organizations becomes explainable. As long as people operate in or create in their minds alternative contexts which challenge the rules of the predominant context, self remains intact. To the extent that self is relinquished, people are unable to prepare counterarguments and thus become cognitively imprisoned by one set of originally extrinsic rules.

Our society encourages each individual to spend a good part of his or her day as a member of a predominant organization. To the extent that the individual accommodates his or her rules to meet the demands of that context, personal rule-organizational role interpenetration occurs, and the individual becomes predictable and thus vulnerable to persuasion. Appropriateness and consistency are the same to this person. His or her source of checks and balances ceases to operate.

Most persons are not so enmeshed in one organization that they lose themselves. On the contrary, each situation in which individuals find themselves offers a different self-context balance. The persuader must determine the extent to which the persuadee perceives himself or herself as an autonomous agent. As mentioned in previous chapters, the level of persuadee self-autonomy influences the success of consistency, appropriateness, or effectiveness appeals. If an individual perceives that he or she has no choice, then consistency appeals are destined to failure. This individual does not consider himself or herself responsible for inconsistent behavior if the context does not allow autonomous behavior. If, however, the appropriateness or effectiveness of the choice can be brought into question, persuasion is possible.

IMPLICATIONS FOR SCIENCE

According to Seibold (1975: 5) a major pitfall of previous persuasion theory has been the "failure to specify theoretically the relationships among messages, underlying attitudes, verbal responses and actions." Seibold considers one challenge facing future theory to be identification and precise specification of the logical relationships among components within the attitude-behavior framework.

The theoretical model proposed in this text, then, must at least begin to meet this challenge. Before attempting to specify component relationships, let us first briefly review what has been proposed. Regulative rules tell a person those combinations of objects, persons, and events (constitutive rules) that render a given behavior sensible (consistent, appropriate, effective). The persuader must determine not only what personal, social, and situation-relevant rules exist in the persuadee's repertoire, but also the activation or application order of these rules.

Earlier in this text rule relevance and order was described as a function of the self-autonomy-context predominance balance. To the extent that self-autonomy is afforded by the context and valued by the persuadee, personal rule consistency appeals are useful. To the extent that contextual considerations predominate, appropriateness and effectiveness gain importance. When the consistent thing to do is to behave appropriately and effectively, these three normative dimensions collapse. Typically, however, they coexist as three sources of normative pressure influencing behavioral choice.

This tripartite differentiation among rules impinging upon behavior, unlike many earlier theoretical perspectives, suggests an important role for communication. Persuader appeals can be directed at prioritizing personal, social, or situational rules in a manner conducive to the desired behavior change. McDermott (1974: 16) makes a similar claim when she states, "To trigger an actor's rules of relationship, messages may (1) focus on can (personal choice), (2) demonstrate should (social reality), or (3) encourage trying (physical reality)."

In terms of the theoretical model in this text, the persuader's job is effectively to guarantee that a sense of consistency, appropriateness, and/or effectiveness will obtain should the persuadee follow the proposed behavioral prescription. Seibold's (1975) discussion of correlation-depressive mitigating variables suggests that such guarantees may be necessary but not sufficient causes of behavior change. For example, a person's locus of control, prior commitments, and certainty about the message subject can influence his or her reception of consistency appeals. Similarly, receptivity to appropriateness appeals may be influenced by persuadee status, persuader credibility, visibility, and importance of the significant others involved. Finally, the reception of effectiveness appeals may be mitigated by the relevance of the situation, time involved, and consequent desirability.

McGuire's (1973) reception-response tendencies dichotomy is useful here. People may receive information regarding behavioral consistency, appropriateness, and effectiveness directly, but they process it as it relates to other important considerations. These process biases influence the extent to which two response tendencies—verbal and behavioral—are correlated, a condition further mitigated by the cognitive effort involved in the realignment of constructs and rules proposed in the message.

The model in Figure 11.1 provides a framework for viewing the interrelationships of those theoretical components introduced in this text. The scientist must determine through observation and subject report which of those variables specified have the most relevance to his or her specific investigation. For example, if the context under study is highly formal (athletic team, military group), appeals to personal consistency are likely to exert less influence on effort than appropriateness appeals. Moreover, operational definitions for each must be rigorously determined and intersubjective agreement derived so that the confusion among variables characteristic of early research is not regenerated.

THE IMPORTANCE OF RULE PRECISION

The model proposed in this chapter assumes the presence of one very important prerequisite to message development. The researcher must be familiar with the context under study so that he or she may determine which rules must be subordinated to the preferred rule. Context familiarity is not something we have required of social scientists. Our uncritical acceptance of student subject pools may be at fault. As we move out into more interesting contexts, however, familiarity with rule systems becomes a necessity. Philipsen's (1975) "Speaking Like a Man in Teamsterville:

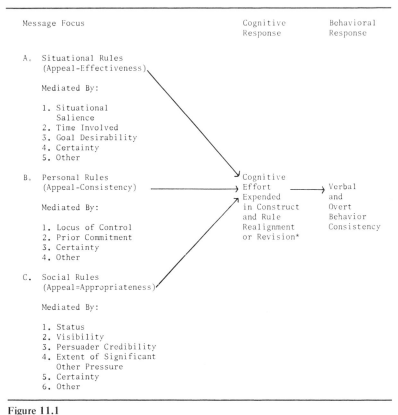

Figure 11.1

NOTE: See Seibold (1975) for discussion of situational and effort thresholds.

Culture and Patterns of Role Enactment in an Urban Neighborhood"
provides an example of the type of preinvestigation research requisite to
the construction of effective persuasive messages. The researcher must
make it his or her business to know the rules of community under study.

This requirement of rule familiarity brings us to one major limitation of
rules theory. Hewes (1978) sees rules theories as facing the problem of
"imprecision in specifying a set of criteria independent of the rules
themselves which distinguish those behaviors, acts, or interaction
sequences representative of underlying rules from those which are due to
accident or choice (see Kaufer, 1976). Hewes claims that "without a
precise set of criteria for specifying the domain of observations amenable

to rules explanation, all rules theories are inherently unfalsifiable; that is, any counter-examples can be dismissed as having been the result, either of choice not to follow the rule, or accident."

At the very least the theoretical framework proposed in this text affords the ground rules for rule rejection. First, "accidents" imply a lack of responsibility for action. According to the framework introduced in previous chapters, such absence of responsibility occurs infrequently. What appears accidental is often the result of discrepancy in researcher and subject construals of the antecedent conditions. Accidents, in the purest sense, are rare in communication behavior, even if the actor claims them as an account. What the researcher considers an accident may actually be purposeful following of a rule. In short, accidents in Hewes's terms are really the result of rule subordination. To the extent that many people subordinate the expected rule to another rule, the researcher expectation is falsified. His or her hypothesis is rejected. People do not misconstrue antecedent conditions in large numbers. To the extent that their construals are similar but differ from that of the researcher, it is the researcher who has had an "accident." To the extent that the researcher and the majority of the subjects agree, the accident (although perhaps very logical to the actor) belongs to the subject who followed an alternative (deviant) rule.

Rules, like gravity, are fictions that constrain behavior. When gravity is defied by astronauts we do not deny the existence of gravity, nor do we refer to the behavior of the astronauts as "accidental"—unusual, perhaps, but definitely purposeful and, from their perspective, rational. When a woman dresses for comfort rather than "for success" can we deny that a rule for appropriate dress exists? We can only assume that she did not know the rule or chose to deny it. Even when a rule is applied inappropriately, at the time of its application it may have seemed rational to the actor. Once the actor recognizes that certain previously unseen conditions render the choice inappropriate, ineffective, or inconsistent, he or she may refer to the action as an accident, when in all probability it was not.

What I believe Hewes wants from rules theorists is some agreement concerning the point at which a rule can be considered inoperative. This is where rule theorists have been negligent. By considering rules personal as well as consensual we have made it possible to explain everything as a result of rules. When consensus is not obtained the rules theorist merely says, "Oh, well, no problem. My subjects have merely chosen to follow their personal rules." The scope conditions of rules theory are thus nonexistent.

This cannot go on if rules theory is to remain within the domain of science and a useful scalpel for dissecting the persuasion process. Hewes is correct in his call for some set of criteria for specifying the domain of observations amenable to rules explanation.

Let us consider for a moment a rule with high consensus. Assume that you have entered an elevator with an unfamiliar person. As the two of you ascend to the fortieth floor the stranger ceases to look up at the numbers and begins to talk about the weather. Would this be sufficient grounds for denying the existence of the elevator silence rule common in our society? Probably not. However, should five other persons enter the elevator and each in turn begin to speak to you, your elevator behavior rule might be in jeopardy. Should five more enter and do the same, the case might be closed. In this example, the set of criteria called for by Hewes is provided by the elevator context. Typically, elevators afford little self-autonomy when dealing with strangers. This generality of application raises the invalidation threshold. Without numerous deviations, the rule cannot be invalidated. It is the obligation of the researcher to be sufficiently familiar with the extent of autonomy afforded by the context under study to set a reasonable invalidation threshold. Invalidation will not deny the existence of the rule, but rather its appropriateness in the specific context or type of context. Similarly, familiarity with a particular individual or type of individual allows us to designate behavior consistency thresholds. The statement, "That's not at all like you," indicates that some rule typically followed by the person to whom the statement is addressed has been violated.

The invalidation threshold for situations involves numbers or percentages of persons in disagreement. The rule invalidation thresholds for an individual involves the number of deviations by that individual. If my friend speaks to all persons entering the elevator, I may assume that the elevator rule is either not in his repertoire or substantially subordinate to other rules. I cannot assume that the rule does not exist for society in general. If he stops talking to me when others enter the elevator, then I may assume that he only uses the silence rule when there are more than two persons in the elevator. I may then qualify the range of convenience of that rule so that his behavior will not surprise me in the future. By incorporating this contextual consideration, I increase the determinancy of the silence rule.

Hewes (1981: 49) argues that any adequate description of human behavior and cognition requires the acceptance of "a range of indeterminancy." He explains further that "no individual can reasonably be expected to have complete control of his or her social environment, especially the other people in that environment." The question facing rules theorists is, How extensive can that range of indeterminancy be before a rule is designated inoperable? The larger question is, Just how much indeterminancy can any theory incorporate before it no longer fits into the realm of science?

Another problem facing the rules theorist concerns mediating variables. If individuals cannot completely control their social environments, it follows that researchers cannot do so either. The rules theorist must determine how to deal with mediating variables previously given as reasons for the absence of significant rule effects. Hewes suggests that we turn to stochastic theories to deal with intraindividual variables, such as attitudes, beliefs, and expectations. He explains that such theories can accommodate the influences of mediating variables, such as environmental factors, and can map out the probabilities of a closed set of behaviors under a specified set of conditions.

Hewes further suggests that we designate regions of acceptance, rejection, and neutrality when predicting behavior. Each region defines evaluatively similar behavior with similar probabilities of, in terms of the persuasion model in this text, rule activation or application. Hewes explains that the choice probabilities are unstable within each region (so close as to inhibit accurate prediction), whereas the probability of change between regions is quite stable and therefore predictable, given certain circumstances. The tripartite perspective on persuasion advanced herein suggests that those "circumstances" involve persuadee perceptions of behavioral inconsistency, inappropriateness, and/or ineffectiveness.

As discussed in Chapter 2, rules specify *types* of behavior and can thus be viewed as specifying regions of acceptance (obligatory, preferred, and permissible behaviors), neutrality (irrelevant behaviors), and rejection (prohibited behaviors) as well. To know the persuadee's cognitive linkages between context and rule repertoire can facilitate a priori identification of regions of acceptance, neutrality, and rejection.

As a researcher becomes familiar with a given subject population and context, he or she is likely to find that some behaviors belonging to the region of acceptance of one rule also belong to logically adjacent rules. Figure 11.2 depicts this condition. Such instances pose prediction problems, but a knowledge of rule arrangement should nevertheless improve our present ability to anticipate behavioral choices accurately.

Rule Adjacency Model

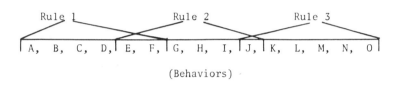

Rule Repertoire

for

Context Q

with

Desired Consequent P

(Behaviors)

Figure 11.2   Rule Adjacency Model

Specifying regions of acceptance, neutrality, and rejection is equivalent to determining what has been referred to in this text as the "range of convenience" of a rule. The researcher must determine when a behavior is too deviant (clearly outside the region predicted) to consider it within the range of convenience of a particular rule. In this way, rules may be designated inoperable for the context or person under study.

CONTEXTUAL CONSIDERATIONS

Linking rules to contexts is one of the toughest tasks facing the persuader and researcher. Nevertheless, context is the key to appropriate designations of ranges of acceptance, neutrality, and rejection. Hewes (1981), in his own stochastic theory of the behavioral effects of message campaigns, recognized that historical processes can influence linkages between messages and behavioral choices. Strong links between context and rule activation or application in one decade can be weak in the next. The researcher is thus obligated to "keep on top of the situation" by knowing as much about the way subjects see a context of action as he or she can.

Ellis (1980: 104-105) defines situation as "an intact assembly of people, objects, time, and space." He adds that "the configurations of these people and objects in time and space contrains behavior," and he suggests that interactions vary in the configuration of situational components.

Ellis's definition breaks situation down a bit, so that we might consider certain aspects of the situation as the reason for its predominance or lack thereof. Time or spacial requirements may render some personal behavioral preferences irrational. For example, a relationship may be too new for a woman to propose marriage, or the rules of the larger societal context may define that behavior as indicative of unfeminine agressiveness. Her self-autonomy is thus constrained, unless she wishes to take the risk that her partner will find such deviance delightfully refreshing.

What this text has proposed is a model of human behavior that combines both person and environment. It is a model that assumes people will continue to cogitate and emote no matter how much the natural scientist in us wishes to deny it. We must free ourselves from a blind commitment to one-sided objectivity, which, by its very nature, is subjective. We must learn to understand under what conditions people rely predominantly on their own personal rules for behavioral choice and when they allow or are forced to accept context predominance. We must train ourselves to utilize the subjects' versions of reality and to recognize how those versions are derived. Finally, we must be willing to set rule invalidation thresholds.

Whether this is a sufficient response to Hewes's call for rules theory to specify its domain is not yet clear. It does appear to be a start. As we continue to develop situational and relationship taxonomies while at the same time attempting to allow the subjects to become active members in the discovery process, imposed and induced approaches may become complementary. The selection of one over the other will be the researcher's choice, explainable in terms of his or her research questions.

Another challenge facing rules theorists lies in discovering how to utilize subject input to determine the extent to which self-autonomy influences consensual rules. The methods discussed by Fairhurst in Chapter 10 hold some promise but reflect primarily imposed approaches to persuasion study. If used appropriately, verbal reports may provide a means of checking and balancing these experimenter-imposed versions of reality. Let us take a closer look at this controversial procedure.

SELF-AUTONOMY AND THE
PROBLEM OF PREDICTION

Throughout this text we have postulated that people impose organization on their environments. For this reason, external reality can never be
known directly. As Kant (1952) suggests, a sensory barrier comes between
us and the palpability of matter. He refers to reality as the "noumenal"
and experienced reality as the "phenomenal." He compares our experience
of reality to the wearing of spectacles. On our side of the spectacles is the
phenomenal realm, and on the other side is the noumenal realm. The
spectacles have an organizing power that can be compared to the organizing power of constructs and rules. They help us to see, but they prevent us
from seeing what is supposedly really "out there." They also enable us to
consider two diverse aspects of reality as similar. Rychlak (1977) proposes
that people use tautologies in their reasoning to make one thing also
another. He explains that those who consider all redheads to be hotheaded
have created a tautological relationship that simplifies reality for them.
Obviously, this opinion is not as extrospectively tautological as the statement, "All bachelors are unmarried males," but it serves as a tautological
relationship for the person who believes it. People create tautologies so
that they can deal with experience. The scientist who decides to ignore all
fallacious tautologies believed by his or her subjects is acting like a doctor
who denies that a patient has swallowed sand because it is such a ridicu-
lous thing to do. People develop ways of categorizing their worlds for their
own use. The experimenter must identify these modes of categorization
because people are often committed to them, despite any hint of fallacy.

Assuming, then, that behavior is predicated on the modes of cognitive
organization utilized by an individual, it is reasonable to expect that
certain of these modes of organization will be dominant. These dominant
premises must be identified by persuaders, since they are likely to exert
the greatest influence on behavioral selection. In Chapter 5, this hierarchi-
cality was described in terms of superordinate constructs which, together
with desired consequents, impose an order on behavioral options. The
persuader's primary task is to determine whether these constructs are
predominantly context- or self-oriented so that he or she may determine
whether to use appeals to appropriateness, consistency, or effectiveness.

In this section we shall focus on the methods researchers might use to
deal with those contexts in which self-autonomy is allowed or even predominant. At the outset it should be mentioned that the self can itself be a
type. In other words, to suggest that an individual is behaving in a
self-autonomous manner means that he or she has placed "borrowed" rules

in a subordinate position to those he or she perceives as "owned." The word *perceives* is very important here. The perception of rule ownership is a prerequisite to having a sense of self. Whether others perceive that a particular role also "belongs" to them does not deny the individual ownership rights. Rules can have many owners. Moreover, it is possible that ownership of one rule implies ownership of one or more others. To the extent that people share rules or rule sets, they are homophilous.

Before embarking on an investigation into types of persons based on reports of similar rules, it is important to recognize that knowledge of rule ownership alone does not provide sufficient information to predict behavior. People can differ in the priorities they assign to those rules, or what was referred to in Chapter 2 as the underlying logic of rule application. This logic may be inferred from the context, but when the self is allowed to operate as a generative mechanism, it is necessary that researchers determine whether the subject sees the interaction of self and situation as they do. At this juncture verbal reports become important.

An article by Ericsson and Simon (1980), "Verbal Reports as Data," provides an optimistic note in an otherwise pessimistic medley of verbal report attacks. Ericsson and Simon (1980: 216) explain that the "notion that verbal reports provide possibly interesting but only informal information to be verified by other data has had a significant effect on the ways in which verbalizations are collected and analyzed." Perhaps out of a reluctance to accept verbal reports, we have been sloppy in our dealings with them. The authors begin their classification of different species of verbalizations by proposing that they may be concurrent with task performance or retrospective. They explain that concurrent generalizations can influence the course and structure of cognitive processes if subjects are asked to verbalize information that (1) would not otherwise be heeded in the normal course of processing, or (2) could not easily be coded in a verbal code.

If, for example, a researcher attempting to uncover the reasons behind the application of a particular rule were to request of the subject information not readily available to him or her during the actual application of the rule (due, perhaps, to the functional autonomy of the rule from its logic as a result of years of application), incomplete or inaccurate accounts are likely to result and influence the course of future action and cognitive processing. Studies by Gagné and Smith (1962) and Wilder and Harvey (1971) indicate that instructions to verbalize reasons for behavior induce more detailed planning. The likely result is an artificial series of behaviors not reflective of uninterrupted action and thus of little use in providing a basis for prediction.

Given the problems associated with concurrent verbalizations, a researcher might choose to use retrospective verbalizations. Here, too, however, problems arise. Ericsson and Simon explain that time lapses between actual behavior and verbal accounts often render the information available in short-term memory during concurrent verbalizations unavailable for retrospective reporting. Also, if the questions put to subjects provide background information or imply a correct answer, subjects are likely to generate answers without consulting their own memories.

It appears then that both concurrent and retrospective verbal reporting have their limitations and require careful attention to the conditions under which researchers can expect accurate reporting. Ericsson and Simon's model specifically rejects the use of verbal reports to discover how subjects believe they would have acted under different experimental conditions, or why they behaved differently from another subject. Such information is not likely to be stored in memory, and so responses are by necessity fabrications. Fabrication is less likely to be a problem when high-consensus rule accounts are requested than when low-consensus accounts are requested.

The problems with verbal reports described by Ericsson and Simon are actually problems with their users. Asking subjects for information that has no relation to what they are or were actually thinking at the time of the behavior in question cannot lead to veridical reports. Expecting verbalizations to render complete accounts for behavior is often unrealistic, especially since some very familiar behaviors may move from cognitively controlled to what Ericsson and Simon refer to as "automatic status." In such cases, complete and accurate accounts may be more available to the researcher than to the subject. This places the burden on the researcher to discover just how much information he or she can expect to derive from verbal reports and how much must come from his or her own observations. Ericsson and Simon (1980: 241) consider incompleteness insufficient grounds for rejecting verbal reports: "Incompleteness of reports may make some information unavailable, but it does not invalidate the information that is present."

When the behavior(s) in question have been followed for years, the cognitive connection of behavior to its logic is likely to be fuzzy for the actor. Those new to the context under investigation may be capable of providing more complete accounts than their experienced associates, since they are in the rule-learning phase (Reardon et al., 1980). Ericsson and Simon consider the novice a better source of information in those cases where behavior has become "automatic."

If the researcher is interested in hypothetical behavior (e.g., What would you do if . . .?), then his or her task is complicated by the fact that the subject's memory may not contain a reference to the situation described. The response the subject gives may be derived from a memory of a remotely similar context. Unless the researcher is sufficiently familiar with the subject population or willing to invest time in a series of important pretests, the likelihood of creating realistic hypothetical situations is minimal and the accuracy of prediction, therefore, threatened. Unfortunately, this usually leads to an attack on verbal reports rather than a critique of their users.

CONCLUSION

The goal of this chapter is not to advocate the use of verbal reports. As Capella (1977) and Hewes (1978) contend, adoration of any one methodology is "the only sin." Hewes believes that the way to circumvent increases in law-of-the-hammer approaches is to have many hammers, in the same way that a person needs enmeshments in several contexts to avoid the pitfalls of myopic cognitive logic. The purpose of this chapter is to assist researchers in avoiding methodological myopia not reflective of the subject matter under investigation. As Hewes (1978: 165) says, "any test of a theory is really a test of the assumptions of that theory and the assumptions of the methodology used in the study."

Seibold (1979: 35) has described the field of communication as characterized by a critical absence of "weedpullers—critics from within or outside the scientific community who make public their scrutiny of the field's findings and fallacies." This chapter has exposed some of the weeds of rules theory and communication science in general. It is unproductive to become so infatuated with weed-pulling that we destroy the entire garden. There is always value in past work, as there is fault in the present.

In this text, criticism of past and present work has been accomplished without uprooting the garden. In an effort to locate the best of persuasion study, some weeds were pulled and some seeds planted, but the task remains incomplete. What I have perceived as plants may be seen as weeds by others. The import accorded to self- and context-balance in the selection of persuasion strategy and scientific method, the definition of persuasion as a reciprocal activity, the emphasis placed on underlying logics varying in their accessibility, the integrations of past and present theories, and the extensions of my colleagues' ideas to other contexts are all, as yet, untested. While I sit back now to appreciate and criticize this garden, other weeds will no doubt pop up and previously unnoted ones will become apparent. Such is the process of science. What was once my garden is now a community garden As Kuhn (1975: 210) suggests, "scientific knowledge, like language, is intrinsically the common property of a group or else nothing at all."

It is wise to remember that gardens reflect, but are not, reality. Nature does not place flowers and plants together in the same way that humans do. Humans select the plants that impress them most, and, remembering the season, the climate, and the terrain, they arrange their selections in some personally meaningful order. Scientists, like gardeners, borrow ideas and create some of their own, but the result can only be a "rendezvous with reality," not a possession of it. In this text much has been borrowed and some created. Whether one accepts or rejects the configuration does not deny the existence of persuasion. It is the reality upon which the theoretical model in this text was advanced and the core of human social existence, a fact which no amount of planting or weed-killing can alter.

BIBLIOGRAPHY

Abelsen, R. P. and Rosenberg, M. J. Symbolic psycho-logic: A model of attitudinal cognition. Behavioral Science 3 (1958), 1-13.

Adorno, T. E., Frenkel-Brunswick, D. L., and Sanford, R. The Authoritarian Personality. New York: Harper & Row, 1950.

Ajzen, I. and Fishbein, M. The prediction of behavioral intentions in a choice situation. Journal of Experimental Social Psychology 5 (1969), 400-416.

Ajzen, I. and Fishbein, M. Attitudes and normative beliefs as factors influencing behavioral intentions. Journal of Personality and Social Psychology, 27 (1973), 41-57.

Alderton, S. M. Group decisions on responsibility for socially deviant behavior: Locus of control in situation and attributor. Presented at the International Communication Association, Philadelphia, 1979.

Alpert, M. I., and Anderson, W. T. Optimal heterophily and communication effectiveness—Some empirical findings. Journal of Communication 23 (1973), 328-343.

Allport, G. W. The Nature of Prejudice. Reading, MA: Addison-Wesley, 1954.

Andersen, P. A., Garrison, J. P., and Andersen, J. F. Implications of a neurophysiological approach for the study of nonverbal communication. Human Communication Research 6 (1979), 74-89.

Anderson, K. and Clevenger, T. A summary of experimental research in ethos. In The Process of Social Influence, ed. T. D. Beiseker and D. W. Parson. Englewood Cliffs, NJ: Prentice-Hall, 1972, 223-247.

Anderson, N. H. Integration theory and attitude change. Psychological Review 78 (1971), 171-206.

Argyris, C. Interpersonal Competence and Organizational Effectiveness. Homewood, IL: Irwin. 1962.

Argyris, C. Integrating the Individual and the Organization. New York: John Wiley, 1964.

Aronson, E. Dissonance theory: Progress and problems, in Theories of Cognitive Consistency: A Sourcebook, ed. R. P. Abelson et al. Skokie, IL: Rand McNally, 1968.

Atkin, C. Parent-child communication in supermarket breakfast cereal selection. In Effects of Television Advertising on Children, Report 7. East Lansing: Michigan State University, October, 1975a.

Atkin, C. Survey of children and mothers' responses to television commercials. In Effects of Television Advertising on Children, Report 8. East Lansing: Michigan State university, December, 1975b.

Atkinson, J. W. Motivational determinants of risk-taking behavior. Psychological Review 64 (1957), 359-372.

Baird, J. E., Jr. and Bradley, P. H. Study of management and communication: A comparative study of men and women. Communication Monographs 46 (1979), 101-111.

Bannister, D. Psychology as an exercise in paradox. Bulletin of the British Psychological Society 19 (1966), 21-26.

Bannister, D. The myth of physiological psychology. Bulletin of the British Psychological Society 21 (1968).

Bannister, D. and Fransella, F. Inquiring Man. New York: Penguin Books, 1977.

Bannister, D. and Mair, J.M.M. The Evaluation of Personal Constructs. New York: Academic Press, 1968.

Barrett, J. H. Individual Goals and Organizational Objectives. Ann Arbor, MI: Institute for Social Research, 1977.

Bartlett, F. C. Remembering: A Study in Experimental and Social Psychology. Cambridge, England: Cambridge University Press, 1967.

Bateson, G. Steps to an Ecology of Mind. New York: Ballantine, 1972.

Bauchner, J. E. Accuracy in detecting deception as a function of level of relationship and communication history. Doctoral dissertation, Michigan State University, 1978.

Bauchner, J. E., Brandt, D. R., and Miller, G. R. The truth/deception attribution: Effects of varying levels of information availability. In Communication Yearbook 1, ed. B. Rubin. New Brunswick, NJ: Transaction, 1977.

Bauer, R. A. and Greyser, A. A. Advertising in America: The Consumer View. Boston: Harvard Business School, 1968.

Baxter, L. An investigation of the convergent and construct validity of nonmetric multi-dimensional scaling analysis of source credibility. Doctoral dissertation, University of Oregon, 1975.

Beach, W. A. A reflexive analysis of conversational sequencing in group systems. International Communication Association Convention, Acapulco, 1980.

Bem, D. J. An experimental analysis of self-persuasion. Journal of Experimental Social Psychology 1 (1965), 199-218.

Bem, D. J. Attitudes as self-descriptions: Another look at the attitude-behavior link. In Psychological Foundations of Attitudes, ed. A. G. Greenwald et al. New York: Academic Press, 1968, 197-215.

Bem, D. J. Self-perception theory. In Advances in Experimental Social Psychology, ed. L. Berkowitz. New York: Academic Press, 1972, 1-62.

Bem, D. J. and McConnell, H. K. Testing the self-perception explanation of dissonance phenomena: On the salience of premanipulation attitudes. Journal of Personality, 14 (1970), 23-41.

Berger, C. R. Toward a role enactment theory of persuasion. Speech Monographs 39 (1972), 260-276.

Berger, C. R. The acquaintance process revisited: Explorations in initial interacrion. Speech Communication Association Convention, New York, 1973.

Berger, C. R. Proactive and retroactive attribution processes. Human Communication Research 2 (1975), 33-50.

Berger, C. R. Interpersonal communication theory and research: An overview. In Interpersonal Communication: A Relational Perspective, ed. W. Morse and L. Phelps. Minneapolis: Burgess, 1979, 3-16.

Berger, C. R. Self-consciousness and the adequacy of theory and research into relationship development. Western Journal of Speech Communication 44 (1980), 93-97.

Berger, C. R. and Calabrese, R. Some explorations in initial interaction and beyond: Toward a developmental theory of interpersonal communication. Human Communication Research 1 (1975), 99-112.

Berkowitz, L. and Cottingham, D. The interest value and relevance of fear-arousing communications. Journal of Abnormal and Social Psychology 60 (1960), 37-43.

Berlo, D. K., Lemert, J. B., and Mertz, R. I. Dimensions for evaluating the acceptability of message sources. Public Opinion Quarterly 33 (1970), 563-576.

Berlyne, D. E. Conflict, Arousal, and Curiosity. New York: McGraw-Hill, 1960.

Berlyne, D. E. Motivational problems raised by exploratory and epistemic behavior. In Psychology: A Study of a Science, Volume 5, ed. S. Kotch. New York: McGraw-Hill, 1963.

Bitzer, L. F. The rhetorical situation. Philosophy and Rhetoric 1 (1968), 1-14.

Blankenship, J. The influence of mode, sub-mode, and speaker predilection on style. Speech Monographs 41 (1974), 85-118.

Bochner, A. P. Conceptual frontiers in the study of communication in families: An introduction to the literature. Human Communication Research 2 (1976), 381-397.

Bodaken, E. M., Plax, T. G., Piland, R. N., and Weiner, A. N. Role enactment as a socially relevant explanation of self-persuasion. Human Communication Research 5 (1979), 203-214.

Bogardus, E. S. Measuring social distance. Journal of Applied Sociology 9 (1925), 299-308.

Bostrom, R. N., Baschart, J. R., and Rossiter, C. M., Jr. The effects of three types of profane language in persuasive communication. Journal of Communication 23 (1973), 461-475.

Bowers, J. W. Language intensity, social introversion, and attitude change. Speech Monographs 30 (1963), 345-352.

Bowers, J. W. Some correlates of language intensity. Quarterly Journal of Speech 50 (1964), 415-420.

Bowers, J. W. and Osborn, M. M. Attitudinal effects of selected types of concluding metaphors in persuasive speeches. Speech Monographs 33 (1966), 147-155.

Bradac, J., Bowers, J. W., and Courtright, J. Three language variables in communication research: Intensity, immediacy, and diversity. Human Communication Research 5 (1979), 257-269.

Brehm, J. W. and Cohen, A. R. Explorations in Cognitive Dissonance. New York: John Wiley, 1962.

Brierly, D. W. Children's use of personality constructs. Bulletin of British Psychological Society 19 (1966).

Brock, T. C. Effects of prior dishonesty on post-decision dissonance. Journal of Abnormal and Social Psychology 66 (1963), 325-331.

Brooks, R. D. The generality of early reversal of attitudes toward communication sources. Speech Monographs 37 (1970), 152-155.

Brooks, R. D. and Scheidel, T. M. Speech as a process: A case study. Speech Monographs 35 (1968), 1-7.

Brooks, W. D. Speech Communication. Dubuque, IA: Wm. C. Brown, 1971.

Brown, J. R. Children's uses of television. In Children and Television, ed. J. R. Brown. Beverly Hills, CA: Sage, 1976.

Buck, R. Human Motivation and Emotion. New York: John Wiley, 1975.

Buck, R. Nonverbal behavior and the theory of emotion: The facial feedback hypothesis. Journal of Personality and Social Psychology 38 (1980), 811-824.

Burgoon, M. The effects of response set and race on message interpretation. Speech Monographs 37 (1970), 264-268.

Burgoon, M. The unwillingness-to-communicate scale: Development and validation. Communication Monographs 43 (1976), 60-69.

Burgoon, M. and Chase, L. J. The effects of differential linguistic pattern in messages attempting to induce resistance to persuasion. Speech Monographs 40 (1973), 1-7.

Burgoon, M., Cohen, Miller, M.D., and Montgomery, C. An empirical test of a model of resistance to persuasion. Human Communication Research 5 (1978), 27-39.

Burgoon, M., Jones, S. B., and Stewart, D. Toward a message-centered theory of persuasion: Three empirical investigations of language intensity. Human Communication Research 1 (1974), 240-256.

Burgoon, M. and Miller, G. R. Prior attitude and language intensity as predictors of message style and attitude change following counterattitudinal advocacy. Journal of Personality and Social Psychology 20 (1971), 246-253.

Burgoon, M. and Stewart, D. Empirical investigations of language intensity: The effects of sex source, receiver, and language intensity on attitude change. Human Communication Research 1 (1974), 244-248.

Byrne, D. Attitude and attraction. In Advances in Experimental Social Psychology, Volume 4, ed. L. Berkowitz. New York: Academic, 1969, 30-89.

Capon, N. and Kuhn, D. The development of consumer information processing strategies. Harvard University. (unpublished)

Carbone, T. Stylistic variables as related to source credibility: A content analysis approach. Speech Monographs 42 (1975), 99-106.

Cartwright, D. Some principles of mass persuasion: Selected findings of research on the sale of U.S. war bonds. In The Process and Effects of Mass Communications, ed. W. Schramm and D. F. Roberts. Chicago: University of Illinois Press, 1971.

Cartwright, D. and Harary, F. "Structural balance: A generalization of Heider's theory. Psychological Review 63 (1956), 277-293.

Chapanis, N. and Chapanis, A. Cognitive dissonance: Five years later. Psychological Bulletin 61 (1964), 1-22.

Chein, I. Behavior theory and the behavior of attitudes: Some critical comments. Reprinted in Attitude Theory and Measurement, ed. M. Fishbein. New York: John Wiley, 1967, 51-57.

Christie, R. Some consequences of taking Machiavelli seriously. In Handbook of Personality Theory and Research, ed. E. F. Borgatta and W. W. Lambert. Skokie, IL: Rand McNally, 1968.

Clark, A. C. and Delia, J. G. Topoi and rhetorical competence. Quarterly Journal of Speech 65 (1969), 187-206.

Clark, R. A. Suggestions for the design of empirical communication studies. Central States Speech Journal 30 (1979a), 51-66.

Clark, R. A. The impact on selection of persuasion strategies of self-interest and desired liking," Communication Monographs, 46 (1979b), 257-273.

Clark, R. A. and Delia, J. Cognitive complexity, social perspective-taking, and functional persuasive skills in second to ninth grade children. Human Communication Research 3 (1977), 128-134.

Cody, M. J. The dimensions of persuasion situations: Implications for communication research and assignments of taxonomy construction methodologies. Doctoral dissertation, Michigan State University, 1978.

Cody, M. J. and McLaughlin, M. L. Perceptions of compliance-gaining situations: A dimensional analysis. Communication Monographs 47 (1980), 132-148.

Cogswell, B. E. Variant family forms and lifestyles: Rejection of the traditional nuclear family. In Advances in Family Psychiatry. International Universities Press, 1979, 53-76.

Comstock, G. and Cobbey, R. Television and the children of ethnic minorities. Journal of Communication 29 (1979), 104-115.

Cook, P. D. and Flay, B. R. The persistence of experimentally induced attitude change: An evaluative review. Advances in Experimental Social Psychology (1978).

Cooper, J. and Scalise, C. Dissonance produced by deviations from life styles: The interaction typology and conformity. Journal of Personality and Social Psychology 29 (1974), 566-671.

Cooper, J. and Worchel, S. Role of undesired consequences in arousing cognitive dissonance. Journal of Personality and Social Psychology 16 (1970), 199-206.

Cooper, J., Zanna, M., and Goethals, G. Mistreatment of an esteemed other as a consequence affecting dissonance reduction. Journal of Personality and Social Psychology 10 (1974), 224-233.

Corner, J. Mass in communication research. Journal of Communication 29 (1979), 26-32.

Courtright, J. A., Millar, F. E., and Rogers-Millar, L. E. Domineeringness and dominance: Replication and expansion. Communication Monographs 46 (1979), 179-192.

Cox, D. F. The audience as communicators. In Measuring Advertising Effectiveness, ed. J. T. Wheatley. Homewood, IL: Irwin, 1969, 201-213.

Crockett, W. H. Cognitive complexity and impression formation. In Progress in Experimental Research, ed. B. A. Maher. New York: Academic Press, 1965.

Cronen, V. Unwanted repetitive episodes. International Communication Association Convention, Philadelphia, 1979.

Cronen, V. and Pearce, W. B. The logic of the coordinated management of meaning: An open systems model of interpersonal communication. International Communication Association, Chicago, 1978.

Cronen, V., Pearce, W. B., and Harris, L. The coordinated management of meaning: Foundation for a communication-centered critique of the social orders. International Communication Association Convention, Acapulco, 1980.

Cronen, V., and Pearce, W. B., and Snavely, L. A theory of rule-structure and types of episodes and a study of perceived enmeshment in undesired repetitive patterns (URPS). In Communication Yearbook 3, ed. D. Nimmo. Transaction, 1979.

Cronen, V. and Reardon, K. The Relationship of Nonverbal Messages to Hierarchical and Temporal Contexts. Falls Church, VA: Speech Communication Association, 1981.

Cronkhite, G. Effects of rater-concept-scale interactions and use of different procedures upon evaluative factor structures. Human Communication Research 2
(1976), 316-329.

Culley, J. D., Lazer, W., and Atkin, C. K. The experts look at children's television.
Journal of Broadcasting 20 (1976), 3-21.

Cummings, R. Double play and replay: Living out there in television land. In Inter
Media, ed. G. Gumpert and R. Cathcard. New York: Oxford University Press,
1979.

Cushman, D. P. The rules perspective as a theoretical basis for the study of human
communication. Communication Quarterly 25 (1977), 30-45.

Cushman, D. P., Valentinsen, B., and Whiting, G. Self-concept as a generative
mechanism in interpersonal communication. International Communication Association Convention, Acapulco, 1980.

Daly, J. A. Talkativeness as a central dimension of person perception. Eastern
Communication Association Convention, Philadelphia, 1979.

Daly, J. A., Richmond, V. P., and Leth, S. Social communicative anxiety and the
personnel selection process: Testing the similarity effect in selection decisions.
Human Communication Research 6 (1979), 18-32.

D'Andrade, R. G. Cultural Construction of Reality. In Cultural Illness and Health, ed.
L. Nader and T. W. Marekzke. Washington, DC: American Anthropological Association, 1973.

Danes, J. E., Hunter, J., and Woefel, J. Mass communication and belief change: A test
of three mathematical models. Human Communication Research 4 (1978),
243-252.

Danowski, J. A. An information theory of communication function: A focus on
information aging. Doctoral dissertation, Michigan State University, 1975.

Darwin, C. The Expressions of Emotions in Man and Animals. Chicago: University of
Chicago Press, 1965.

Davidson, J. and Kiesler, S. Cognitive behavior before and after decisions. In Conflict,
Decision and Dissonance, ed. L. Festinger. Stanford, CA: Stanford University
Press, 1964, 10-19.

De Charmes, R. Personal Causation. New York: Academic Press, 1968.

Delia, J. G. Some tentative thoughts concerning the study of interpersonal relationships and their development. Western Journal of Speech Communication 49
(1980), 97-15.

Delia, J. G. Constructivism and the study of human communication. Quarterly
Journal of Speech 63 (1977), 66-83.

Delia, J. G., and Clark, R. A. Cognitive complexity, social perception, and the
development of listener-adapted communication in six-, eight-, ten-, and twelve-
year-old boys. Communication Monographs 44 (1977), 326-345.

Delia, J. G., Kline, S. L., and Burleson, B. R. The development of persuasive
communication strategies in kindergarteners through twelfth-graders. Communication Monographs 46 (1979), 241-256.

Delia, J. D., Clark, R. A., and Switzer, D. E. Cognitive complexity and impression
formation in informal social interaction. Speech Monographs 41 (1974), 209-308.

Deutsch, M. and Krauss, R. M. The effect of threat upon interpersonal bargaining.
Journal of Abnormal and Social Psychology 61 (1960), 181-189.

Deutsch, M., Krauss, R. M., and Rosenau, N. "Dissonance or Defensiveness?" Journal
of Personality, 30 (1962), pp. 16-28.

Deutsch, M. and Krauss, R. M. Theories in Social Psychology. New York: Basic Books, 1965.

Dimitrovsky, L. "The Ability to Identify the Emotional Meanings of Vocal Expressions at Successive Age Levels." In The Communication of Emotional Meaning. Edited by J. R. Davitz, New York: McGraw-Hill, 1964.

Doob, L. W. The behavior of attitudes. Psychological Review 54 (1947), 135-156.

Doob, L. W. The behavior of attitudes. Reprinted in Readings in Attitude Theory and Measurement, ed. M. Fishbein. New York: John Wiley, 1967.

Dray, W. H. The historical explanation of actions reconsidered. In Philosophy and History, ed. S. Hook. New York: New York University Press, 1963, 105-135.

Dubin, R. Industrial workers' worlds: A study of the 'central life interests' of industrial workers. Social Problems 3 (1956), 131-142.

Duck, S. W. Personal Relationships and Personal Constructs. New York: John Wiley, 1973.

Duck, S. W. Personal relationships research in the 1980's: Toward an understanding of complex human sociality. Western Journal of Speech Communication 44 (1980), 114-119.

Duval, S. and Wicklund, R. A Theory of Objective Self-Awareness. New York: Academic Press, 1972.

Eagly, A. and Himmelfarb, S. Attitudes and opinions. Annual Review of Psychology 29 (1978), 517-554.

Eagly, A. H., Wood, W., and Fishbaugh, L. Sex differences in conformity: Surveillance by the group as a determinant of male nonconformity. Amherst: University of Massachusetts, 1980.

Edwards, A. L. Techniques of Attitude Scale Construction. Englewood Cliffs, NJ: Prentice-Hall, 1957.

Edwards, C. N. Interactive styles and social adaptation. Genetic Psychology Monographs 87 (1973), 123-174.

Ekman, P., and Friesen, W. V. Detecting deception from the body or face. Journal of Personality and Social Psychology 29 (1974a), 288-298.

Ekman, P., and Friesen, W. V. Unmasking the Face. Englewood Cliffs, NJ: Prentice-Hall, 1974b.

Elms, A. C. Role playing, incentive, and dissonance. Psychological Bulletin 68 (1967), 132-148.

Ericsson, K. A. and Simon, H. A. Verbal reports as data. Psychological Review 87 (1980).

Fairhurst, G. E. Using the functional prerequisites to communication rules as a structure for rule-behavior research. International Communication Association, Acapulco, 1980.

Falcione, R. L., McCroskey, J. C., and Daly, J. A. Job satisfaction as a function of employees' communication apprehension, self-esteem, and perceptions of their immediate supervisors. In Communication Yearbook 1, ed. B. Rubin. New Brunswick, NJ: Transaction, 1977, 363-366.

Farace, R. V., Taylor, J. A. and Stewart, J. P. Criteria for evaluation of organizational communication effectiveness: Review and synthesis. In Communication Yearbook 2, ed. B. Rubin. New Brunswick, NJ: Transaction, 1978, 271-292.

Feffer, M. Developmental analysis of interpersonal behavior. Psychological Review 77 (1970).

Feldman, A., Wolf, A., and Warmouth, D. Parental concern about child-directed commercials. Journal of Communication 27 (1977), 125-137.

Festinger, L. A. A theory of social comparison processes. Human Relations 7 (1954), 117-140.

Festinger, L. A. A Theory of Cognitive Dissonance. Evanston, IL: Row Peterson, 1957.

Festinger, L. A. and Maccoby, N. On resistance to persuasive communication. Journal of Abnormal and Social Psychology 68 (1964), 359-366.

Festinger, L. A. and Walster, E. Post-decision regret and decision reversal. In Conflict, Decision, and Dissonance, ed. L. Festinger. Stanford, CA: Stanford University Press, 1964, 100-112.

Fishbein, M. An investigation of the relationships between beliefs about an object and an attitude toward that object. Human Relations 16 (1963), 233-240.

Fishbein, M. Readings in Attitude Theory and Measurement. New York: John Wiley, 1967.

Fishbein, M. and Ajzen, I. Belief, Attitude, Intention and Behavior: An Introduction to Theory and Research. Reading, MA: Addison-Wesley, 1975.

Fisher, B. A. Perspectives on Human Communication. New York: Macmillan, 1978.

Fitzpatrick, M. A. A typological approach to communication in relationships. In Communication Yearbook 1, ed. B. Rubin. New Brunswick, NJ: Transaction, 1977, 263-275.

Fitzpatrick, M. A. and Best, P. Dyadic adjustment in relational types: Consensus, cohesion, affectional expression, and satisfaction in enduring relationships. Communication Monographs 46 (1979), 167-178.

Fitzpatrick, M. A. and Winke, J. You always hurt the one you love: Strategies and tactics in interpersonal conflict. Communication Quarterly 27 (1979), 3-11.

Ford, R. N. Motivation Through the Work Itself. New York: American Management Association, 1969.

Forgas, J. P. The perception of social episodes: Categorical and dimensional representations of two different social milieus. Journal of Personality and Social Psychology 34 (1976), 199-209.

French, M. The Women's Room. New York: Harcourt Brace Jovanovich.

Frentz, T. S. A generative approach to episodic structure. Western Speech Association Convention, San Francisco, 1976.

Friedman, H. The concept of skill in nonverbal communication: Implications for understanding social interaction. In Skill in Nonverbal Communication: Individual Differences, ed. R. Rosenthal. Cambridge, MA: Oelgeschlager, Gunn and Hain Publishers, 1979.

Frost, J. H. and Wilmot, W. W. Interpersonal Conflict. Dubuque, IA: Wm. C. Brown, 1978.

Gagné, R. H. and Smith, B. C. A study of the effects of verbalization on problem-solving. Journal of Experimental Psychology 63 (1962), 12-18.

Gantz, W., Gartenberg, H., and Rainbow, C. Approaching invisibility: The portrayal of the elderly in magazine advertisements. Journal of Communication 30 (1980), 56-60.

Gerbner, G. Mass media and human communication theory. In Human Communication Theory, ed. F. E. Dance. New York: Holt, Rinehart & Winston, 1967, 40-57.

Gerbner, G. The dynamics of cultural resistance. In Hearth and Home: Images of Women in the Mass Media, ed. G. Tuchman et al. New York: Oxford University Press, 1978, 46-50.

Gillig, P. M. and Greenwald, A. G. Is it time to lay the sleeper effect to rest? Journal of Personality and Social Psychology 29 (1974), 132-139.

Goethals, G. R., and Cooper, J. The role of intention and postbehavioral consequences in the arousal of cognitive dissonance. Journal of Personality and Social Psychology 23 (1972), 293-301.

Goethals, G. R., and Cooper, J. When dissonance is reduced: The timing of self-justificatory attitude change. Journal of Personality and Social Psychology 32 (1975), 361-367.

Goffman, E. Interaction Ritual. New York: Doubleday, 1967.

Goldberg, P. Are women prejudiced against women? Transaction 5 (1968), 28-31.

Gollin, E. S. Organizational characteristics of social judgment: A developmental investigation. Journal of Personality 26 (1958), 139-154.

Gordon, G. N. Persuasion: The Theory and Practice of Manipulative Communication. New York: Hastings House, 1971.

Gottlieb, G. The Logic of Choice. New York: Macmillan, 1968.

Graen, G. Role-making processes within complex organizations. In Handbook of Industrial and Organizational Psychology, ed. M. D. Dunnette. Skokie, IL: Rand McNally, 1976, 1201-1245.

Greenberg, B. S. and Miller, G. R. The effects of low-credible sources on message acceptance. Speech Monographs 33 (1966), 127-136.

Greenberg, M. and Gorn, G. Some unintended consequences of TV advertising to children. Journal of Consumer Research 5 (1978), 22-29.

Gross, N., Mason, W., and McEachern, A. Explorations in Role Analysis. New York: John Wiley, 1958.

Gumpert, G. The ambiguity of perception. In Inter Media Interpersonal Communication in a Media World, ed. G. Gumpert and R. Cathcart. New York: Oxford University Press, 1979.

Guterman, S. The Machiavellians. Lincoln: University of Nebraska Press, 1970.

Guttman, L. A basis for scaling qualitative data. American Sociological Review 9 (1944), 139-150.

Haaland, G. A. and Venkatesan, M. Resistance to persuasive communications: An examination of the distraction hypothesis. Journal of Personality and Social Psychology 9 (1968), 167-170.

Haiman, F. S. An experimental study of the effects of ethos in public speaking. Speech Monographs 16 (1949), 190-202.

Hall, J. A. Gender effects in decoding nonverbal cues. Psychological Bulletin 85 (1978), 845-857.

Hamner, W. and Tosi, H. Relationship of role conflict and role ambiguity to job involvement measures. Journal of Applied Psychology 59 (1974), 497-499.

Harre, R. Science as representation: A reply to Mr. MacKinnin. Philosophy of Science 44 (1977), 146-158.

Harris, V. A. and Jellison, J. M. Fear-arousing communications, false physiological feedback, and the acceptance of recommendations. Journal of Experimental and Social Psychology 7 (1971), 269-279.

Hawes, L. C. "Toward a hermeneutic phenomenology of communication." Communication Quarterly 5 (1977), 30-41.

Heath, R. L. Variability in value system priorities as decision-making adaptation to situational differences. Communication Monographs 43 (1976), 325-333.

Heider, F. Social perception and phenomenal causality. Psychological Review 51 (1944).

Heider, F. Attitudes and cognitive organization. Journal of Psychology 21 (1946), 107-112.

Heider, F. The Psychology of Interpersonal Relations. New York: John Wiley, 1958.

Heise, D. R. Causal Analysis. New York: John Wiley, 1975.

Hempel, C. G. The function of general laws in history. Journal of Philosophy 39 (1942), 35-48.

Herman, J. B. Cognitive processing of persuasive communications. Organizational Behavior and Human Performance 19 (1977), 126-147.

Herzberg, F. Work and the Nature of Man. Cleveland: World Publishing, 1966.

Hewes, D. E. Interpersonal communication theory and research: A metamethodological overview. In Communication Yearbook, ed. B. Rubin. New Brunswick, NJ: Transaction, 1978.

Hewes, D. E. An axiomatized, stochastic model of the behavioral effects of message campaigns. In Message-Attitude-Behavior Relationship, ed. D. P. Cushman and R. D. McPhee. New York: Academic, 1981, 43-88.

Hewitt, J. and Stokes, R. Disclaimers. American Sociological Review 40 (1975), 1-11.

Hocking, J., Bauchner, J., Kaminski, E., and Miller, G. Detecting deceptive communication from verbal, visual and paralinguistic cues. Human Communication Research 6 (1979), 33-46.

Hovland, C. Reconciling conflicting results derived from experimental and survey studies of attitude change. American Psychologist 14 (1959), 8-17.

Hovland, C., Janis, I., and Kelley, H. Communication and Persuasion. New Haven, CT: Yale University Press, 1953.

Hovland, C. and Mandel, W. An experimental comparison of conclusion-drawing by the communicator and by the audience. Journal of Abnormal and Social Psychology 47 (1952), 581-588.

Hovland, C. and Weiss, W. The influence of source credibility on communication effectiveness. Public Opinion Quarterly 15 (1951), 635-650.

Hoyt, M., Henley, M., and Collins, B. Studies in forced compliance: The confluence of choice and consequences on attitude change. Journal of Personality and Social Psychology 23 (1972), 205-210.

Huber, G., O'Connell, M., and Cummings, L. Perceived environmental uncertainty—Effects of information and structure. Academy of Management Journal 18 (1975), 725-740.

Hull, C. L. Principles of Behavior. Englewood Cliffs, NJ: Prentice-Hall, 1943.

Hunter, J. E., Levine, R. L., and Sayers, S. E. Attitude change in hierarchical belief systems and its relation to persuasibility dogmatism and rigidity. Human Communication Research 3 (1976), 3-28.

Huseman, R. C., Logue, C. M., and Freshly, D. L. Readings in Interpersonal and Organizational Communication. Boston: Holbrook, 1977.

Insko, C. A. Theories of Attitude Change. Englewood Cliffs, NJ: Prentice-Hall, 1967.

Jackson, J. A conceptual and measurement model for norms and roles. Pacific Sociological Review (1966), 35-47.

Janis, I. and Feshback, S. Effects of fear-arousing communications. Journal of Abnormal and Social Psychology 48 (1953), 78-92.

Janis, L. and Field, P. A behavioral assessment of persuasibility: Consistency of individual differences. Sociometry 19 (1956), 241-259.

Jeeker, J. D. The cognitive effects of conflict and dissonance. In Conflict, Decision, and Dissonance, ed. L. Festinger. Stanford, CA: Stanford University Press, 1964, 21-30.

Jones, E. and Davis, K. From acts to dispositions: The attribution process in person perception. In Advances in Experimental Psychology, ed. L. Berkowitz. New York: Academic, 1965, 220-266.

Jones, E. and Nisbett, R. The Actor and the Observer: Divergent Perceptions of the Causes of Behavior. New York: General Learning Press, 1971.

Kahn, R. L., Wolfe, D. M., Quinn, P., Snoek, J. D., and Rosenthal, R. A. Organizational Stress. New York: John Wiley, 1964.

Kaminski, E., McDermott, S., and Boster, F. The use of compliance-gaining strategies as a function of Machiavellianism and situations. Presented at Central States Speech Association Convention, Southfield, Michigan, 1977.

Kant, I. The critique of pure reason. In Great Books of the Western World, Volume 42, ed. R. M. Hutchins. Chicago: Encyclopedia Britannica, 1952, 1-250.

Karlins, M. and Abelson, H. How Attitudes and Opinions Are Changes. New York: Springer, 1970.

Katz, D. The functional approach to the study of attitudes. Public Opinion Quarterly 24 (1960), 163-204.

Katz, D. and Kahn, R. The Social Psychology of Organizations. New York: John Wiley, 1966.

Kaufer, D. Developing a rule theoretic approach to communication as opposed to a dictionary of rules: Some considerations and criteria. Presented at the Doctoral Honors Seminar, University of Massachusetts, 1976.

Keasey, C. Young children's attribution of intentionality to themselves and others. Child Development 48 (1977), 261-264.

Kelly, G. The Psychology of Personal Constructs. New York: Norton, 1955.

Kelly, G. Europe's matrix of decision. In Nebraska Symposium, ed. M. R. Jones. Lincoln: University of Nebraska Press, 1979.

Kelman, H. C. Processes of open change. Public Opinion Quarterly 25 (1961), 57-78.

Kelman, H. C. Attitudes are alive and well and gainfully employed in the sphere of action. American Psychologist 29 (1974), 310-324.

Kelman, H. C. and Hovland, C. I. Reinstatement of the communicator in delayed measurement of opinion change. Journal of Abnormal and Social Psychology 48 (1953), 327-335.

Kennedy, J. J. An Introduction to the Design and Analysis of Experiments in Education and Psychology. Washington, DC: University Press of America, 1978.

Kenny, D. Correlation and Causality. New York: John Wiley, 1979.

Kiesler, S. and Mathog, R. Distraction hypothesis in attitude change: Effects of effectiveness. Psychological Reports 23 (1968), 1123-1133.

Kipnis, D. The Power-Holders. New York: Academic Press, 1976.

Knapp, M. and Comadena, M. Telling it like it isn't: A review of theory and research on deceptive communications. Human Communication Research 5 (1979), 270-285.

Knapp, M., Stahl, C., and Reardon, K. K. Memorable messages. 1980. (unpublished)

Kohlberg, L. A. A cognitive developmental analysis of children's sex-role concepts and attitudes. In The Development of Sex Differences, ed. E. Maccoby. Stanford, CA: Stanford University Press, 1966.

Kohlberg, L. A. The cognitive developmental approach to socialization. In Handbook of Socialization Theory and Research, ed. D. Goslin, Skokie, IL: Rand McNally, 1969.

Korzenny, F. and Neuendorf, K. Television viewing and self-concept of the elderly. Journal of Communication 30 (1980), 71-80.

Kramer, C. Women's speech: Separate but unequal? Wuarterly Journal of Speech 60 (1974a), 14-24.

Kramer, C. Folklinguistics. Psychology Today 8 (1974b), 82-85.

Kuhn, T. The Structure of Scientific Revolutions. Chicago: University of Chicago Press, 1975.

Lapiere, R. G. A Theory of Social Control. New York: McGraw-Hill, 1954.

LaPiere, R. T. Attitudes versus actions. In Readings in Attitude Theory and Measurement, ed. M. Fishbein. New York: John Wiley, 1967, 26-31.

Larson, C. and Sanders, R. Faith, mystery, and data: An analysis of 'scientific' studies of persuasion. Quarterly Journal of Speech 61 (1975), 178-194.

Lashbrook, W. B. Program ARISTOTLE; Computerized technique for the simulation and analysis of audiences. Presented at the annual meeting of the Central States Speech Association, Chicago, 1976.

Lashbrook, W. B., Snavely, W. B., and Sullivan, D. L. The effects of source credibility and message information quantity on the attitude change of apathetics. Communication Monographs 44 (1977), 252-262.

Lehmann, S. Personality and compliance: A study of anxiety and self-esteem in opinion and behavior change. Journal of Personality and Social Psychology 15 (1970), 76-86.

Leventhal, H. Findings and theory in the study of fear communications. In Advances in Experimental Social Psychology, ed. L. Berkowitz. New York: Academic Press, 1970.

Leventhal, H. and Niles, P. Field experiment on fear arousal with data on the validity of questionnaire measures. Journal of Personality 32 (1964).

Leventhal, H., Singer, R., and Jones, S. Effects of fear and specificity of recommendations upon attitudes and behavior. Journal of Personality and Social Psychology 2 (1965), 20-29.

Leventhal, H. and Watts, J. C. Sources of resistance to fear-arousing communications on smoking and lung cancer. Journal of Personality 34 (1966), 155-175.

Levinson, D. J. The seasons of a man's life. New York: Ballantine, 1978.

Likert, R. A. Technique for the measurement of attitudes. Archives of Psychology 140 (1932).

Lin, N. Information flow, influence flow, and the decision-making process. Journalism Quarterly 48 (1971), 33-40.

Liska, A. E. Emergent issues in the attitude-behavior consistency controversy. American Sociological Review 39 (1974), 261-272.

Little, B. R. Psychological man as scientist, humanist, and specialist. Journal of Experimental Research in Personality 6 (1972), 95-118.

Livesley, W. J. and Bromley, D. B. Person Perception in Childhood and Adolescence. New York: John Wiley, 1973.

Locke, E. A. Toward a theory of task motivation and incentives. Organizational Behavioral Human Performance 3 (1968), 157-189.

Loevinger, L. The ambiguous mirror: The reflective-projective theory of broadcasting and mass communication. In InterMedia, ed. G. Gumpert and R. Cathcart. New York: Oxford University Press, 1979, 243-260.

London, H. Psychology of the Persuader. Morristown, NJ: General Learning Press, 1973.

Lumsden, D. An experimental study of source-message interaction in a personality impression task. Communication Monographs 44 (1977), 121-129.

Magnussen, D. An analysis of situational dimensions. Perceptual and Motor Skills 32 (1971), 851-867.

Mair, J. The derivation, reliability and validity of grid measures: Some problems and suggestions. Bulletin of the British Psychological Society 17 (1964).

Marwell, G. and Schmitt, D. Dimensions of compliance-gaining behavior: An empirical analysis. Sociometry 30 (1967), 350-364.

McCroskey, J. Scales for the measurement of ethos. Speech Monographs 33 (1966), 65-72.

McCroskey, J. A summary of experimental research on the effects of evidence in persuasive communication. Quarterly Journal of Speech 55 (1969), 169-175.

McCroskey, J. A critique of the top five papers in interpersonal and small group communication. Speech Communication Association Convention, San Antonio, 1979.

McCroskey, J. and Burgoon, M. Establishing predictors of latitude of acceptance-rejection and attitude intensity: A comparison of assumptions of social judgment authoritarian personality theories. Speech Monographs 41 (1974), 421-426.

McDermott, V. The development of a functional message variable: The locus of control. Presented at the Speech Communication Association, Chicago, 1974.

McDougall, W. An Introduction to Social Psychology. London: Methuen, 1908.

McCroskey, J. and Richmond, V. Communication apprehension as a predictor of self-disclosure. Communication Quarterly 25 (1977), 40-43.

McEwen, W. J. Counterattitudinal encoding effects on message style and performance. Doctoral dissertation, Department of Communication, Michigan State University, 1969.

McEwen, W. J., Watt, J. H., and Shea, C. G. Content and style attributes as predictors of TV commercial recall. International Communication Association Convention, Berlin, 1977.

McGarry, J. and Hendrick, C. Communication credibility and persuasion. Memory and Cognition 2 (1974), 82-86.

McGuire, W. and Papageorgis, D. The relative efficacy of various types of prior belief-defense in producing immunity against persuasion. Journal of Abnormal and Social Psychology 62 (1961b), 327-337.

McGuire, W. J. The effectiveness of supportive and refutational defenses in immunizing and restoring beliefs against persuasion. Sociometry 24 (1961a), 184-197.

McGuire, W. J. Inducing resistance to persuasion: Some contemporary approaches. In Advances in Experimental Social Psychology, Volume 1, ed. L. Berkowitz. New York: Academic, 1964.

McGuire, W. The nature of attitudes and attitudinal change. In Handbook of Social Psychology, ed. G. Lindzey and E. Aronson. Cambridge, MA: Addison-Wesley, 1969, 136-314.

McGuire, W. Personality and susceptibility to social influence. In Handbook of Personality Theory and Research, ed. E. F. Borgatta and W. W. Lambert. Skokie, IL: Rand McNally, 1970, 1130-1187.

McGuire, W. Persuasion, resistance, and attitude change. In Handbook of Communication, ed. I. Pool et al. Skokie, IL: Rand McNally, 1973, 216-252.

McKelvey, W. H. Expectational noncomplementarity and style of interaction between professional and organization. Administrative Science Quarterly (1969).

McLaughlin, M. L. Relationships of situational preference to self-disclosure and predisposition to communicate. Communication Quarterly 27 (1979), 3-11.

McQuail, D. Alternative models of television influence. In Children and Television, ed. R. Brown. Beverly Hills, CA: Sage, 1979, 343-359.

Merton, R. K. Social Structure and Social Theory. New York: Free Press, 1957.

Miles, R. H. An empirical test of causal inference between role perceptions of conflict and ambiguity and various personal outcomes. Journal of Applied Psychology 60 (1975), 334-339.

Miles, R. H. Role-set configuration as a predictor of role conflict and ambiguity in complex organizations. Sociometry 40 (1977), 150-163.

Miller, G. R. The current status of theory and research in interpersonal communication. Human Communication Research 14 (1978), 164-178.

Miller, G. R. On rediscovering the apple: Some issues in evaluating the social significance of communication research. Central States Speech Journal 30 (1979), 14-24.

Miller, G. R. On being persuaded: Some basic distinctions." In Persuasion: New Directions in Theory and Research, ed. G. Miller and M. Roloff. Beverly Hills, CA: Sage, 1980.

Miller, G. R., Boster, F., Roloff, M. E., and Seibold, D. Compliance-gaining message strategies: A typology and some findings concerning effects of situational differences. Communication Monographs 44 (1977), 37-51.

Miller, G. R. and Burgoon, M. New Techniques of Persuasion. New York: Harper & Row, 1973.

Miller, G. R. and Burgoon, M. Persuasion research: Review and commentary. In Communication Yearbook 2, B. Rubin. New Jersey: Transaction, 1978, 29-47.

Miller, G. R. and Hewgill, M. A. The effects of variations in nonfluency on audience ratings of source credibility. Quarterly Journal of Speech 50 (1964), 36-44.

Miller, G. R. and Steinberg, M. Between People: A New Analysis of Interpersonal Communication. Chicago: Science Research Associates, 1975.

Miller, M. and Burgoon, M. The relationship between violations of expectations and the induction of resistance to persuasion. Human Communication Research 5 (1979), 301-313.

Miller, N., Maruyama, G., Beaber, R. J., and Valone, K. Speed of speech and persuasion. Journal of Personality and Social Psychology 34 (1976), 615-624.

Mills, C. W. Situational actions and vocabularies of motives. American Sociological Review 5 (1940), 904-913.

Millman, S. Anxiety, comprehension, and susceptibility to speech influence. Journal of Personality and Social Psychology 9 (1968), 251-256.

Mischel, H. Sex bias in the evaluation of professional achievements. Journal of Educational Psychology 2 (1974), 157-160.

Moltz, H. and Thistlewaite, D. Attitude modification and anxiety reduction. Journal of Abnormal and Social Psychology 50 (1955).

Mulac, A. The effects of obscene language upon three dimensions of listener attitude. Communication Monographs 43 (1976), 300-307.

Nel, E., Helmreich, R. K., and Aronson, E. Opinion change in the advocate as a function of the persuasibility of his audience: A clarification of the meaning of dissonance. Journal of Personality and Social Psychology 12 (1969), 117-124.

Newcomb, T. M. An approach to the study of communicative acts. Psychological Review 60 (1953), 393-404.

Newcomb, H. Toward a television aesthetic. In Television: The Critical View, ed. H. Newcomb. New York: Oxford University Press, 1979a.

Newcomb, H. Television: The Critical View. New York: Oxford University Press, 1979b.

Newcomb, T. M. The consistency of certain extrovert-introvert behavior patterns in 51 problem boys. In Contributions to Education 382. New York: Teachers College, Columbia University, 1929.

Nietzke, A. The American obsession with fun. In Mass Media Issues, ed. L. Sellers and W. Rivers. Englewood Cliffs, NJ: Prentice-Hall, 1977, 337-345.

Norton, R. Foundation of a communicator style construct. Human Communication Research 4 (1978), 99-112.

Norton, R., Mulligan, A., and Petronio, S. Strategies to elicit self-disclosure. International Communication Association Convention, 1975.

Norton, R. and Pettegrew, L. Attentiveness as a style of communication. Communication Monographs 46 (1979), 13-26.

Novak, M. Television shapes the soul. In Mass Media Issues, ed. L. Sellers and W. Rivers. Englewood Cliffs, NJ: Prentice-Hall, 1977, 41-56.

Nunally, J. and Bobren, H. Variables concerning the willingness to receive communications on mental health. Journal of Personality 27 (1959), 38-46.

O'Keefe, B. J. The theoretical commitments of constructivism. Speech Communication Association Convention, 1978.

O'Keefe, D. and Delia, J. Construct comprehensiveness and cognitive complexity as predictors of the number and strategic adaptation of arguments and appeals in a persuasive message. Communication Monographs 46 (1979), 231-256.

Osgood, C. Some effects of motivation on style in encoding. In Style in Language, ed. T. Seboek. Cambridge, MA: MIT Press, 1960.

Osgood, C., Suci, G., and Tannebaum, P. The Measurement of Meaning. Urbana: University of Illinois Press, 1957.

Osgood, C. and Tannebaum, P. The principle of congruity in the prediction of attitude change. Psychological Review 62 (1955), 42-55.

Osterhouse, R. A. and Brock, T. C. Distraction increases yielding to propaganda by inhibiting counterarguing. Journal of Personality and Social Psychology 15 (1970), 344-358.

Parsons, T. The Social System. New York: Free Press, 1951.

Pearce, W. B. The coordinated management of meaning: A rules-based theory of interpersonal communication. In Explorations in Interpersonal Communication, ed. G. R. Miller. Beverly Hills, CA: Sage, 1976, 17-36.

Pearce, W. B. and Conklin, F. A model of hierarchial meanings in coherent conversation and a study of "Indirect Responses," Communication Monographs 46 (1979), 75-88.

Pearce, W. B. and Cronen, V. E. Communication Meaning and Action: The Creation of Social Realities. New York: Praeger, 1978.

Petty, R., Wells, G., and Brock, T. Distraction can enhance or reduce yielding to propaganda: Thought disruption versus effort justification. Journal of Personality and Social Psychology 34 (1976), 874-884.

Philipsen, G. Speaking like a man in Teamsterville: Culture and patterns of role enactment in an urban neighborhood. Quarterly Journal of Speech 61 (1975), 13-22.

Philipsen, G. Linearity of research design in ethnographic studies of speaking. Communication Quarterly 24 (1977), 42-50.

Piaget, J. The Moral Judgment of the Child. London: Routledge & Kegan Paul, 1932.

Piaget, J. The Construction of Reality in the Child. New York: Basic Books, 1954.

Piaget, J. Comments on Vygotsky's Critical Remarks. Cambridge, MA: MIT Press, 1962.

Piaget, J. The Child's Conception of the World. Totowa, NJ: Littlefield, Adams, 1969.

Plutchik, R. and Ax, A. F. A critique of "Determinants of Emotional State" by Schachter and Singer (1962). Psychophysiology 4 (1967), 79-82.

Ray, M. Marketing communication and the hierarchy of Effects. In New Models for Communication Research, ed. P. Clarke. Beverly Hills, CA: Sage, 1973.

Reardon, K. Conversational deviance: A structural model. Falls Church, VA: Speech Communication Association.

Reardon, K. and Carilli, T. Elderly tactile communication: A rejoinder to a gospel of delusion. University of Connecticut, 1979. (unpublished)

Reardon, K., Noblet, C., Carilli, T., Shorr, M., and Beitman, M. A theoretical model of rules invalidation: A study of new faculty. International Communication Association Convention, Acapulco, 1980.

Reardon-Boynton, K. Conversational deviance: a developmental perspective. Doctoral dissertation, University of Massachusetts, 1978.

Reardon-Boynton, K. and Fairhurst, G. Elaboration on the concept rule: A case study with the military. International Communication Association Convention, Philadelphia, 1978.

Reynolds, P. D. A Primer in Theory Construction. Indianapolis: Bobbs-Merrill, 1975.

Richmond, V. P. and McCroskey, J. C. Whose opinion do you trust? Journal of Communication (1975), 42-50.

Roberts, D. F. Approaches to the study of mass communication effects: Attitudes and information. In The Process and Effects of Mass Communication, ed. W. Schramm and D. F. Roberts. Urbana: University of Illinois Press, 1972, 389-398.

Robertson, T. S. Parental mediation of television advertising effects. Journal of Communication 29 (1979), 12-25.

Robertson, T. S. and Rossiter, J. R. Children's responsiveness to commercials. Journal of Communication 27 (1977), 101-106.

Rogers, E. and Agarwala-Rogers, R. Communication in Organizations. New York: Free Press, 1976.

Rogers, E. and Shoemaker, F. Communication of Innovations: A Cross-Cultural Approach. New York: Free Press, 1971.

Rokeach, M. The Open and Closed Mind. New York: Basic Books, 1960.

Rokeach, M. and Rothman, G. The principle of congruence and the congruity principle as models of cognitive interaction. Psychological Review 72 (1965), 129-156.

Roloff, M. E. Self-awareness and the persuasive process. In Persuasion: New Directions in Theory and Research, ed. M. Roloff and G. Miller. Beverly Hills, CA: Sage, 1980, 29-66.

Rosenberg, M. J. Discussion: On reducing inconsistency between consistency theories. In Theories of Cognitive Consistency: A Sourcebook, ed. R. P. Abelson et al. Skokie, IL: Rand McNally, 1968, 801-803.

Rosenthal, P. The concept of the paramessage in persuasive communication. Quarterly Journal of Speech, 1972.

Rosenthal, R. and DePaulo, B. M. Sex differences in accommodation of nonverbal communication. In Skill in Nonverbal Communication: Individual Differences, ed. R. Rosenthal. Cambridge, MA: Oelgeschlager, Gunn & Hain, 1979.

Rosten, L. The intellectual and the mass media: Some rigorously random remarks. In Mass Media Issues, ed. L. Sellers 1977. and W. Rovers. Englewood Cliffs, NJ: Prentice-Hall, 1977.

Rothenberg, B. B. Children's social sensitivity and the relationship to interpersonal comfort, and intellectual level. Developmental Psychology 2 (1970), 335-350.

Rotter, J. B. Social Learning and Clinical Psychology. Englewood Cliffs, NJ: Prentice-Hall, 1954.

Rotter, J. B. Generalized expectancies for internal versus external control of reinforcement. Psychological Monographs 80 (1966).

Rubin, R. B. The effect of context on information seeking across the span of initial interactions. Communication Quarterly 27 (1979), 13-20.

Rychlak, J. F. The Psychology of Rigorous Humanism. New York: John Wiley, 1977.

Sarason, I. G., Smith, R. E., and Diener, E. Personality research: Components of variance attributable to the person and the situation. Journal of Personality and Social Psychology 32 (1975), 199-204.

Schachter, S. The Psychology of Affiliation: Experimental Studies of the Source of Gregariousness. Stanford, CA: Stanford University Press, 1959.

Schachter, S. The interaction of cognitive and physiological determinants of emotional states. In Advances in Experimental Social Psychology, ed. L. Berkowitz. New York: Academic, 1964.

Schachter, S. Cognitive effects on bodily functioning: Studies of obesity and eating. In Neurophysiology and Emotion, ed. D. C. Glass. New York: Rockefeller University Press, 1967.

Schenck-Hamlin, W. J., Wiseman, R. L., and Georgacarakas, G. N. A typology of compliance-gaining strategies and the logic of their underlying relationships. Presented at the International Communication Association, Acapulco, 1980.

Schlenker, B. R. and Riess, M. Self-presentations of attitudes following commitment to proattitudinal behavior. Journal of Human Communication Research 5 (1979), 325-334.

Schramm, W. and Roberts, D. F. The Process and Effects of Mass Communication. Urbana: University of Illinois Press, 1972.

Schuler, R. Role perceptions, satisfaction and performance: A partial reconciliation. Journal of Applied Psychology 60 (1975), 683-687.

Scott, M. B. and Lyman, S. M. Accounts. In Symbolic Interaction, ed. J. G. Manis and B. M. Meltzer. Boston: Allyn & Bacon, 1974.

Sears, D. O. and Freedman, J. L. Selective exposure to information: A critical review. Public Opinion Quarterly 31 (1967), 194-213.

Seibold, D. R. Communication research and the attitude verbal-overt behavior relation: A critique and theoretic reformulation. Communication Research 2 (1975), 3-32.

Seibold, D. R. Criticism of communication theory and research: A critical celebration. Central State Speech Journal 30 (1979), 25-39.

Shapiro, D. and Crider, A. Psychophysiological approaches in social psychology. In Handbook of Social Psychology, Volume 3, ed. G. Lindsey and E. Aronson. Reading, MA: Addison-Wesley, 1968.

Shatz, M. The relationship between cognitive processes and the development of communication skills. In Nebraska Symposium on Motivation, ed. H. E. Howe, 1977.

Sheahy, G. Passages. New York: Dutton, 1976.

Sheikh, A. A. and Moleski, L. M. Conflict in the family over commercials. Journal of Communication 27 (1977), 152-157.

Sherif, M. and Sherif, C. W. The own category procedure in attitude research. In Readings in Attitude Theory and Measurement, ed. M. Fishbein. New York: John Wiley, 1967.

Shimanoff, S. B. Communication Rules. Beverly Hills, CA: Sage, 1980.

Shroder, H., Driver, M., and Streufert, S. Human Information Processing. New York: Holt, Rinehart & Winston, 1967.

Shulman, G. An experimental study of the effects of receiver sex, communicator sex, and warning on the ability of receivers to detect deception. Masters thesis, Purdue University, 1973.

Shweder, R. A. How relevant is an individual difference theory of personality? Journal of Personality 37 (1975), 455-484.

Shweder, R. A. Illusory correlation and the MMPI controversy. Journal of Consulting and Clinical Psychology 47 (1977), 917-924.

Simons, H. Persuasion: Understanding, Practice and Analysis. Reading, MA: Addison-Wesley, 1976.

Singer, R. The effects of fear-arousing communication on attitude change and behavior. Doctoral dissertation, University of Cincinatti, 1965.

Smith, T. J. Communication and multiple generative mechanisms: A theoretical extension. Michigan State University, East Lansing. (unpublished)

Snyder, D. P. Modal Logic and Its Applications. New York: Litton, 1971.

Snyder, M. Self-monitoring of expressive behavior. Journal of Personality and Social Psychology 30 (1974), 526-537.

Staats, A. An outline of an integrated learning theory of attitude formation and function. In Readings in Attitude Theory and Measurement, ed. M. Fishbein. New York: John Wiley, 1967.

Staats, A. Learning, Language, and Cognition. New York: Holt, Rinelart & Winston, 1968.

Starbuck, W. H. Organizations and their environments. In Handbook of Industrial and Organizational Psychology, ed. M. D. Dunnette. Skokie, IL: Rand McNally, 1976, 1069-1123.

Stewart, J. B. Repetitive Advertising in Newspapers: A Study in Two New Products. Boston: Harvard Business School, 1964.

Swanson, D. L. and Delia, J. G. The Nature of Human Communication. Science Research Associates, 1976.

Sypher, H. E. Illusory correlation in communication research. Human Communication Research 7 (1980), 83-87.

Sypher, H. E. and O'Keefe, D. The comparative validity of several complexity measures as predictors of communication-relevant abilities. International Communication Association Convention, Acapulco, 1980.

Tannenbaum, D. and Norris, E. Effects of combining congruity principle strategies for the reduction of persuasion. Journal of Personality and Social Psychology 3 (1966), 233-238.

Thibaut, J. W. and Kelly, H. H. Interpersonal Relations: A Theory of Interdependence. New York: John Wiley, 1978.

Thompson, J. D. Bureaucracy and Innovation. University, AL: University of Alabama Press, 1967.

Thurstone, L. L. Theory of attitude measurement. Psychological Review 36 (1929), 222-241.

Thurstone, L. L. and Chave, E. J. The Measurement of Attitude. Chicago: Chicago University Press, 1929.

Tittle, C. R. and Hill, R. J. Attitude measurement and prediction of behavior: An evaluation of conditions and measurement techniques. Sociometry 30 (1967), 199-213.

Tolman, E. C. Purposive Behavior in Animals and Men. Englewood Cliffs, NJ: Prentice-Hall, 1932.

Tosi, H. Organizational stress as a moderator of the relationship between influence and role response. Academy of Management Journal 14 (1971), 7-20.

Toulmin, S. E. The Uses of Argument. Cambridge, England: Cambridge University Press, 1958.

Triandis, H. C. Exploratory factor analysis of the behavioral component of social attitudes. Journal of Abnormal and Social Psychology 68 (1964), 420-430.

Triandis, H. C. Attitude and Attitude Change. New York: John Wiley, 1971.

Tuchman, G. The symbolic annihilation of women by the mass media. In Hearth and Home: Images of Women in the Mass Media, ed. G. Tuchman et al. New York: Oxford University Press, 1978, 3-38.

Underwood, B. J. and Shaughnessy, J. J. Experimentation in Psychology. New York: John Wiley, 1975.

vandenberg, S. and Watt, J. Changes in audience perceptions of sex and violence on television. University of Connecticut, 1977, 1978. (unpublished)

vonBertanlannfy, L. General Systems Theory. New York: George Brazitler, 1968.

Vohs, J. L. and Garrett, R. L. Resistance to persuasion: An integrative framework. Public Opinion Quarterly 32 (1968), 445-452.

Wackman, D. B. and Ward, S. The development of consumer information processing skills: Contributions of cognitive development theory. In Advances in Consumer Research, ed. B. B. Anderson. Cincinnati: Association for Consumer Research, 1976.

Walster, E. The temporal sequence of post-decisional processes. In Conflict, Decision and Dissonance, ed. L. Festinger. Stanford, CA: Stanford University Press, 1964, 112-127.

Walster, E. H., Bersheid, A., and Walster, G. W. New directions in equity research. Journal of Personality and Social Psychology 25 (1973), 151-176.

Wartella, E. Children Communicating: Media and Development of Thought Speech, Understanding. Beverly Hills, CA: Sage, 1979.

Wartella, E. and Ettema, J. S. A cognitive developmental study of children's attention to television commercials. Communication Research 1 (1974), 46-69.

Wartella, E., Wackman, D. B., Ward, S., Shamir, J., and Alexander, A. The young child as consumer. In Children Communicating: Media and Development of Thought, Speech, Understanding. Beverly Hills, CA: Sage, 1979.

Watson, G. and Johnson, D. Social Psychology: Issues and Insights. Philadelphia: J. B. Lippincott, 1972.

Watt, J. H. and Krull, R. An examination of three models of television viewing and aggression. Human Communication Research 3 (1976).

Weber, M. Theory of Social and Economic Organization. New York: Oxford University Press, 1947.

Weick, K. E. The Social Psychology of Organizing. Reading, MA: Addison-Wesley, 1969.

Weigel, R. H., Vernon, D. T., and Tognacci, L. N. Specificity of the attitudes as a determinant of attitude-behavior congruence. Journal of Personality and Social Psychology 30 (1974), 724-728.

Weimann, J. M. Explication and test of a model of communication competence. Human Communication Research 3 (1977), 195-213.

Weiss, R. F., Rawson, H. E., and Pasamanick, B. Argument strength, delay of argument, and anxiety in "conditioning" and "selective learning" of attitudes. Journal of Abnormal and Social Psychology 67 (1963), 157-165.

Weiss, R. F., Rawson, H. E., and Pasamanick, B. Argument strength in the "conditioning" and "selective learning" of attitudes. In Readings in Attitude Change, ed. S. Himmelfarb and A. H. Eagly. New York: John Wiley, 1974.

Werner, H. Comparative Psychology of Metal Development. New York: Harper Row, 1940.

Werner, H. Comparative Psychology of Mental Development. New York: International University Press, 1957.

Westie, F. R. and DeFleur, M. L. Autonomic responses and their relationship to race attitudes. Journal of Abnormal and Social Psychology 58 (1959), 340-347.

Wheeles, L. R. The effects of attitude, credibility, and homophily on selective exposure to information. Speech Monographs 41 (1974), 329-338.

White, R. W. Motivation reconsidered: The concept of competence. Psychological Review 66 (1959), 297-333.

Wicker, A. W. Attitudes vs. actions: The relationship of verbal and overt behavioral responses to attitude objects. Journal of Social Issues 25 (1969), 41-78.

Wilder, L. and Harvey, D. J. Overt and covert verbalization in problem solving. Speech Monographs 38 (1971), 171-176.

Wolf, M. A. and Hexamer, A. Children and television commercials: A look at the child's frame of reference. International Communication Association, Acapulco, 1980.

Woods, M. M. What does it take for a woman to make it in management? Personnel Journal (January 1975), 38-41.

Zajonc, R. B. The process of cognitive tuning in communication. Journal of Abnormal and Social Psychology 61 (1960), 159-164.

Zajonc, R. B. Cognitive theories in social psychology. In The Handbook of Social Psychology, Vol. 1, ed. G. Lindzey and E. Aronson. Reading, MA: Addison-Wesley, 1968, 320-411.

Zillmann, D. Attribution and misattribution of excitory reactions. Indiana University, 1977. (unpublished)

Zillmann, D., Williams, B. R., Bryant, J., Reardon-Boynton, K., and Wolf. M. A. Acquisition of information from educational television programs as a function of differently paced humorous inserts." Journal of Educational Psychology 72 (1980), 170-180.

Zimbardo, P. and Ebbesen, E. B. Influencing Attitudes and Changing Behavior. Reading, MA: Addison-Wesley, 1970.

Zimbardo, P. G., Ebbesen, E. B., and Maslach, C. Influencing Attitudes and Changing Behavior. Reading, MA: Addison-Wesley, 1977.

ABOUT THE AUTHOR

Kathleen Kelley Reardon is an Assistant Professor of Interpersonal and Mass Media Communication in the Department of Communication Sciences at the University of Connecticut. Dr. Reardon is President of the Connecticut Communication Association. She has been the recipient of several awards for her research, including the 1978 International Communication Association Top Three Graduate Student Paper Award and the 1979 Speech Communication Association Dissertation of the Year Award. Dr. Reardon is also the secretary of the Interpersonal Division of the International Communication Association. Outside of the academic community, she has served as a communication consultant to Connecticut organizations and professional societies as well as for the United States Government Employee Training Program in Washington, D.C. Dr. Reardon has published articles in the areas of interpersonal, mass media, and organizational communication. In addition, she is the co-author of *An Introduction to Communication Science,* a forthcoming Prentice-Hall publication.